Genealogy Online, 6th Edition

Genealogy Online, 6th Edition

Elizabeth Powell Crowe

Osborne/McGraw-Hill

New York Chicago San Francisco
Lisbon London Madrid Mexico City
Milan New Delhi San Juan
Seoul Singapore Sydney Toronto

Osborne/**McGraw-Hill**
2600 Tenth Street
Berkeley, California 94710
U.S.A.

To arrange bulk purchase discounts for sales promotions, premiums, or
fund-raisers, please contact Osborne/**McGraw-Hill** at the above address. For
information on translations or book distributors outside the U.S.A., please see
the International Contact Information page immediately following the index of
this book.

Genealogy Online, 6th Edition

34567890 CUS CUS 0198765432
ISBN 0-07-219465-0

Publisher: Brandon A. Nordin
Vice President & Associate Publisher   Scott Rogers
Acquisitions Editor: Margie McAneny
Project Editor: Katie Conley
Acquisitions Coordinator: Emma Acker
Technical Editor   Terry Morgan
Copy Editor: Marsha Baker
Proofreader: Susie Elkind
Indexer: Jack Lewis
Computer Designers: George Toma Charbak, Tara A. Davis & Melinda Lytle
Illustrators: Michael Mueller & Lyssa Wald
Series Design: Gary Corrigan
This book was composed with Corel VENTURA™ Publisher.

To my mother, Frances Spencer Powell

About the Author

Elizabeth Powell Crowe is the best-selling author of the previous editions of *Genealogy Online*, as well as *Information for Sale* (co-authored with John Everett) and *The Electronic Traveler*. She has been a contributing editor for *Computer Currents* magazine and the author of numerous articles in both popular and technical publications. Crowe has been pursuing genealogy for over 20 years, and served as editor of The Tennessee Valley Genealogical Society's *Valley Leaves* and co-editor of The Spencer Genealogical and Historical Society's *Le DeSpencer*. She lives in Huntsville, Alabama, with her husband and two children.

Contents at a Glance

Part 1

The Basics

1 Beginning a Genealogy Project 3

2 Hardware and Software 21

3 Online Society 51

Part 2

The Internet

4 The World Wide Web 67

5 Search Engines 79

6 Chat: Hail Thy Fellow on the Net! 97

7 Genealogy Mailing Lists and Newsletters 113

8 Usenet 127

Part 3
Specific Online Resources

9 The Library of Congress and the NARA 145

10 The Church of Jesus Christ of Latter-day Saints 159

11 Ellis Island Online: The American Family Immigration
History Center 173

12 Online Library Card Catalogs 183

13 International Genealogy Resources 193

14 Ethnic Genealogy Resources 209

15 The National Genealogical Society 221

16 RootsWeb 227

17 The Ancestry.com Family of Sites 243

18 Everton Publishers 253

19 CompuServe's Genealogy Forums 263

20 America Online's Golden Gate Genealogy Forum 281

21 Around the Web in 80 (or so) Sites 303

Part 4
Appendices

A Genealogical Standards from the National
Genealogical Society 335

B Forms of Genealogical Data 343

C Internet Error Messages 351

Glossary 357
Index 371

Contents

Acknowledgments xvii
Introduction xix

Part 1
The Basics

1 Beginning a Genealogy Project 3
    An Overview of Genealogy 4
        Always Start with Yourself 5
        Keeping Track 6
        Sources That Can Help a Genealogical Researcher 6
        A Baker's Dozen of Free Forms 7
        Line by Line 9
        Queries 10
    Good Practices 12
        Sources and Proof 12
        References to Have at Hand 18
    Scams 19
    Wrapping Up 20

2 Hardware and Software 21
    Getting Set Up 22
        Modems 23
        High-Speed Connections 25

Other Choices 28
Choosing an ISP 30
Baby Steps 31
Software 33
What Makes the Web Tick 33
FTP 35
E-mail 35
The Legislative Front 37
Internet Mail Clients 43
Inoculations 44
Publishing on the Internet 46
Wrapping Up 50

3 Online Society 51
Manners Matter 52
Civil Discourse 54
Danger: *Scams Ahead!* 61
Chat Etiquette 61
Wrapping Up 63

Part 2
The Internet

4 The World Wide Web 67
Browser-speak 68
Which Browser Should I Use? 69
A Guided Tour of a Browser 70
Browser Tips and Tricks 74
FTP 76
Wrapping Up 78
FTP Conventions 78

5 Search Engines 79
Defining Terms 80
Searching with Savoir Faire 82
Using Boolean Terms 83
Search Sites 85
White Page Directories 93
Wrapping Up 95

6 Chat: Hail Thy Fellow on the Net! 97
Can We Talk? 98
Important Warnings About Chat 100

How It Works 101
Security Risks In *IRC* 102
Chat Flavors 103
How to Chat 106
Where to Chat 109
Wrapping Up 111

7 Genealogy Mailing Lists and Newsletters 113
Proper Addressing 114
General Subscribing Tips 115
An In-Depth Visit to ROOTS-L 115
Other Mail List Sites 122
Read-Only Lists 124
Finding More Mailing Lists 125
Wrapping Up 126

8 Usenet 127
Complicated, but *Useful* 128
Usenet's Structure 129
The Software 131
Newsgroups of Interest to Online Genealogists 137
Binary Files on Usenet 139
Newsgroup Frequently Asked Questions (FAQs) Files 140
Net Etiquette and Tips on Usenet 141
Wrapping Up 142

Part 3
Specific Online Resources

9 The Library of Congress and the NARA 145
Library of Congress 146
American Memory 146
National Archives and Records Administration 151
The Genealogy Page 151
NARA Web Databases 152
Prologue 157
Some Experience Helpful 157
Wrapping Up 157

10 The Church of Jesus Christ of Latter-day Saints 159
FamilySearch Internet 160
A Run-Through 161
Other Cool Stuff 165
Library 167
Other Resources 167

How to Use Information from LDS 167
Some Background 168
A Visit to an FHC 170
Wrapping Up 171

11 Ellis Island Online: The American Family Immigration
History Center 173
The Grand Opening 174
A Guided Tour 176
Wrapping Up 182

12 Online Library Card Catalogs 183
Connecting to Card Catalogs by Web Browser 184
A Sample OCC Search 185
Connecting to Card Catalogs by Telnet 188
Where to Find More Online Card Catalogs 190
Wrapping Up 191

13 International Genealogy Resources 193
A Success Story 194
Where to Look 199
LDS Research Guides 199
WorldGenWeb 201
Other Good Starting Places 202
South America 206
Australia 206
Africa 207
North America 207
Wrapping Up 208

14 Ethnic Genealogy Resources 209
African American 211
Arab 213
Australian Aborigines 213
Caribbean 214
Creole/Cajun 214
Cuban 215
Doukhobors 216
Gypsy, Romani, Romany, and Travellers 216
Hmong 216
Jewish 216
Native American 217
Métis 219
Melungeon 219
Wrapping Up 220

15 The National Genealogical Society 221
       National Genealogical Society 222
          Wrapping Up 225

16 RootsWeb 227
       The Merger 228
          RootsWeb Leads to a Reunion 229
       What You'll Find at RootsWeb 230
          Other Search Engines 234
          Message Boards and Mailing Lists 234
          Newsletters 238
          Web Pages at RootsWeb 239
          The HelpDesk 241
          More and More 242
          Wrapping Up 242

17 The Ancestry.com Family of Sites 243
       Ancestry.com 244
       FamilyHistory.com 246
          Message Boards 247
          World Tree 248
          Society Hall 248
       MyFamily.com 248
          Family Tree 250
          History 251
          Chats 251
          Other Features 252
       A Nice Collection of Sites 252
          Wrapping Up 252

18 Everton Publishers 253
          Databases 254
          Online Classes 256
          Other Features 259
          Subscribing 261
          Wrapping Up 261

19 CompuServe's Genealogy Forums 263
          Web Access 264
          Plenty to Offer 265
          A Quick Overview 266
          GO Genealogy 267
          Forums 268
          Forum Decorum 271
          Grand Tour 273

        Profile: Dick Eastman, Genealogy Forum Manager 278
        Wrapping Up 279

20 America Online's Golden Gate Genealogy Forum 281
        Member Welcome Center 284
        Beginners' Center 286
        Messages 290
        Surnames 294
        Resources 294
        Reunions 295
        Search the Forum 295
        Chats 295
        Library 297
        Columnists 298
        Features and Events 298
        The Staff of the Genealogy Forum 299
        Wrapping Up 302

21 Around the Web in 80 (or so) Sites 303
        True Story: The Web Helps a Mobility-Challenged
            Genealogist 304
        Four Score and Seven Sites to See 305
        A Closer Look 321
        AfriGeneas 322
        DearMYRTLE 325
        Genealogy Home Page 327
        USGenWeb 328
        GENSERV 331
        Wrapping Up 332

Part 4

Appendices

A Genealogical Standards from the National Genealogical Society 335
        Standards for Sound Genealogical Research 336
        Guidelines for Using Records, Repositories, and Libraries 337
        Standards for Use of Technology in Genealogical Research . . 338
        Standards for Sharing Information with Others 340
        Guidelines for Publishing Web Pages on the Internet 341

B Forms of Genealogical Data 343
        GEDCOMs, Ahnentafels, and Tiny Tafels 344
        GEDCOMs 344
        Ahnentafels 344
        Tiny Tafels 346

C Internet Error Messages 351
   Browser Error Messages 352
   FTP Error Messages 354
   Usenet Error Messages 355
   E-Mail Error Messages 356
   Smiley (Emoticon) Glossary 366

   Glossary 357
   Index 371

Acknowledgments

As with any book, this one was made possible by the efforts of many people besides the author. First, I'd like to thank each and every person mentioned in this book, as I obviously couldn't have done it without all of you.

Special thanks go to DearMYRTLE, Jean Henry, Terry Ann Morgan, Nick Pawluck, Cricket Grilliot, Peg Zitko, Gale Fuller, Liz Kelley Kerstens, Margie McAneny, Emma Acker and all the staff at Osborne/McGraw-Hill. And to Leah Bailey, who took me out of town when I most needed a break!

Great gratitude is due to all my family and friends, who were more than patient with me while I was writing this book.

But most of all I want to thank my mother, Frances Spencer Powell, who urged and encouraged me, proofread and researched for me, traveled and travailed with me throughout the entire process from initial idea to final galleys.

Introduction

"I've gotten more genealogy done in one year on Prodigy than I did in 20 years on my own!" my mother exclaimed. This quote, from a 30-year genealogy veteran, shows how technology has changed even this popular hobby. The mind-boggling deluge of data needed to trace one's family tree has finally found a knife to whittle it down to size: the computer.

This edition covers the incredible new resources that have been made available to online genealogists in the recent past. The potential for finding clues, data, and other researchers looking for your same family lines has increased exponentially since the last edition of this book was published. One of the most significant recent contributions to the world of online genealogy is the Ellis Island records database, which was published online in early 2001 by the Statue of Liberty Foundation (with help from The Church of Jesus Christ of Latter-day Saints). This searchable database, which represents roughly 60 percent of all United States immigration records, contains data on over 20 million people who immigrated to the United States from other countries during peak immigration years. In the time since we published the last edition, major genealogy Web sites Ancestry.com, Genealogy.com, Everton.com, and FamilySearch.org have all added more data and made their sites more user-friendly. Even if you've never used the Internet before, these sites can help you get started with online genealogy. And now more software programs than ever can help you track your genealogy and share it with others, such as the newest version of Personal Ancestral File, which lets you carry your pedigree around with you on your Palm Pilot. In short, online genealogy is just getting better and it's a good time to try your hand at it!

A reader of a previous edition of *Genealogy Online* wrote to me:

> Libbi, I can't begin to tell you how much benefit I've gotten from Genealogy Online! After reading your book, I began an online search for John's and my ancestors. Since both of our mothers also had an interest in genealogy and had already prepared quite a bit of information that they passed to us, I was starting with most branches of our combined families in the early 1800s and working backwards from there, when records were sparse.
>
> With the knowledge I gained from your book, I've been able to trace many branches of our combined family back several more generations! I've found out that my husband and kids are related to George Washington and Wild Bill Hickok. The Hickok connection was always in the family folklore, but I've been able to provide the missing link.
>
> I've traced one line back to the 1400s in England and have recently learned that another line is available back to the 800s. I've traced our roots back to the very same rural county in Virginia where John's brother now lives, just a short distance from the original family farm. Through the Internet, I've made connections with two of my mother's cousins and two of John's fourth cousins, and we are collectively working to share family information and document our heritage.
>
> I've had so much fun, but I've had to learn to be patient when searching. Sometimes the most obscure reference is the one that provides the missing link you're searching for. Without *Genealogy Online*, I wouldn't have even known where to get started on my search. With the help of your book, we now have several hundred more years' worth of family history!
>
> —Linda Hanson

This book will help you understand that a rich community of information is out there—information that can help you find where those missing ancestors are lurking. Some of the sources are free, some cheap, some dear. Until you know about them, however, they're worthless to you. Once you know, you can decide for yourself whether to use them.

Where Computers Come in

Databases, online services, online card catalogs, and bulletin boards are changing the *brick wall syndrome,* that frustrating phase of any lineage search where the information needed seems unavailable. Genealogists who have faced the challenges and triumphed are online, helping others.

The Church of Jesus Christ of Latter-day Saints (the Mormons) has collected an extensive bank of genealogical data (official registers of births, marriages, and deaths, and related documents), probably the greatest such collection in existence. Church members use these records to bring their ancestors posthumously into the church. The index to their information is now on the Internet.

The federal government has recently started to put much of its data, such as death records, veterans' records, and so on in machine-readable databases, which could then be accessible via an Internet. The Bureau of Land Management, the Library of Congress, and the National Archives and Records Administration are just a few examples of government sites that can help the family historian.

The United States alone has numerous genealogical societies that trace people's descent. Some of these are national, but many more are local or regional, such as the Tennessee Valley Genealogical Society or the New England Historical Society. Others are specific to certain names. Many patriotic organizations, such as the Daughters of the Confederacy, limit membership to descendants of a particular historical group.

A recent cover article in *CompuServe* magazine highlighted the uses of its online forum for genealogy, where forum leader Dick Eastman said thousands of users visit a week. The article then describes how the forum helped one woman find her natural father, how stories about ancestors are swapped, and the sort of informational files uploaded to the library.

There's no denying that the computer has changed nearly everything in our lives, and the avocation and vocation of genealogical research is no exception. Further, a wonderful new resource for computers, the Internet, has come into being and is still developing at a dizzying pace. This book explores many different networks, services, and Web sites that can help you in your pursuit of your ancestry.

Stories about how online communities have helped people in their genealogical research abound. Here are some examples:

DearMYRTLE Finds a Patriot

DearMYRTLE, a daily genealogy columnist on the Internet (see Chapter 7 or www.DearMYRTLE.com/), was helping a friend move files, data, and programs from an old computer to a new one. In the course of the conversation, DearMYRTLE's friend wondered aloud what online genealogy could do for him, but expressed doubt anything useful could turn up online.

Then the conversation turned to the first of the new United States quarters, the one with the Delaware patriot Cesar Rodney on the reverse.

"Who was he?" asked DearMYRTLE's friend.

"All right," DearMYRTLE replied, "let's run a test. Your wife here will look up Cesar Rodney in the *Encyclopaedia Britannica.* You look him up on your old computer using Microsoft Encarta 97. I'll look him up on the Internet with your new computer."

The friend and his wife both found short-text mentions that Rodney had signed the Declaration of Independence and led the Delaware Militia (the wife slightly tore a page in the book in the process). In the same amount of time, DearMYRTLE had found the Web site of the Historical Society of Delaware (www.hsd.org/washington_letter.htm) with a short biography on him and a copy of a letter from George Washington to Rodney discussing troop movements, along with two others written by Delaware patriots Caesar Rodney and Jacob Broom (see Figure I-1).

Nancy's Story

Nancy is a friend of mine from high school who knows more about computers and the Internet than I do, but not quite so much about genealogy. When her stepmother died recently, Nancy got a large box of her father's memorabilia and photos. One day I showed her some good genealogy sites on the Internet on her laptop computer.

I didn't think much more about it until she called me a few weeks later in considerable excitement. She had not only found the USGENWEB (www.usgenweb.org) site for her father's home county in Texas, but also that the moderator of the site had known both her father and her grandfather. She was scanning in the old photos and e-mailing them to

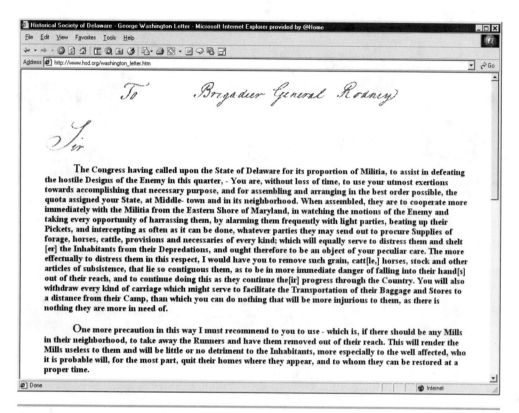

FIGURE I-1. *Online research leads to treasures, such as this letter from George Washington to Cesar Rodney.*

the fellow, and he was identifying people in them left and right. One was of Nancy's grandfather as a child. Another showed her father as a teenager. Every day, the USGENWEB sysop was helping her fill in more holes in her family history.

What's a Hoosier? Genealogy Has the Answer

Randy Hooser, of Huntsville, Alabama, has been working on his genealogy for years. One result has been his work with a University of Indiana professor to publish a white paper to prove his family is the origin of the nickname "Hoosier." A fascinating story, the migration of Randy's family involves religious and political movements of this nation's history. You

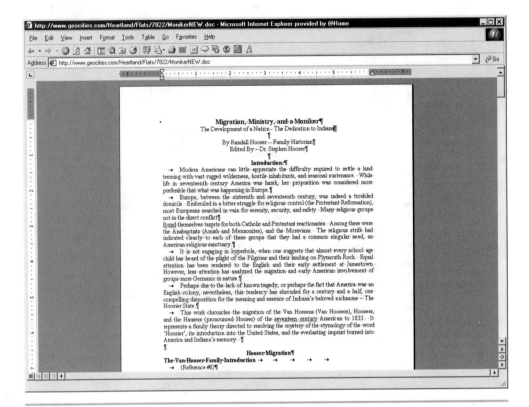

FIGURE I-2. *Randy Hooser has posted his study on the nickname "Hoosier" on his Web site.*

can see the results of his research on his Web site, www.geocities.com/ Heartland/Flats/7822/, as shown in Figure I-2. In it, Randy postulates that his pioneer ancestors, being usually the farthest west of civilization, were the origin of the nickname "Hoosier."

This isn't the only use for Randy's Web site, though. Randy used it to plan a big family reunion in Indiana in 2000, to exchange genealogical data among the cousins, and to publish a newsletter. An e-mail list with all Randy's known relatives keeps everyone up-to-date on births, marriages, and deaths among those living and provides similar data on ancestors as the family historians find them. This is just one example of how genealogists are using online resources to gather and disseminate information.

A Quick Look at This Book

This book gives you a basic education in the online world. Nevertheless, please be aware that what is written here was current as of late 2001. Since that time, commercial online services and the Internet will have added to, expanded, revised, and changed what they offer, as well as how and when they offer it. The only constant in the online world for the last five years has been change, and at an exponential rate. So, be prepared for adventures!

Part 1: The Basics

Chapter 1: Beginning a Genealogy Project—A quick primer on how to get started.

Chapter 2: Hardware and Software—A look at the basic tools for online research.

Chapter 3: Online Society—The ins and outs of getting along online.

Part 2: The Internet

Chapter 4: The World Wide Web—An overview of how to use the Internet.

Chapter 5: Search Engines—How to get the most out of search engines.

Chapter 6: Chat: Hail Thy Fellow on the Net! —The most addictive part of the Web. How it can help you find other genealogists.

Chapter 7: Genealogy Mailing Lists and Newsletters—Worldwide, continual discussions on all genealogy topics via e-mail.

Chapter 8: Usenet—The mother of all messaging systems.

Part 3: Specific Online Resources

Chapter 9: The Library of Congress and the NARA —How to use the resources these institutions offer online.

Chapter 10: The Church of Jesus Christ of Latter-day Saints—A wonderful Web site—plus local Family History Centers. You'll learn how to use both.

Chapter 11: Ellis Island Online—A new online resource that lets you search ships' passenger lists for the most active years of the Ellis Island Immigration Center.

Chapter 12: Online Library Card Catalogs—How to find out if a library has the book you need before you leave home.

Chapter 13: International Genealogy Resources—Once you find that initial immigrant in a family line, you need to search in "the old country." Here's how to get started online.

Chapter 14: Ethnic Genealogy Resources—Special pages and resources to help with researching genealogy of many different groups.

Chapter 15: The National Genealogical Society—How to learn about genealogy.

Chapter 16: RootsWeb—The grand old lady of genealogy Web sites.

Chapter 17: The Ancestry.com Family of Sites—A family of sites for researching genealogy.

Chapter 18: Everton Publishers—The venerable genealogy publisher has a useful Web site.

Chapter 19: CompuServe's Genealogy Forums—The Roots Forum is now available online, as well as to CompuServe subscribers.

Chapter 20: America Online's Golden Gate Genealogy Forum—The Golden Gate Genealogy Forum has some of the best offerings online.

Chapter 21: Around the Web in 80 (or so) Sites—A compilation of sites you shouldn't miss!

Part 4: Appendices

Appendix A: Genealogical Standards from the National Genealogical Society

Appendix B: Forms of Genealogical Data

Appendix C: Internet Error Messages

Glossary

I hope you'll find in this book the tools you need to get started or to continue pursuing your genealogy with online resources, to share data with other genealogists online, and to participate in the online society in its many facets. Happy hunting!

Part 1

The Basics

Chapter 1

Beginning a Genealogy Project

Many folks come to online genealogy after years of doing it the old-fashioned way. They know what they're looking for and simply want to use online tools to help them in their search. However, perhaps you are as new to genealogy as you are to the online world. In that case, here's some background information before you begin.

An Overview of Genealogy

My opinion is that humans became civilized as a result of pedigrees because, when people began to divide themselves into clans based on bloodlines, genealogy begat civilization. To keep track of who belonged in which clan, knowing one's family history was essential. Before people could write down their genealogies, they would pass down family stories to their children by word of mouth. Such storytelling has been important throughout all eras of human history and could even be considered the beginning of all literature. The endurance of this tradition shows we all care who we are and from where our people came.

When clans formed into tribes and tribes formed into nations, genealogy became an essential part of society. Laws were enacted because the division of wealth and power depended largely on inheritance laws, especially regarding thrones and landholdings. Genealogy was used in land transactions, taxation, lawsuits, and not a few feuds and wars. What were the Wars of the Roses about if not genealogy?

In feudal times, the difference between a freeman and a villein was birthright: Those whose forebears worked free land were free to move about as they pleased. Those whose forebears worked the land owned by lords were bound to stay there unless the lord gave them leave. Courts were kept busy with lords trying to prove families were beholden and families trying to prove they weren't, based on genealogy. Religion, too, has long found the study of genealogy important, from Judaism to Shintoism to today's Shi'ite Muslims and the Mormons.

By the late 1800s, genealogy had become a popular hobby in the United States. The establishment of groups such as the First Families of Virginia, the Daughters of the American Revolution, and so on gave impetus to the trend. To join these civic-minded groups, one had to prove one's ancestors and their participation in the various wars, settlements, and other historical events of interest. By the time Alex Haley's genealogical saga *Roots* came along in 1976, people who'd been feeling rootless in the twentieth century were ready to embrace the study of family history.

Then came the personal computer. It didn't take long for genealogy groups to form on mail lists, Usenet, chat servers, and the first commercial online services, such as CompuServe and Prodigy. People began swapping success stories, looking up data in libraries for one another, and sharing information online by 1980. Once the Internet became accessible to the general public, online genealogy increased exponentially.

Many genealogists see the hobby as a way to understand where they came from and where they're going. This certainly is a fun and interesting way to make history come alive. When you see an account of the Battle of Saratoga, or the potato famine in Ireland, or the French Revolution, knowing your ancestors were present makes history much more interesting.

This also proves, of course, that history is all about *you*.

Always Start with Yourself

Begin with what you know for certain: your own vital statistics and those of the people living with you. Collect the documentation that proves your birth, marriage, graduation, and things you own. Such documents are considered primary sources because they reflect data recorded close to the time and place of an event. Write down family stories, legends, and events as you remember them. Gather up photos and identify the people in them (and the date the photos were taken, if possible).

> **Note**
>
> *A primary source is an original piece of information that documents an event: a death certificate, birth certificate, marriage license, and so forth. A secondary source is a source that might cite an original source, but isn't the source itself, such as a newspaper obituary or birth notice, a printed genealogy, a Web site genealogy, and so forth.*

Sources That Can Help a Genealogical Researcher

Vital records: Birth, death, marriage records, and the Social Security Death Index: Many states didn't require these before the twentieth century.

Court records: Wills, adoptions, land and property bills of sale, tax rolls, deeds, naturalization, even lawsuits.

Church records: Baptisms, marriages, burials, and so forth.

Newspapers, magazines: Not only obituaries, marriage and birth notices, but also social news: perhaps parents, siblings, or cousins are mentioned.

Military records: Enlistment, commission, muster rolls, veterans' documentation.

Fraternal organizations: Many clubs such as the Lion's Club, the Masons, and so forth keep records on members. Such records can help you pinpoint an ancestor's location at a certain time.

Ships' passenger lists: Not only for immigrants to your country, but travel within. Also, some rivers, such as the Tennessee, were the site of many pioneer marriages.

Keeping Track

Now, determine how you'll keep track of all this information. You can fill out family group sheets or pedigree charts, record the data in a genealogy software program, use index cards, or whatever method suits you. An example of an index card is shown in Figure 1-1.

Most people feel that finding a good genealogy program, which enables them to record sources (as noted in Chapter 2), is the way to go. Paper sources can be scanned into digital form and/or stored in good old-fashioned filing cabinets. Remember to keep a record of all your research findings, even those pieces of information that seem unrelated to your family lines. You never know when you can use such information or pass it on to someone else who needs it.

Even if you decide to do the bulk of your research on a computer, you might still need some paper forms to keep your research organized. The following box lists some Web sites where you can find forms to use

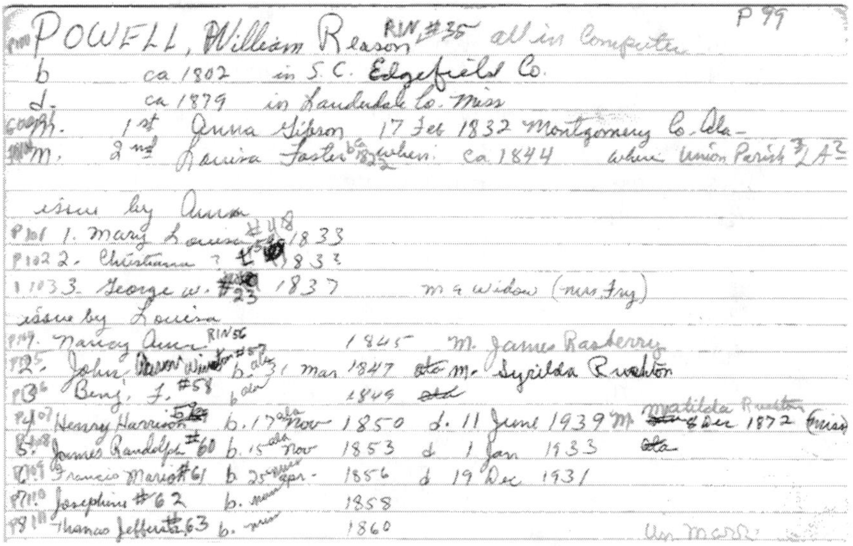
POWELL, William Reason RIN #35 all in Computer P 99
b ca 1802 in S.C. Edgefield Co.
d. ca 1879 in Lauderdale Co. Miss
m. 1st Anna Gibson 17 Feb 1832 Montgomery Co. Ala
m. 2nd Louisa Foster ca 1844 where Union Parish
issue by Anna
1. Mary Louisa #48 1833
2. Christiana ? 1833
3. George W. #23 1837 m a widow (mrs. Fry)
issue by Louisa
1. Nancy Ann RIN 56 1845 m. James Rasberry
2. John b. 31 mar 1847 m. Syrilda Rushton
3. Benj. F. #58 1849
4. Henry Harrison b. 17 Nov 1850 d. 11 June 1939 m. Matilda Rushton 8 Dec 1872
5. James Randolph #60 b. 15 Nov 1853 d. 1 Jan 1933
6. Francis Marion #61 b. 25 Apr. 1856 d 19 Dec 1931
7. Josephine #62 b. 1858
8. Thomas Jefferson #63 b. 1860 Un marr.

FIGURE 1-1. *Index cards can be used to record data and where it was found, as well as provide backup to your computer data.*

as you research censuses and other records, so you can document your findings and sources. There's more about documentation later in this chapter.

A Baker's Dozen of Free Forms

You can find free, downloadable forms to record and track your research. Here are a few places you can find them:

At FamilySearch (www.familysearch.org) click the Search tab | Research Helps | Sorted by Document Type | Click Form. You'll find a list of forms from charts to time lines to census worksheets. These files are in PDF format. You must have *Adobe Acrobat* (a free downloadable file reader) to read and print these files.

Several members of RootsWeb (www.rootsweb.org) have posted their most useful forms on its site. Under "Research and Resources," for example, you can find PDF files of family group sheets and a census summary chart.

Ontario GENWEB's site (www.rootsweb.org/~canon/genforms.html) has a collection of forms useful for recording Canadian research: census, vital statistics, and so on.

PBS.org has a section on PBS's Ancestors Series that includes PDF files for research questions, source notes, and charts. Search for Ancestors Series and then charts.

The site Genealogy.com (www.genealogy.com) contains a chart to keep track of your correspondence.

At Ancestry.com (www.ancestry.com) you can find PDF files of useful forms, such as a research calendar and source summary.

The Mid-Continent Public Library has a whole section on genealogy and four PDF files to help you record research at www.mcpl.lib.mo.us/ge/forms.

The Genealogy Mall (www.genealogy-mall.com) has lots of books and resources for sale, but also has a set of free forms at www.genealogy-mall.com/freechar.htm. These are HTML files, which you can save to your disk or print for copying later. You can also buy sets of these forms from the mall if you find them useful.

Mary (Hagstrom) Bailey and Duane A. Bailey are two generous genealogists who have posted forms they developed for their own use at www.cs.williams.edu/~bailey/genealogy. These forms are free for nonprofit use.

Another generous genealogist, Judith Haller, has developed templates for spreadsheets and word processing programs. She offers them free for personal use at www.io.com/~jhaller/forms/forms.html.

The Genealogical Society of Washtenaw County, Michigan, Inc., has a page at www.hvcn.org/info/gswc/links/toolforms.htm, with links to forms and articles discussing how to use them.

You can find out what forms to use for records at the National Archives and Records Administration (NARA) at www.nara.gov/research/ordering/ordrfrms.html. Several are available for printing and downloading.

The Roots Forum (CompuServe) has a set of Genealogy Research Forms in Word for Windows 6.0 and Word Perfect formats. The file for Word is GENERA.ZIP and the one for Word Perfect is WPFRMS.ZIP These forms were uploaded by Clyde Jones and are

> free for personal use. Go to www.rootsforum.com, click Genealogy
> Techniques Forum, and then click Files. In the keyword search, enter
> **Forms**, and the files will be in the list. Right-click to download them.

Most of the genealogy programs on the market today print family group sheets, as well as other report formats and blank forms. Then you can take them to the library or a genealogy conference for quick reference, or display them at family reunions. Many can also handle video and sound recordings. Whichever program you choose, be certain you record a source for each fact and keep families together in your system. I recommend keeping printed copies of research findings in case of a computer crash or failure, as well as giving duplicates to family or friends in case of a fire, flood, or other disaster.

✍ *Note*

A PDF file is an Adobe Portable Document Format file. This is a file with text, and sometimes pictures, saved so it can be displayed the same way no matter what type of computer or operating system you use. With a free program called Adobe Acrobat Reader software, you can view and print Adobe PDF files. You can download the reader at www.adobe.com.

Line by Line

The next step is picking a surname to pursue. As soon as you have a system for storing and comparing your research findings, you're ready to begin gathering data on that surname. A good place to begin is interviewing family members: parents, aunts, uncles, cousins, and in-laws. Ask them for stories, names, dates, and places of the people and events in the family. When it's possible, get documents to back up what you're told. Family Bibles, newspapers, diaries, wills, and letters can help here.

A good question to ask at this point is whether any genealogy of the family has been published. Understand that such a work is still a secondary source, not a primary source. If published sources have good documentation included, you might find it a great help.

Visit a Family History Center (FHC) and the FamilySearch (www.familysearch.org) site, which has indexes to The Church of Jesus Christ of Latter-day Saints' (LDS) genealogy information (see Chapter 14). This includes the following:

♦ **IGI** The event-based International Genealogical Index (The largest single database in the world. Use with care, though, because sometimes mistakes are included.)

♦ **Ancestral File (AF)** A patron-submitted pedigree format genealogy.

♦ **Old Parochial Register (OPR)**

All the previous databases are made up of research done by LDS members, but might include data on people who aren't members.

Record all you find in your system of choice. This is tedious, but necessary. Get someone to proof your entries (typing 1939 when you meant to type 1993 can easily happen!).

Once you take the first few steps of gathering official documents, choosing a system to organize your project, and interviewing family members, you'll have enough information to start asking intelligent questions in queries to magazines and mail lists (this is covered in Chapter 7). You'll also have enough data to answer questions in chat rooms and Usenet groups, discussed in Chapters 6 and 8. And, most of all, you'll have enough names, dates, and places to start using search engines to find Web sites and FTP sites, covered in Chapter 4.

Queries

A *query*, in genealogy, is a request for data on a specific person, or at least clues to where to find data on that person. Queries might be sent to one person in a letter or electronic mail message and to someone else in an online site, a magazine, a mail list, or some other forum that reaches many people at one time.

Note

Never send a letter query that says, "Send me everything you have on the Jones family," or words to that effect. It is rude and unfair to ask for someone to just hand over years of research. You must have some data to exchange and a specific genealogy goal to fulfill when you query for information. And offer to pay copying and/or postage costs.

Writing a good query isn't hard, but you do have to stick to certain conventions for it to be effective.

- Make the query short and to the point. Don't try to solve all your genealogical puzzles in one query. Zero in on one task at a time.

- List at least one name, at least one date or time period, and at least one location to go with the name. Don't bother sending a query that doesn't have all three of these elements. No one can help you without a name, a date, and a place. If you aren't certain about one of the elements, follow it with a question mark in parentheses.

- Capitalize all surnames, including the maiden name and previous married names of female ancestors. Include all known relatives' names: children, siblings, and so forth. Use complete names, including any middle names, if known. Proofread all the names.

- Give complete dates as far as you know. Follow the format DD Month YYYY, as in 20 May 1865. If the date is uncertain, use "before" or "about" as appropriate, such as "Born circa 1792" or "Died before October 1850." Proofread all dates for typos; this is where transpositions can really get you!

- Give town, county, and state (or province) for North American locations; town, parish (if known) and county for United Kingdom locations, and so on. In other words, start with the specific and go to the general, including all divisions possible.

- Include how you wish to be contacted. For a letter query, or one sent to a print magazine, you will want to include your full mailing address. For online queries, you want to include at least an e-mail address.

So, a sample query that could go in to a print or online venue is as follows:

I need proof of the parents of Diadama CRIPPEN born 11 Sept 1794 in (?), NY. I believe her father was Darius CRIPPEN son of Samuel CRIPPEN and her mother was Abigail STEVENS CRIPPEN, daughter of Roger STEVENS, both from CT. They lived in Egremont, Berkshire County, MA and Pittsfield, Rutland County, VT before moving to Bastard Township, Ontario, Canada. I will exchange information and copying costs. [Here you would put your regular mail address, e-mail address, or other contact information.]

True Story: A Beginner Tries the Shotgun Approach

Just two months ago, my mother shared some old obits with me that intrigued me enough to send me off on a search for my family's roots. I started at the Roots Web site with a metasearch, and then sent e-mails to anyone who had posted the name I was pursuing in the state of origin cited in the obit. This constituted over 50 messages. A real shotgun approach. I received countless replies indicating there was no family connection. Then, one day, I got a response from a man who turned out to be my mother's cousin. He himself had been researching his family line for the last two years. He sent me census and marriage records, even a will from 1843 that gave new direction to my search.

In pursuing information on my father, whom my mother divorced when I was two months old (I never saw him again), I was able to identify his parents' names from an SS 5 application and, subsequently, track down state census listings containing not only their birth dates, but also the birth dates of their parents. All of which has aided me invaluably in the search for my family's roots.

Having been researching only a short while, I have found the online genealogy community to be very helpful, and am more than willing to share information with newbies like myself. The amount of information online has blown me away.

—Sue Crumpton

Good Practices

As you gather more and more information, you want to check what you find against what's considered good practice for genealogists. The National Genealogical Society (NGS) has a set of standards for research, as shown in Appendix A. You can also find these on the Web at the NGS Web site located at www.ngsgenealogy.org.

Sources and Proof

Most serious genealogists who discuss online sources want to know if you can "trust" what you find on the Internet. Many professional genealogists I know simply don't accept what's found on the Internet as proof of genealogy, period. Their attitude is this: A source isn't a primary source unless you've held the original document in your hand. And a primary source isn't proof unless it's supported by at least one other original document you've held in your hand. To them, seeing a picture of a scanned original on the Internet isn't "proof." For example, as you can see in Figure 1-2, *The Mayflower* passenger list has been scanned in at Caleb Johnson's site, Mayflower Passenger List members.aol.com/calebj/passenger.html. Would you consider this a "primary source?" A "secondary source?" Or simply a good clue?

Some genealogists get annoyed with those who publish their genealogy data on the Internet without citing each source in detail. Once, when I was teaching a class on how to publish genealogy on the Internet at a conference, a respected genealogist took me to task over dinner. "Web pages without supporting documentation are lies!" she

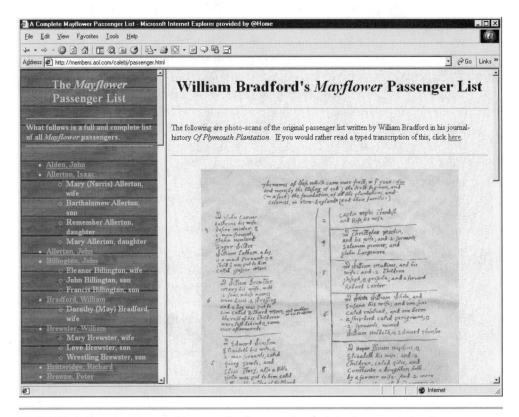

FIGURE 1-2. *Is a scanned image of a document an original source to you?*

insisted. "You're telling people to publish lies because if it's not proven by genealogical standards, it might not be true!"

I have to admit I don't see it that way. In my opinion, you must evaluate what you find on the Internet, just as you evaluate what you find in a library, courthouse, or archive. Many a genealogy book has been published with errors and the same is true of online genealogies. On the Web, no real editors exist. You can find all kinds of information and sources on the Internet—from casual references in messages to documented genealogy to original records transcribed into HTML. The range is astounding. But the same can be true of vanity-published genealogies found in libraries.

You can find some limited primary materials online. People are scanning and transcribing original documents onto the Internet, such as the Library of Virginia and the National Park Service. You can also find online a growing treasure trove of indexes of public vital records, scanned images of Government Land Office land patents at www.glorecords.blm.gov and more (see Figure 1-3).

Don't be put off by those who sneer at the Internet, saying nothing of genuine value can be found there. This might have been true only a few years ago, but not today. Now you can find scanned images of census records are going online at both the Census site (www.census.gov) and volunteer projects, such as the USGenWeb Digital Census Project. Looking at these records in HTML is as good as, or better than, looking at them in microfilm or microfiche, in my opinion.

Nevertheless, secondary sources are much easier to find than primary sources. The main value of these secondary sources on the Internet is finding other genealogists who are researching the same lines. Additionally, you might uncover leads to finding primary and secondary sources offline, and, rarely, get a glance at an actual data source, perhaps even a primary source. Simply knowing a source *exists* can be a breakthrough.

Other people are putting their family trees online. While many of these data files don't have the disk space available to include complete documentation, most people who publish online are willing to provide pertinent details to anyone who has data to exchange with them.

Therefore, I still believe in publishing and exchanging data over the Internet. However, you must use good judgment.

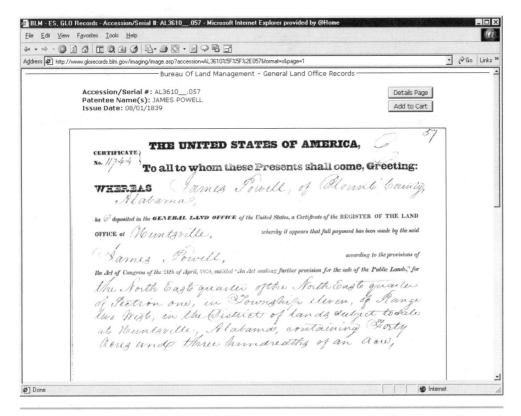

FIGURE 1-3.   *The Bureau of Land Management can show you land patents online at www.glorecords.blm.gov.*

How to Judge

The criteria for the evaluation of resources on the Web must be the same criteria you would use for any other source of information. Be aware that just because something is on a computer, this doesn't make it infallible. Garbage in, garbage out. With this in mind, ask yourself some questions in evaluating online genealogy sites.

Who created it?   You can find resources on the Internet from libraries, research institutions, and organizations such as the NGS, not to mention government resources and those from universities. Sources such as these give you more confidence in their data than, say, resources from a hobbyist. Publications and software companies also publish genealogical information, but you must read the site carefully to determine whether they've actually researched this information or simply accepted anything their customers threw at them. Finally, you can find tons of "family traditions" and, while traditions usually have a grain of truth to them, they're usually not unvarnished.

How long ago was it created?   The more often a page is updated, the better you can feel about the data it holds. Of course, a page listing the census for a certain county in 1850 needn't be updated every week, but a pedigree put online should be updated as the author finds more data.

Where does the information come from?   If the page in question doesn't give any sources, you'll want to contact the page author to acquire the necessary information. If sources *do* exist, of course, you must decide if you can trust them, for many a genealogical error has been printed in books, magazines, and online.

In what form is the information?   A simple GEDCOM published as a Web page can be useful for the beginner but, ideally, one wants an index to any genealogical resource, regardless of form. If a site has no search function, no table of contents, or not even a *document map* (a graphic leading you to different parts of the site), this is much less useful than it could be.

How well does the author use and define genealogical terms?
Does the author clearly know the difference between a yeoman farmer and a yeoman sailor? Does the author seem to be knowledgeable about genealogy? Another problem with online pages is whether the page author understands the problems of dates, both badly recorded dates and the 1752 calendar change. Certain sites can help you with calendar problems.

Does the information make sense compared to what you already know?   If you have documentary evidence that contradicts what you see on a Web page, treat it as you would a mistake in a printed genealogy or magazine: Tell the author about your data and see whether the two versions can be reconciled. If you have documentary evidence that contradicts what you see on a Web page, treat it as you would a mistake in a printed genealogy or magazine: tell the author about your data and see whether the two versions can be reconciled. And, this sort of exchange, after all, is what online genealogy is all about!

For example, many online genealogies have a mistake about one of my ancestors because people didn't stop to analyze the data and made erroneous assumptions.

In Figure 1-4, you can see a transcription of the 1850 Census of Lake County, Indiana. The column labeled HN is household numbered in order of visit; the column labeled FN is for families numbered in order of visitation. You can see Abraham (age 58) and Diadama (age 56, her name is misspelled on the census form) Spencer have children Stephen through Elisabeth, and underneath are Amanda, age 27, and then three children under the age of 5.

Some assume Amanda and the following children are also offspring of Abraham and Diadama but, if you look at the ages and how the families are listed—with Amanda and the younger children under the youngest of Abraham and Diadama's children—you see this doesn't make sense. If you were to look at the mortality schedule for the county for that year, you see Orsemus Spencer, Amanda's husband and

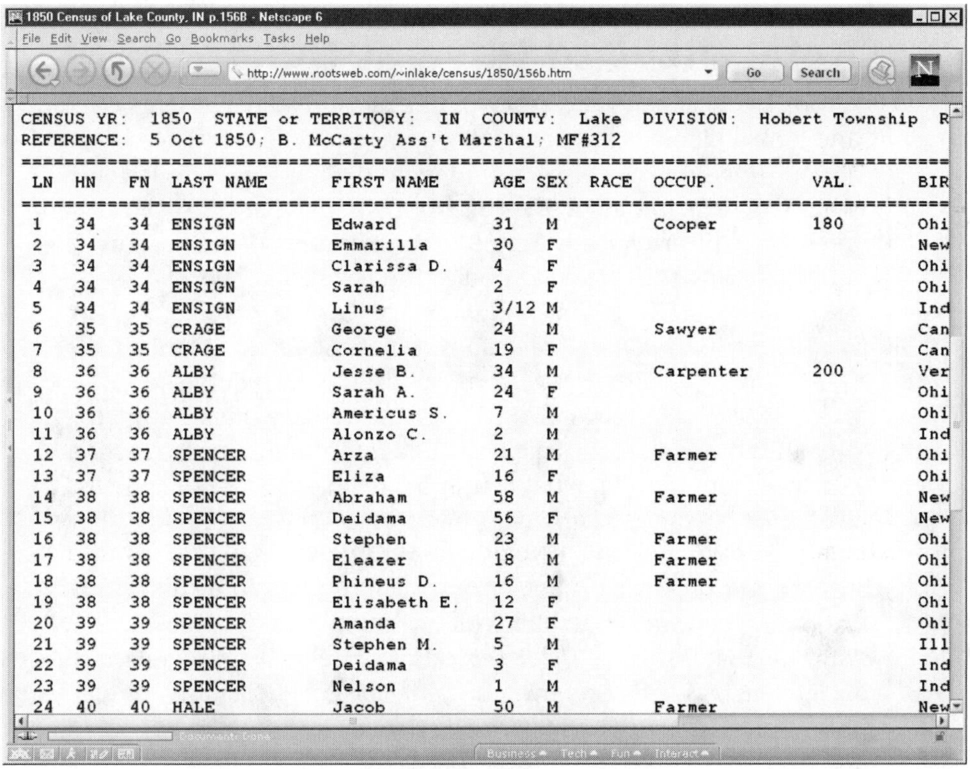

CENSUS YR: 1850 STATE or TERRITORY: IN COUNTY: Lake DIVISION: Hobert Township R
REFERENCE: 5 Oct 1850; B. McCarty Ass't Marshal; MF#312

LN	HN	FN	LAST NAME	FIRST NAME	AGE	SEX	RACE	OCCUP.	VAL.	BIR
1	34	34	ENSIGN	Edward	31	M		Cooper	180	Ohi
2	34	34	ENSIGN	Emmarilla	30	F				New
3	34	34	ENSIGN	Clarissa D.	4	F				Ohi
4	34	34	ENSIGN	Sarah	2	F				Ohi
5	34	34	ENSIGN	Linus	3/12	M				Ind
6	35	35	CRAGE	George	24	M		Sawyer		Can
7	35	35	CRAGE	Cornelia	19	F				Can
8	36	36	ALBY	Jesse B.	34	M		Carpenter	200	Ver
9	36	36	ALBY	Sarah A.	24	F				Ohi
10	36	36	ALBY	Americus S.	7	M				Ohi
11	36	36	ALBY	Alonzo C.	2	M				Ind
12	37	37	SPENCER	Arza	21	M		Farmer		Ohi
13	37	37	SPENCER	Eliza	16	F				Ohi
14	38	38	SPENCER	Abraham	58	M		Farmer		New
15	38	38	SPENCER	Deidama	56	F				New
16	38	38	SPENCER	Stephen	23	M		Farmer		Ohi
17	38	38	SPENCER	Eleazer	18	M		Farmer		Ohi
18	38	38	SPENCER	Phineus D.	16	M		Farmer		Ohi
19	38	38	SPENCER	Elisabeth E.	12	F				Ohi
20	39	39	SPENCER	Amanda	27	F				Ohi
21	39	39	SPENCER	Stephen M.	5	M				Ill
22	39	39	SPENCER	Deidama	3	F				Ind
23	39	39	SPENCER	Nelson	1	M				Ind
24	40	40	HALE	Jacob	50	M		Farmer		New

FIGURE 1-4. *You must analyze what you find before you make conclusions.*

Abraham's son, died in February before the census taker arrived in October. Amanda and her children moved in with her in-laws after her husband's death. They are part of the household, but they aren't Abraham Spencer's children.

With this in mind, becoming familiar with the National Genealogical Society's Standards for Sharing Information with Others, as shown in Appendix A, would help. Judge what you find on the Internet by these standards. Hold yourself to them as you exchange information and help keep the data on the Internet as accurate as possible.

After you have these standards firmly in mind, a good system to help you track what you know, how you know it, and what you don't know, and the surnames you need, is simply a matter of searching for the facts regarding each individual as you go along.

References to Have at Hand

As you begin to send and receive messages, read documents online, and look at library card catalogs, you need some reference books at your fingertips to help you understand what you've found and what you're searching for. Aside from a good atlas and, perhaps, a few state or province gazetteers (a geographic dictionary or index), having the following books at hand can save you a lot of time in your pursuit of family history:

The Handybook for Genealogists: United States of America, 9th Edition, by George B. Everton (Editor) (Everton Publishers, ISBN: 1890895032). DearMYRTLE says she uses this reference about 20 times a week. This book has information such as when counties were formed, what court had jurisdiction where and when, listings of genealogical archives, libraries, societies and publications, dates for each available census index, and more.

The Source : A Guidebook of American Genealogy, by Loretto D. Szucs and Sandra H. Luebking (Editors) (MyFamily.com, Inc., ISBN: 0916489671), or *The Researcher's Guide to American Genealogy, 3rd Edition,* by Val D. Greenwood (Genealogical Publishing Company, ISBN: 0806316217). These are comprehensive, how-to genealogy books. Greenwood's is a little more accessible to the amateur; Luebking's is aimed at the professional, certified genealogist.

Cite Your Sources: A Manual for Documenting Family Histories and Genealogical Records, by Richard S. Lackey (Editor), (University Press of Mississippi, ISBN: 0878052860) or *Evidence!: Citation & Analysis for the Family Historian*, by Elizabeth Shown Mills, (Genealogical Publishing Company, ISBN: 0806315431). These books can help you document what you found, where you found it, and why you believe it. The two books approach the subject differently: the first is more amateur-friendly, the second is more professional in approach.

Scams

In the twenty-first century, genealogy is an industry. Entire companies are centered on family history research and resources. Not surprisingly, you can find people willing to take your money and give you little or nothing in return in genealogy, just as in any industry. Many of them started long before online genealogy became popular and they simply followed when genealogists went online. Halberts of Ohio is one notorious example. Dick Eastman covered this in the March 2001 edition of his online newsletter (see Chapter 7) and it's worth looking up at www.ancestry.com/library/view/columns/eastman/3538.asp.

Books with titles such as The World Book of [YOUR SURNAME] and Three Centuries of [YOUR SURNAME], sold via junk mail flyers as well as online, often turn out to be nothing you couldn't find in a telephone book. You have to read such pitches carefully and, before you send any money, ask on the mail lists, chat rooms, and Usenet groups whether anyone has had experience with this company. Also, go online and check the company's name and sales pitch against these sites, which list common genealogy scams:

♦ **Black Sheep** (blacksheep.rootsweb.org/halberts.htm)
   This page describes the Halberts' scam and imitators.

♦ **Cyndi's List** (www.cyndislist.com/myths.htm)   Cyndi Howells keeps on top of myths, lies, and scams in genealogy on this page.

♦ **Ancestor Detective Watchdog** (www.ancestordetective.com/watchdog.htm)   Liz Kelley Kerstens, CGRS, CGL investigates reports of genealogy Web sites with questionable pitches and posts the results to this page.

Wrapping Up

♦ To begin your genealogy project, start with yourself and your immediate family, documenting what you know.

♦ Look for records for the next generation back, by writing for vital records, looking for online records, posting queries, and researching in libraries and courthouses.

♦ Gather the information with documentation on where, when, and how you found it.

♦ Organize what you have and look for what's needed next.

♦ Repeat the cycle.

♦ Beware of scams!

Chapter 2

Hardware and Software

Online genealogy is only different from the old-fashioned kind in the type of tools you use. Instead of using a photocopier, you make copies on your printer. Instead of sending queries in an envelope, you send them by e-mail. Instead of reading an article in a magazine, you read it in a browser. And, instead of going to the library in person, you might visit it by computer connection!

Please understand, I don't mean to imply you won't ever do things the old-fashioned way again. Of course you will! But you'll use these online techniques often, sometimes even before you try to do research the traditional way. These are new tools for age-old genealogical tasks.

You'll need to learn the ins and outs of hardware, software, and techniques for online information exchange to get the most out of the experience. This chapter covers hardware considerations and software you might want to use, as well as online techniques and tips you should know.

Getting Set Up

In this chapter, you will learn what you need to get connected to the Internet. To use the Internet, you need a way to connect your computer to the wires. You can do this through a modem (which now comes automatically with every new computer) or through a digital data service such as an ISDN or a digital subscriber line (DSL), which requires different equipment. In my experience, most people start out with a modem. Digital connections, which are covered in the next section, are coming on fast, but most people begin with a good old dial-up connection.

Note

Telephone lines have little electrical resistance. You should always disconnect your modem from the phone line and your computer from an electrical outlet during a thunderstorm. If you don't, your modem, computer, and printer could be damaged by a lightning strike. The added measure of installing a surge protector on your phone and electrical lines wouldn't hurt either.

Modems

A *modem* is a gadget that converts the data of your computer system into sounds, which are then sent via a phone line (or a cable physically connecting two computers) to another computer. That's *modulation*. The other computer, with its modem, translates these sounds back into computer-readable signals. That's *demodulation*. The modulator/demodulator, or modem, makes it possible for computers to "talk to each other."

Note

A modem, incidentally, changes the data from digital to analog and back to digital. If you have a digital connection, this isn't necessary, but you still have to get the data from your computer into the wire. Therefore, we have the seeming oxymoron, a digital modem, more often called a cable modem, DSL modem, or ISDN modem.

Most modems that come with a computer are capable of receiving information at up to 56,000 bits of data per second (56 Kbps) and transmitting it at up to 36 Kbps. The reason it's faster coming in than going out is the wiring in your house ends and begins with analog transmission. Once it gets to your phone company's equipment, it becomes all digital.

A modem compresses the data according to a protocol. The protocol used must be the same for both the devices sending and receiving the data. When such protocols are grouped together and approved by the International Telecommunications Union, they become a *standard*. When you buy a modem, be sure it meets the V.92 ITU standard. Although this is the latest technology, it includes past technologies within it. So a V.92 modem can talk to other V.92 modems, as well as to older modems that don't have the standard yet.

Note

A protocol is a standard set of formats and procedures for the exchange of information between systems. Many modem protocols have existed in the past, with the latest being V.92.

Your new computer usually comes with an *internal modem*—that is, it fits into a slot inside your computer. Some people prefer *external modems,* which means the modem is housed in a case outside your computer, sits on your desk, and has lights on the front to show you the status of various functions. External modems have their own power supply along with the case, so they tend to be slightly more expensive than internal modems. An external modem also requires a high-quality cable to connect it to the communications port on your computer. Be sure to ask if such a cable is included when you purchase an external modem. If not, make sure you buy one. Other important features to consider when selecting a modem include the following:

- **Fax capabilities, fax speed, and fax software** Being able to send and receive faxes can be a convenience if the software is user-friendly. Many modems have this built-in and include software to run it. Also, Windows 95 and Windows 98 can be installed with Windows Fax functions. Unless you also have a scanner, you won't be able to fax anything you didn't create on your computer. But, even without a scanner, you can use your fax modem as a printer and send anything you create on your computer as a fax. This can be a real convenience.

- **Flash Upgrade Modem technology** Since their emergence 15 years ago, modems have been constantly changing and evolving. Customers, however, soon got tired of being told every 18 months that their modems were obsolete, with the only solution being to shell out another $200 for a new one. As a result, the flash upgrade was developed. This is a special program that rewrites the chip in the modem called read-only memory (ROM). The ROM holds permanent information for the modem, such as the V.92 standard. Someday that standard will be replaced by a newer one and, if your modem has flash upgrade capability, you can upgrade without getting a new modem. This will definitely be much more expedient!

- **Bells and whistles** Extras such as software or hardware that allow two computers to use one modem or that enable two computers to connect to share data.

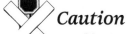

Caution

> *Disable your call-waiting service before connecting to your ISP.*
> *That way, if you're online and a call comes in, you won't be*
> *disconnected. With many phone systems, you enter *70 and a comma*
> *for a short pause in your dialup routine before the number your*
> *software dials for Internet access. You can enter that in your dial-up*
> *connection settings.*

High-Speed Connections

The modem isn't the only way to connect to Internet services and it
isn't the fastest way either. The alternatives, ISDN, DSL, and cable
modems are more expensive, but so much faster that many think
they're worth it.

Cable Modems

At the beginning of 2001, I signed up for a cable modem service, and
cancelled the second phone line we had installed for dial-up Internet
service. Because of the sign-up special (first month free, the cable
modem for one-third the usual cost), the yearly expense compared to
the old way turned out to be a wash, but the service was, to my
amazement, exponentially better. I hadn't expected to become so
quickly addicted to high-speed downloads, an always-on connection,
and media that truly streams instead of sputtering.

A cable modem setup isn't that different from a dial-up modem
setup. The one I have is connected to my computer through a network
card. Other models connect through a USB port and still others are
internal—no connection required. The software for TCP/IP through
the cable modem was included in the package and it took less than
30 minutes to install. The service has been as reliable as the dial-up ISP
I'd been using. Some services include setup and installation in the price,
so you needn't even bother with that.

I'd heard that as more and more people in my neighborhood signed
up for the same cable ISP, my service would get slower. That hasn't
happened yet.

> ### Caution
>
> *With all digital connections, two things are true: first, they offer continuous connection to the Internet. Second, because of this continuous connection, you are vulnerable to certain attacks on your system. Because of the second fact, you must have virus protection software, and you should have firewall software and/or hardware.*

ISDN

Integrated Services Digital Network (ISDN) is a kind of connection that has three channels (A, B, and Data) to carry your signals. Phone companies have been promising for years that ISDN would replace our old (and reliable) analog phone lines. With an ISDN line hooked up to your PC, phone, fax, and what-have-you, you can send and receive nearly any kind of data—voice, documents, graphics, sound, even the full-motion video necessary for movies or teleconferencing—over the line at speeds up to 64,000 bits per second (bps).

Another selling point is versatility. With the right equipment and software on your end, a single ISDN line can support two phone numbers. In effect, you could get a video phone call from Grandma on one line, while transmitting a report to your company on the other. ISDN also lets your phone be a little smarter because the "ring" sent down an ISDN line could tell your phone who's calling, the type of call (data or speech), the number dialed, and so on. Your intelligent phone could analyze this information and act appropriately. For example, your phone could be programmed to answer calls from certain numbers only or to answer specific calls on specific lines, such as all fax calls on line two.

The phone companies currently marketing ISDN to their customers would like you to believe that faster is better and that that's the only issue to consider. Unfortunately, ISDN isn't cheap, although prices are falling each month. Even though you'd treat an ISDN line like your old analog phone line—being billed for long-distance charges, call waiting features, and so on—it comes with a passel of complications.

Although an ISDN line costs as little as $20 a month in California, it's considerably more expensive on the East coast. Moreover, installation runs about $200. An ISDN line would eliminate the need for a modem—after all, a MODulator-DEModulator is designed to turn digital data into analog and back again, and ISDN is all-digital. Yet hooking up your PC to an ISDN line requires a special adapter that can cost up to $1,000 or more, depending on the application. Moreover, using your existing fax machine, telephone, and so on requires buying bridging devices and still more software. The alternative is to buy all new, ISDN-smart equipment. 3COM, Adtran, and many other companies are starting to offer consumer-priced equipment like this. So, if you shop hard enough, you might find something in your price range.

Many communities that have adopted ISDN are often isolated digital islands in an analog sea. Still, the web of ISDN communities is growing, so sending and receiving data at blinding speeds from point A to point B across the country might be possible fairly soon.

Criticizing ISDN is easy—after all, adopting it involves more than a few leaps of faith. Many companies you'd expect to be taking the ISDN leap—such as commercial online services—are moving slowly to implement it. You're lucky if you can find an Internet service provider (ISP) who has an ISDN link. Nevertheless, ISDN may be coming to a town near you.

xDSL

Then there's xDSL, with the x being a letter that designates a type. Types include asymmetric, rate adaptive, very high, single line, and all sorts of other flavors. Some people will advise you to dump your modem. Forget ISDN. Leave the cable attached to your TV. If you believe the boosters, we could all be merrily surfing the Net at megabits per second using some form of DSL.

What all the various DSL versions have in common is they're much faster than modems. They use plain old telephone lines to carry data at up to 51 megabits per second (Mbps) and they're not cheap (yet).

How does DSL do its magic? Naturally, you need DSL modems at both ends of the connection. Using everything from digital signal processing to fancy compression algorithms, DSL shoots data over your phone line at a much different frequency than the frequency used by voices and standard modems. And, while DSL is using your existing phone line to transmit data, it also lets you talk over it because your voice is travelling at different frequencies than the data.

As you might suspect, getting on the DSL track requires new hardware and services from your local phone company. Although you needn't order a new physical line, you do have to order DSL service from your local Bell (assuming it offers DSL; many don't). You also need to buy a DSL modem and, in some cases, a *splitter,* which lets the phone line carry both DSL data transmissions and your voice. For

Internet access, you need to order a DSL account from your local ISP. (America Online, for example, offers DSL access.)

But don't rush out and sign up just yet. For starters, make sure your phone company offers DSL. Second, make sure your ISP offers matching service. (I suspect most will go the ADSL light route.) Third, make sure the DSL modem you buy is appropriate to the service you're getting: Different flavors of DSL require different modems.

Don't forget that DSL speeds can vary wildly due to local conditions. That 52 Mbps line might only deliver 13 Mbps. Remember, too, that various standards have yet to be ironed out. Most versions of DSL are incompatible with each other. Also, no doubt bugs will be in the DSL hardware and in Windows' attempts to work with DSL. Besides, it won't be cheap.

Note

To learn more about DSL, check out the ADSL Forum at www.adsl.com and TeleChoice at www.telechoice.com.

Other Choices

Hand-held Internet access devices and cell phones with e-mail access are popping up all over. The latter can offer you convenience when traveling, but cost will be a big factor.

Palmtop Computers

The palm-top computer (especially those models with Internet connections) has become popular with genealogists. In addition to its usefulness in note-taking, retrieving e-mail, and, if it has the proper port, uploading and downloading information to desktop or laptop computers, some surprisingly functional software for these devices is available.

Some examples are:

♦ The PAF 5.1 from FamilySearch.org has Palm capability, which is handy for storing work until you can upload it to your computer.

♦ The GEDStar (www.gedpalm.com) lets you browse a GEDCOM (see the Glossary) and could be useful for trips to the library. See Figure 2-1 for some screen shots. The program even has its own discussion list (www.rootsweb.com/ ~ jfuller/ gen_mail_ software.html#GenPalm).

- MyRoots (www.tapperware.com/MyRoots) is a genealogical database that can be accessed using a Palm Pilot.

- Relations 2.3 (members.home.net/msdsoft/relations2.html) is a database configured for Newton palm devices.

- A list of Palm programs is maintained on Cyndi's List (www.cyndislist.com/software.htm#Palm).

Cell Phones

Connection to the Internet through a cell phone is slow, expensive, and hard on the eyes. This isn't something I recommend to genealogists for an everyday Internet connection. Still, if you simply must keep up with a mail list while away from your computer, this is an option.

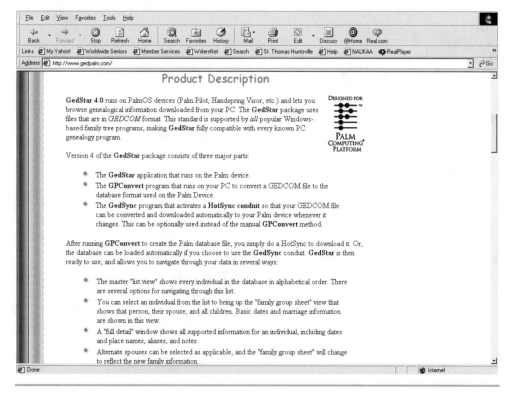

FIGURE 2-1. *GEDStar is just one genealogy program available for personal digital assistants.*

Choosing an ISP

Just as you do when you choose a mate, you should know what you want before you start looking for an ISP. Your choice isn't final, of course—but you don't want to hopscotch from one e-mail address to another, either. So, go into this knowing that Internet providers are as different as dog breeds. All of them will get you on to the Net, but access speeds, services, software, and other goodies vary. Before you put down any cash, ask yourself these basic questions:

- What services do I need?

- How often do I need them?

- How fast do I need them?

- How many hassles am I willing to put up with to save money?

- How much am I willing to pay?

Remember, trade-offs exist no matter what provider you finally choose. For example, you might find a price break exists for slower and less direct connections, or a premium is necessary to dial in to your account from various places in the country. In addition, you might find companies consider support extremely expensive to provide, so if you sign up with a full-service provider, it can cost a bit more.

Note ────────────────────────

You can sign up for a Web-based e-mail, such as Yahoo!, Bigfoot, and others that can send your e-mail to another address.

You might save money by choosing only what you need. In the end, though, you might find you need the whole shebang. While some users are happy with just electronic mail, to uncover all the genealogical treasures out there, you'll need considerably more features, such as a Web browser to fetch sound, pictures, and online animation. Consequently, you'll also need a provider that offers high-speed Internet connections.

When it comes to services, insist on the whole range: e-mail, telnet, Usenet news groups, FTP, gopher, and more—in short, everything the Internet has to offer. Even if the ISP service is basic, it should at least come with a technical support service.

Baby Steps

As mentioned earlier, the commercial online services offer Internet access as well as their proprietary content, which always includes at least one genealogy discussion group. For your first online forays, these are probably your best bet. Once online with MSN, CompuServe, America Online, or a similar service, you can quickly learn the ropes and familiarize yourself with what's out there, after which, you might decide you want an ISP instead. To find a local ISP, look in your Yellow Pages. Or, use AOL, CompuServe, or Prodigy to find one of several sites that let you search for an ISP by area, cost, or other factors. The following are two such sites:

- ◆ www.isps.com: From a publisher called CMP Net. Lets you search for an ISP by area code, name, price, and national and toll-free services.

- ◆ www.thelist.com: From Meckler Media. This is a buyer's guide to ISPs.

Go Shopping

Make a list of two or three ISPs, contact them, and ask these questions:

- ◆ Does the ISP offer 56 Kbps and faster access? The answer should be Yes. The faster the better, because the amount of genealogical information out there is immense.

- ◆ If you decide digital access is for you, ask the ISP if such access is available for your neighborhood. If so, what is the cost?

- ◆ For dial-up accounts, will you get busy signals if you call during prime time in the evening? In other words, how many high-speed lines does the provider have? How many customers log in on average during prime time? (And test them on their answer: dial them up just after supper!) Their response should be this: you can get on any time you want. The ISP should have enough lines or enough ISDN capability to handle their current customer base.

- Does the ISP offer anything else besides Internet access, such as BBS echoes and file collections? The answer should be Yes. This is part of support.

- Can a graphical third-party front-end like Netscape access the ISP's system? Does it provide this software? Both answers should be Yes. If the first answer is No, then you have to deal with a text-oriented UNIX system and the provider should supply a written manual. If no manual or menu system exists, this should be a really cheap service.

- Which message readers can you use with Usenet newsgroups? The answer should be a client that runs on your machine, which they can provide you. If the answer is pine, rn, or nn, beware! These are arcane UNIX newsreaders, text-based and a real pain to use. Windows and Mac-based user-friendly readers like Free Agent or Outlook Express are better. New browsers such as Microsoft Internet Explorer (IE) and Netscape Navigator include newsreaders as part of the program.

- What's the capacity of private e-mail boxes? Here, the answer should be at least 100K of space. Bigger is better. If you subscribe to even a few genealogical mail lists and Newsgroups, your mailbox could be stuffed quickly. Even worse, if your mailbox is limited to 100 messages, you might miss important mail.

- Will your connection be Serial Line Internet Protocol (SLIP) or Point-to-Point Protocol (PPP)? PPP is better: it's newer, faster, and more reliable than SLIP, but if SLIP is all you can get, take it.

- Does the ISP provide access to all Usenet newsgroups or only to a selection? The answer should be All. This is extremely important when it comes to some of the more arcane genealogical ones.

- When does the ISP schedule downtime for maintenance? How heavily loaded is the system? Good luck getting straight answers to either question, but the ISP should at least reassure you that downtimes are, somehow, announced in advance. For the real scoop, nose around Internet discussion areas and ask users of the service for the low-down.

- Does the ISP have Points of Presence (POPs) across the country, so if you're on the road, you can still reach them with a local (or toll-free) call? You hope the answer is Yes, but reality could dictate you get Internet accounts from two different providers—one for home and one for the road, unless you use a national provider such as Mindspring, AOL, or CompuServe.

♦ How does the ISPcharge? A flat monthly fee for unlimited connect time is the ideal answer. The second best answer is a flat fee with a generous allotment of online time and a low hourly fee ($1 to $3) for use beyond that allotment. Beware of hourly based connect charges, which can add up in a hurry.

Really smart ISPs offer a complete manual, training classes, and online news featuring phone number changes, service enhancements, and other information of interest to users. With prices ranging from $10 a month for telnet access to $260 a month for an always-open direct line, something is out there for everyone. The trick is knowing what you want, asking tough questions of prospective ISPs, and finding a company that can give you what you need. Don't forget to compare the answers to these questions with the national ISPs and to check up on how prices have changed every few months.

Software

Once you have your hardware in place and you know how you're going to connect, you need to look at your software. As noted before, many ISPs include software as part of the package. AOL, CompuServe, Prodigy, Mindspring, Netcom, and most other national ISPs have front-end software that includes the communications software, browser, FTP, e-mail, and other programs you need.

The software you use to access the web is often called *clients*. These programs send signals to other computers, called *servers,* instructing them to display files and information to you or to run programs for you. The resulting display might be e-mail, a Web page, or a GEDCOM you want to download. The program the clients run might be a search engine or a chat site.

What Makes the Web Tick

Your communications software is what makes a modem work. Think of it as the inner workings of a watch. The watch displays the time, which to you is the whole point of the thing but, to a watchmaker, the workings determine the value of the watch. So it is with the software: For the most part, you just want the clients to contact the servers and tell you what you want to know. Nevertheless, you should also know a little bit about how these things tick.

Transmission Control Protocol/Internet Protocol (TCP/IP) is the chief communications format for the Internet, proving the standard way of connecting one computer to another. An example of using TCP/IP in Windows 98 is shown in Figure 2-2.

In many cases, you needn't worry about finding communications software for your modem; it will find you. Most of the commercial services have front-end software to connect to their service. America Online, CompuServe Information Service, Prodigy Internet, and other

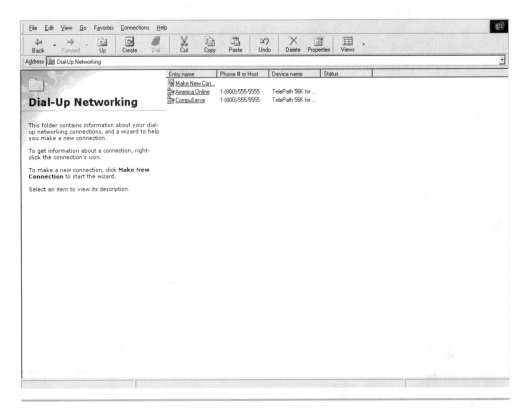

FIGURE 2-2. *Dial-Up Networking in Windows 98 is handled through your TCP/IP stack.*

ISPs (and many cable modem companies) and probably the other fast-access companies usually supply you with the software you need.

The best ISPs include a package of software, manuals, and handholding to get you started.

FTP

File Transfer Protocol (FTP) is how files are sent and received from many places on the Internet. When receiving a file, such as a photograph or a program, your browser handles that fine. No worries. However, if you want to upload (send) a file, you should use an FTP program. Some browsers can handle sending, but an FTP program does it faster and easier. Most browsers include FTP in their program code.

You can also use a separate program. Programs for FTP abound on the Internet. Some of the more popular ones include CuteFTP, ActifFTP, and LeechFTP. My favorite has always been WS_FTP. You can try the limited edition free if it's for home, educational, or nonprofit use.

E-mail

Reading mail is the biggest part of online life. Some of the best information, and even friendships, come through e-mail. If you're on any ISP, a mail reader makes life much easier. The mail readers in browsers tend to have fewer features than the stand-alone mail clients.

General Techniques

To get the most out of electronic mail, or e-mail, you need to get a few techniques under your belt.

Filters   A *filter* is an action you want the mail program to take when a message matches certain conditions. You can have an e-mail program reply to, copy, move, or destroy a message based on such things as the sender, the subject line, or words found in the text. You can have the e-mail program do all that before you read your mail or even before the e-mail gets downloaded from the ISPs mail server.

If you've never dealt with e-mail, this might seem like a lot of bells and whistles but, believe me, when you start getting involved in active mail lists (see Chapter 7), you'll want to sort your mail by geography, surname, and time period, at least!

Furthermore, there'll be some people you don't want to hear from. You can have your mail filters set up to delete mail from those people, which brings up the next important topic: spam protection.

Spam Protection   Long ago (okay, less than ten years ago) only academics and researchers used the Internet and they liked it that way. They didn't want the general public and, most of all, general businesses to get to play on the Web. Once the Internet was open to the public, they warned, the demons of advertising would hound us. Ads would flood our mailboxes, clog the bandwidth with their shilling and hawking, and make the Internet much less useful and fun. Well, we opened Pandora's box anyway and the result was junk e-mail. The old Netheads were right after all, and the spammers are now on us.

Spammers is the Net slang term for people who send unsolicited e-mail to advertise. Spammers get their name from an old Monty Python skit where people in a restaurant are prevented from having a normal conversation because some folks at the next table insist on loudly praising Spam. The uninvited e-mail advertisements you receive are often called spam because, as in the skit, they rudely interrupt you during more enjoyable activities. The Hormel folks, understandably, don't like the term and prefer the more accurate and official unsolicited bulk e-mail (UBE) to describe this annoyance.

UBE could constitute endless messages regarding get-rich-quick ideas, pyramid schemes, vitamins, you name it. Sometimes the pitch is disguised as a newsletter and might include some bogus return address. But, whatever the guise, the purpose is the same: they are using your paid online account for their own advertising.

Why You Get Spam   Any time you post a message to a newsgroup, use a public chat room on America Online, CompuServe, or the Internet, or supply an online service with your profile, the UBE guys are there collecting your e-mail address and any other information they can find. Then they sort the addresses and sell them, causing you to get junk e-mail.

Naturally, they know not everyone is going to be pleased to hear from them, so they disguise themselves with bogus From: and Reply to: lines. You can try to reply and remove or unsubscribe yourself from their lists, but this seldom works. The return addresses either don't exist or aren't designed to receive mail. To reach the culprits and get off their lists, you must do some detective work.

What to Do About Spamming   Frankly, I'm intensely opposed to this noxious form of telemarketing (can you tell?). The first step is for everyone who uses the Internet to write to Congress and have this practice stopped. If Washington can pass a law controlling junk faxes, why can't it do the same for junk e-mail?

Second, learn to protect yourself. One extreme measure would be never to use chat, post to Usenet, use a forum on AOL or CompuServe or a bulletin board on Prodigy, or post your member profile online. But then, online life would be pretty dull, wouldn't it?

A less-harsh solution is to create two e-mail accounts: one public and one private. You use the public one for Usenet, chat, anonymous FTP, and so on. The other you keep hidden like an unlisted phone number, only giving it out to people you truly want to hear from. Then, all you have to do is check your private e-mail box whenever you feel like it and ask your ISP to delete any mail that comes to the public one. (It's more like doing it yourself—highlighting each letter and pressing DELETE before you read it.)

If you use an e-mail program like Eudora or Pegasus, you can filter out all the junk. Both programs can, based on a message's address, subject line, or body text, drop e-mail into specific folders. Whenever I get junk e-mail, I copy the address, header, and any catch phrase like "money-making opportunity" to a filter. The next time I get a message from the spammer, it's dumped into my Trash folder and deleted. (In Eudora, for example, select Tools | Filters, enter the e-mail address, check the Transfer To box and select Trash.) And what about America Online and CompuServe users? AOL can now automatically intercept incoming e-mail from known UBE senders, thanks to a recent court decision. The controls are set by default. To turn them off, use the

---

The Legislative Front

UBE is sent by folks who claim it's their First Amendment right to use a service you paid for to advertise their stuff to you. Congress is currently considering that claim and whether they can protect us from these twerps. You can keep abreast of it at the Center For Democracy and Technology's "Junk E-mail" pages, URL: www.junkemail.org/bills. See Figure 2-3 for the home page.

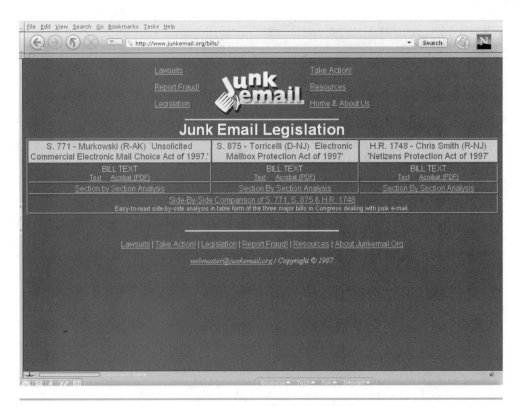

FIGURE 2-3.   *Junk E-mail Legislation is a site where you can get involved in the fight against UBE.*

keyword: PREFERRED MAIL. Of course, AOL's action keeps out only so much UBE. If you get junk e-mail from an AOL account, forward it to TOSSPAM. AOL's staff then tells that person to stop sending you e-mail. You can also control what you get by entering the keyword: MAIL CONTROLS. Click the icon that says Set Up Mail Controls and choose the screen name, clicking Edit.

The Mail Controls window gives you several options:

Allow all e-mail, Allow e-mail only from AOL members, and Block all e-mail are the first three choices. I don't use these because the first is too open, and the second and third are too restrictive. Plus, many UBE senders use AOL screen names.

Allow e-mail from all AOL members, and only from the listed Internet domains and addresses. This is the one I use because I need to receive e-mail from AOL's ever-changing public relations staff. Allow e-mail from the listed AOL members, Internet domains and addresses is the best choice for most people. The drawbacks are you're limited to 100 such names and this filters out e-mail based on the From: field (not the subject or the text of the message). Still, I find this workable. You can insert a specific address like Libbic@prodigy.net in the list. In addition, if you know a certain domain (such as RootsWeb.com or Ancestry.com) will only send you mail you want, you can simply put the part of the address after the @ and any mail from that ISP will get through. You can even put in a top-level domain, for example, any address that ends in .gov or .edu is allowed on my list. I figure if I receive any UBE from a government or educational institution, I can quickly report it and have it taken care of!

The last choice, Block e-mail from the listed AOL members, Internet domains, and addresses is almost useless because of the 100-name limit on the list. Considering hundreds of thousands of UBE senders are out there, this would be like trying to plug a fire hydrant with a golf tee. If you want to block a specific person who is annoying or repeatedly pesters you, you might use this option, as well as report that person to AOL.

CompuServe doesn't offer as many options for blocking UBE, but it's always been against the rules for CIS members to send advertising to other CIS members. If you do, CIS can terminate your account. As for non-CIS mail, you can set your e-mail preference never to receive or send any Internet mail, but that's hardly a solution.

Desperate Measures   Is junk e-mail still deluging you? You can try to track down the culprits, even though they try to disguise their true whereabouts. Don't look at the From or even the Reply To lines. Look at the lines that say Comments: Authenticated sender is: or Received. These lines will tell you the route of the message from your mailbox back to its origin. Once you have a domain name (such as yxt2@srdinc.com), you at least know on which ISP the message originated. (See the list that follows for examples.)

◆   Return-Path: < xxxxxxxo@freewebemail.com >

◆   Received: from mh2-sfba.mail.home.com ([24.0.95.133])

◆   by femail2.sdc1.sfba.home.com

◆   (InterMail vM.4.01.03.20 201-229-121-120-20010223) with ESMTP

- id <20010607013005.PSBU4140.femail2.sdc1.sfba.home.com@ mh2-sfba.mail.home.com>

- for <xxxxxx@mail.hntsvlle1.al.home.com>;

- Received: from mx2-sfba.mail.home.com (mx2-sfba.mail.home.com [24.0.95.137])

- by mh2-sfba.mail.home.com (8.9.3/8.9.0) with ESMTP id SAA05205

- Received: from bigfoot.com (litemail.bigfoot.com [208.156.39.208])

- by mx2-sfba.mail.home.com (8.11.1/8.11.1) with SMTP id f571U3W03920

- Received: from ntgateway.lamconstruct.com.hk ([202.60.244.109])

- by BFLITEMAIL4.bigfoot.com (LiteMail v3.01(BFLITEMAIL4)) with SMTP id 06Jun2001_BFLITEMAIL4_7352_107559186;

- Wed, 06 Jun 2001 21:35:05 -0400 EST

- Received: from yahoo.com (63.49.236.197) by ntgateway.lamconstruct.com.hk (Worldmail 1.3.167); 7 Jun 2001 01:32:23 -0000

- Message-Id: <8una7sl.2otk6nyla36fo@yahoo.com>

- X-Mailer: Microsoft Internet E-mail/MAPI - 8.0.0.4211

- From: xxxxxxxx@mochamail.com

- Subject: Loopholes Run Rampant! - Investigate via the Internet!

- Date: Wed, 06 Jun 2001 16:29:24 -0100

- Content-Type: text/html;

- charset = "iso-8859-1"

- Content-Transfer-Encoding: 8BIT

Send a message to the ISP using the format postmaster@provider.com. Politely explain that you don't want to receive any more messages from the perpetrator. Do this consistently and the UBE sender's privileges might be revoked.

Caution

Don't insult or scold the ISP. It might not know the client is using the account this way. Assume the ISP is on your side when you write.

At the moment, no surefire, legal way exists to shut these scoundrels up as they fill our e-mail boxes, clog the already crowded Internet, and cost us extra toll charges. Although recent court decisions indicate more controls are coming, who knows when they'll come to pass. Instead, be prepared. Use the strategies previously outlined and, as a result, your e-mail box should have less digital clutter.

Many of my friends, though, don't like to expend that much energy. They use filters and their DELETE keys and let it go at that.

Note

Two frequently asked questions (FAQs) on this subject are posted on the Web. The E-mail Abuse FAQ is at members.aol.com/emailfaq/emailfaq.html#5b. The Net-Abuse FAQ is at www.cybernothing.org/faqs/net-abuse-faq.html.

File Attachments and Formats   Judging from the comments of my readers, nothing causes more gnashing of teeth to new Internet users than file attachments. You get a message that looks like gobbledygook or has some filename like foobar.mim, and you don't know what to do with it.

The Internet is so big and powerful, we sometimes lose sight of its limitations. For example, e-mail—the Net's original reason for being— is limited to transmitting the 128 alphanumeric characters (the ones on your keyboard) of the basic ASCII set. Nearly every computer—large and small—uses ASCII, which is why e-mail (and Usenet newsgroups) are limited to these characters.

Yet how does one send the photograph of an ancestor to a newsgroup? The secret has to do with the processes of encoding and decoding. Like Little Orphan Annie's Secret Decoder Ring, *encoding* schemes turn binary files (such as EXE files, graphics, spreadsheets, and formatted documents) into strings of text that, when properly decoded on the other end, resume their original form.

The downside: An encoded file can be 25 to 100 percent larger than the original file.

Many different encoding schemes are used on the Internet. As with FTPs, you must know which scheme your correspondent used so you can properly decode the file you receive. The key schemes and their file extensions follow. (Usually your ISP or mail program does the coding/unencoding for you, so you may never see these in coded form by the time they reach your mailbox.)

♦ UUENCODE (.UUE, .UU) is one such scheme. Its name comes from UNIX to UNIX Encoding, and it's a common, old method. UUencoded files are deciphered with UUDECODE.

♦ XXENCODE (.XXE) is a slightly different version of UUENCODE, created for later versions of UNIX.

♦ BINHEX (.HQX, .HEX) originated on the Mac, but you can now find BINHEX encoders and decoders for the PC.

♦ MIME (.MME, .MM) or the Multipurpose Internet Mail Extensions specify the kind of file being sent. This allows many e-mail and Web browser programs to recognize what's in a certain MIMEd file and to display its contents with the appropriate helper application.

If your ISP or your mail program lets a coded file slip through, how do you translate it? If you're using a fairly decent e-mail program like Outlook, Pegasus, or Eudora, or you're using AOL and you get a MIME or BINHEX file, you usually don't have to do anything—the software's built-in decoders do the job for you. If you get a file that's been coded with another format, though, you need a third-party program to do the dirty work for you. I noted some sources later in this section.

"But wait!" says a reader. "I sometimes get a coded file that has another coded file within in it. In my e-mail program, I see this huge ream of nonsense text. What do I do?" Look closely and you can see instructions in this mess of text: probably the words "copy below this line" and "copy above this line."

Select the text between these lines and paste it into a word processor. Save the file as text only, with the .UUE file extension (because this is a UUENCODED file). Then run a UUDECODE program and the hidden file will emerge.

> *Note* _____
>
> *Sometimes, a large UUENCODED file is split into a number of e-mail messages, usually labeled FILE1.UUE, FILE2.UUE and so on. Carefully cut and paste the contents of these files, from the first message to the last, into a single file. Then follow the steps in the text.*

Which programs decode (and encode) attached files? You can search the shareware sites for the latest offerings. I recommend the following:

♦ UUE.ZIP (shareware.cnet.com/shareware/0-13628-500-1268763.html?tag = st.sw.13628_501_1.lst.titledetail) is free, simple, fast, and small. It doesn't do anything but deal with UUENCODE.

♦ WinZIP (www.winzip.com) costs $29, but handles many kinds of files, including UUENCODE, and also most compression formats. It's worth the money.

Internet Mail Clients

Mail-reading programs (also known as *clients*) are everywhere and some do quite a bit of fancy stuff. To get you started, I recommend you try one of these:

Eudora 5.1   *Qualcomm Eudora 5.1* lets you choose to pay for all its powerful features, use them free (by putting up with some ads), or install an ad-free lite version .You can find the latest edition at www.eudora.com. Eudora works great with the default settings, but you can tweak the program to do many things automatically.

Pegasus   *Pegasus Mail* has all the features of Eudora and more. In fact, because Pegasus Mail has so many more features, it's a little harder to learn at first. Once you get the hang of it, though, Pegasus Mail is wonderful. This is an extremely intuitive, great-looking mail program with integrated address books and mailing lists. The program itself is free, but if you want a printed manual to help you learn all the features, it costs $40.

To download Pegasus mail, go to the Pegasus home page at www.pmail.com.

Microsoft Outlook Express   *Microsoft Outlook Express* not only reads e-mail, but also Usenet (see Chapter 8) and it can keep track of e-mail addresses, just like Pegasus and Eudora. It comes free with Microsoft IE. The filtering capabilities are as good as Eudora's, and the sorting of messages into folders and subfolders is superior. You can color-code as well as file, save, delete, copy, or forward messages with the filters.

The main drawback to using this program is most of the e-mail-based viruses are written to exploit Microsoft's features. If you're going to use Outlook, you have no choice but to use a virus protection program that checks e-mail (and to keep that virus program updated weekly). Indeed, no matter what e-mail program you use, you need to check all attachments for viruses.

With this nifty segue, it's time to discuss virus protection software.

Inoculations

No journey is without risk. Whenever you enter the jungle of cyberspace, that dreaded microorganism, the computer virus, might be lurking about. Not only that, but your activities could attract Trojan horses and worms, too, so keep a sharp eye out.

A *virus* is a program hidden on a disk or within a file that can damage your data or computer in some way. Some viruses simply display a message or a joke, while others can wipe out all the information you saved to the hard drive. Therefore, I strongly recommend you inoculate your computer before using any mode of electronic travel.

One breed of computer virus is the Trojan horse. This is a program that seems to be useful and harmless when it first arrives but, secretly, might be destroying data or breaking down the security on your system. The Trojan horse differs from a virus only because it doesn't propagate itself as a virus does.

A *worm* is a program that causes your computer to freeze or crash as it sucks up all your available resources, like system memory. A worm can make copies of itself and spreads through connected systems.

Programs to detect and remove these exotic virtual creatures are in your local computer store and on various online services. Some are shareware, while others are more costly, but if the program manages to delete a virus before it harms your system, it's worth the price.

The two major virus protection suites are Norton AntiVirus and McAfee AntiVirus, which include one free year of virus updates, available to you once or twice a month. Whatever program you buy, however, be sure to keep it updated.

Even if you have virus protection software, you need to take precautions. Make a backup of everything important to you: data, letters, and so on and resave it no less than once a month. The virus protection software offers to make a recover disk; do so. This can save you much time and trouble later on down the line if your system needs to be restored. Generally, when you download, look for an indication that the files have been checked for viruses. If not, reconsider downloading from that site. If someone mails or hands you a floppy disk with data, always run a virus check on the disk before you do anything else. Once a virus is copied on to your hard disk, removing it can be a major headache. In addition, make sure you run a virus check on your hard drive at least twice a month, just to be certain. This should be part of your regular tune-up and maintenance.

Caution

Unless the subject line indicates the message is about genealogy, don't open a message from someone you don't know.

Virus protection is good, but if you opt for a high-speed, continuous connection such as DSL or cable Internet, you also need a firewall to help protect you from crackers, Trojan horses, and worms. A *firewall* is a piece of software, hardware, or combination of both that forms an electronic boundary preventing unauthorized access to a computer or network. It can also be a computer whose sole purpose is to be a buffer between your main computer and the Internet. A firewall controls what goes out and what comes in, according to how the user has set it up. Example firewall programs are ZoneAlarm by Zone Labs, BlackICE Defender from NetworkICE, or Internet Security 2000 by Symantec Corp. A detailed description of how firewalls work can be found on Shields Up, a Web site devoted to broadband security created by programmer Steve Gibson, head of Gibson Research Corp. (www.grc.com) of Laguna Hills, Calif. Run the tests. You'll be surprised.

Note

A hacker is a person who likes to work with computer codes and security systems. A cracker is a hacker who tries to break into other people's systems.

Publishing on the Internet

Sooner or later you're going to want to share what you've found, perhaps by publishing it on the Internet. To do this, you need a server; most ISPs allot some disk space on their servers for their users. Check with your ISP to see how much you have.

Furthermore, dozens of sites are out there offering up to ten megabytes of space free: AOL's Hometown, Yahoo!, Xoom, Angelfire, and more. Most of these are free, as long as you allow them to display an ad on the visitor's screen.

Finally, genealogy-specific sites exist, such as RootsWeb and MyFamily.com with free space for noncommercial use.

Many genealogy database programs translate your genealogy data into HTML format, so you can publish them on the Web. Furthermore, several Web sites, such as MyFamily.com, will put the information you have into HTML automatically. All you must do is upload the GEDCOM. Finally, you can use an HTML editor to create the layout and design yourself. In short, publishing on the Internet is very doable, as well as enjoyable.

I should warn you, though, that not everyone may be thrilled to be part of your project. Some people get upset at finding their names published online without their written permission. Some genealogists consider anything published, whether it's online or in hard copy, to be false unless the documentation proving it as true is included in the publication. Still others feel sharing their hard work without getting data and/or payment in return is a bad idea. For these and other reasons, you might want to:

1. Publish data only on deceased people.

2. Publish only enough data to encourage people to write you with their own data.

In short, be careful about what you post on the Web and how you post it. The National Genealogical Society recently adopted a set of standards for publishing genealogy on the Internet. With their permission, I included them in Appendix A.

Almost every good genealogy program now includes a way to publish on the Web. Ultimate Family Tree, Family Origins, Family Tree Maker, The Master Genealogist, Generations Family Tree, and Ancestral Quest are only a few of the programs that can turn your genealogical database into HTML. Most of them simply create a standard tree-branching chart with links to the individuals' data. Others may create a set of family group sheets. Many of them let you have "still living" replace the vital statistics for certain people. In many of these programs, the process is as simple as creating a printed report. You simply choose HTML as the format.

Some of the programs, however, don't give you a choice of where you post your data. Family Tree Maker (FTM), for example, publishes your data on its site. Once there, your data becomes part of the FTM database, which is periodically burned on to CD-ROMS and sold in stores. Simply by posting your data on the site, you give them permission to do this. Quite a bit of discussion and debate is ongoing about this privatization of publicly available data. Some say this will be the end of amateur genealogy, while others feel this is a way to preserve data that might be lost to disaster or neglect. Even others say it takes money to store and maintain this data. It's up to you whether you want to post to a site that reuses your data for its own profit.

This is one reason I strongly urge you to visit local genealogy groups that have "show and tell" nights for genealogy software. Try several programs before you buy one. Ask questions about how and where it will publish your work on the Web. Furthermore, some genealogy programs let you record your sources, notes, and anecdotes to go along with your data. This capability to record and cite sources is essential, in my opinion, for any genealogy program. Don't choose one without it.

Notice the programs' metaphors and try to find one that works the way you think. For example, some programs use a scrapbook metaphor where you enter a page per person with details, pictures, even sound clips. Others have an index card metaphor, which feels much like the good old-fashioned way of recording your data. Still others use a family group sheet form. Buy one that uses a format you find easy and comfortable to use.

Then look at the output. Besides HTML, some genealogy programs can output New England Historical and Genealogical Society formats, narratives in a book form, fan charts, even murals with pictures. And, of course, you won't buy any program that doesn't have the capability to export and import GEDCOM files. Be aware, however, that subtle differences exist in how each program handles GEDCOM. Translation from one to another is rarely perfect.

Think about your goals in genealogy and pick a program that can help you meet them.

Turning a GEDCOM into HTML

Some programs are available that take a GEDCOM from any program on the market and turn it into HTML. An inexpensive program ($10) GedPage (www.frontiernet.net/ ~ rjacob/gedpage.htm) turns GEDCOM files into attractive HTML files. You can choose a version for Macintosh or Windows (3.1 and up). The output is formatted as Family Group Sheets, as shown in Figure 2-4.

Note

Because a GEDCOM usually doesn't include sources and citations, this page doesn't conform completely to the NGS guidelines.

Using this program is simplicity itself. First, create a GEDCOM. Then change the files HEADER.HTM and FOOTER.HTM to say what you want, generally your contact information. (You can do this in any text editor. Simply replace the text and leave anything within the < and > brackets alone.) Start GedPage and fill in the blanks for the URL, the e-mail address, and then choose colors if you like. Click Create Page. In a few seconds, a set of pages for the database are created. Then you use an .ftp program to upload the pages to your site.

This program is only one example; others are out there. Check out Cyndi's List for a current list of programs: www.cyndislist.com/software.htm.

Using an HTML Editor

For the real do-it-yourselfer, HTML editors can help you create your own site from the ground up. Most modern HTML editors work just like word processors and, in fact, Word 2000 can save any document file in HTML format, complete with links and graphics. Microsoft IE and Netscape both come with simple, useful HTML editors as part of the package. Microsoft IE can be installed with Front Page Express and Netscape with the Composer module. Both are fairly easy to use. Once you finish, the programs can post the results for you. Simply choose Publish under the File menu.

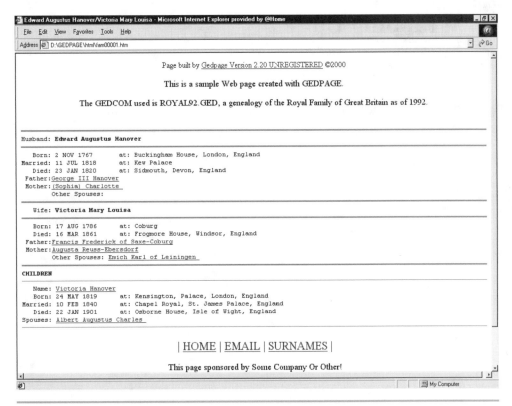

FIGURE 2-4. *GedPage produces a readable, if simple, set of pages from a GEDCOM.*

Using a Web Site to Publish

MyFamily.com (Chapter 17), RootsWeb (Chapter 16), AOL, and other sites give you an opportunity to publish on the Web. You'll learn how in the chapters that cover these sites.

Wrapping Up

To get online, you need the following:

- ◆ A computer (with lots of hard disk space!).
- ◆ A connection device, whether a modem or a digital device.
- ◆ An Internet service provider.
- ◆ The correct software.

Chapter 3

Online Society

You've probably heard the Internet described as an online world. This is an apt description, but the differences between the online world and "the real world" have decreased drastically lately. Still, you'll find a set of norms, often termed "netiquette," that holds sway in the online communities. Indeed, Miss Manners herself has laid down a few laws on proper behavior in cyberspace (see *Wired* magazine's interview with Judith Martin, aka Miss Manners, in the following box), and an entire site on the subject is at www.albion.com/netiquette.

Genealogy communities also have their own special subset of rules, which this chapter discusses.

Manners Matter

by Kevin Kelly

Sit up straight, folks—Miss Manners is here. She has mastered her voicemail, got control of her cell phone, and now she's logged on to the Net.

In real life, Miss Manners's true name is Judith Martin. For years she's written about excruciatingly correct behavior for all those moments when the modem is not on; now she has a few interesting things to say about the wired life. For example, people who don't give a hoot about sending thank-you notes are suddenly bent out of shape when they get an e-mail message typed in ALL CAPS. *Wired* spoke to Miss Manners and asked her, very politely, how etiquette is bringing civility to the online frontier.

Wired: What is it about cyberspace that has rekindled interest in etiquette?

Miss Manners: Freedom without rules doesn't work. And communities do not work unless they are regulated by etiquette. It took about three minutes before some of the brighter people discovered this online. We have just as many ways, if not more, to be obnoxious in cyberspace and fewer ways to regulate them. So, posting etiquette rules and looking for ways to ban people who violate them is the way sensible people are attempting to deal with this.

Wired: Do you find online etiquette rules parallel the rules of etiquette offline?

Miss Manners: Yes. Spamming is the equivalent of boring people or mixing in business. Flaming is the equivalent of being insulting. You may not realize how annoying it is when you ask an obvious question to a group that has been meeting for a while. So etiquette refers you to a FAQ file. I'm delighted people are doing a good job on the Net.

Wired: To sort out the correct behavior when corresponding through technology, you suggest the body is more important than any disembodied communication. Somebody sitting in front of you should take precedence over just a voice—like a phone conversation. And a voice takes precedence over a further disembodied e-mail. The more disembodied the communication is, the less precedence it has. Is that fair?

Miss Manners: Yes. And it is disobeyed flagrantly. The interesting thing is why people think that someone who is not present (a phone ringing) is more important than someone who is. Generally it has taken a person a lot more effort to come to see you than to call you on the telephone.

Wired: Let's see. I need some advice. E-mail has an alarming proclivity to be copied. What are the rules for passing on private e-mail?

Miss Manners: For e-mail, the old postcard rule applies. Nobody else is supposed to read your postcards, but you'd be a fool if you wrote anything private on one.

Wired: Most people are not writing their e-mail that way.

Miss Manners: That's their mistake. We're now seeing e-mail that people thought they had deleted showing up as evidence in court. You can't erase e-mail. As that becomes more commonly realized, people will be a little wiser about what they type.

Wired: You're very much of a stickler for keeping one's business life from intruding upon one's social life. That distinction online is becoming more blurred all the time. There seems to be a deliberate attempt to mix these two up—working at home, for example. Is this the end of civilization as we know it?

> **Miss Manners:** Blurring the two is not conducive to a pleasant life, because it means that the joys of being loved for yourself, and not for how high-ranking you are or what you can do for other people, quickly disappear. People who are downsized, for instance, find they've been dropped by everyone they know because they don't have real friends. They only had business acquaintances. One of the big no-nos in cyberspace is that you do not go into a social activity, a chat group or something like that, and start advertising or selling things. This etiquette rule is an attempt to separate one's social life, which should be pure enjoyment and relaxation, from the pressures of work.
>
> Reprinted with permission from *Wired* magazine, November 1997 issue

Civil Discourse

You can converse on the Internet in several ways. Usenet (see Chapter 8) is a fast-paced way of messaging, where you post messages to a newsgroup and usually within a few minutes a response appears. This isn't as "instant" as chat (see Chapter 6), but you'll find new postings and responses appear more quickly than on a mail list (see Chapter 7). Online message boards, such as CompuServe's Roots Forum, are somewhat more leisurely: a message might get answered within a week.

Still, these are all conversations. And, as they are written conversations, with no body language or facial expression to clue the participants, certain rules and standards have developed so that users can understand each other.

Flames

A *flame* is an argument on a message system—a chat, Usenet newsgroup, mail list, or message board—in which people type insults and angry messages back and forth. Often, these arguments are the result of a misunderstanding where one person misinterprets another, who, in turn, takes offense. Flames accomplish nothing. They never change any minds, and they hurt feelings.

If someone flames you, the best course of action is to a) inform the moderator of the group, list, or chat room, that you've been flamed and b) don't respond to the flamer. Indeed, you might even want to set your e-mail program, chat program, or newsreader program to filter out all messages from that sender. If it happens on a message board, simply stop opening messages from that sender.

The Rules

No, we're not talking about dating, but about conversations online. Sometimes you get flamed because you broke a rule—a rule you were probably unaware even existed. The best way to avoid this is to keep yourself informed of the standards and traditions of the group. You can do this in two ways: one way is to lurk until you get the lay of the land, so to speak. To *lurk* is to read the messages without responding or posting any messages yourself. This isn't considered rude. With the exception of chat, most message systems won't alert others to your presence until you post something. Lurking before you leap is completely acceptable in online genealogy.

Another way to familiarize yourself with online rules is to read the rulebook. Almost always, the rules are contained in a Frequently Asked Questions (FAQ) file. On Usenet, almost every newsgroup posts an FAQ at regular intervals. If you joined in the middle of a cycle, you can find most of them at www.faq.org. The home page of this site has a search box. Type Genealogy in the search box, click search, and you get a list of FAQ files for various groups, as shown in Figure 3-1. You might also want to search the FAQ archive for adoption, family history, and ancestry for related groups.

If you can't find an FAQ message or file for a Usenet newsgroup, make one of your first questions on the group, "Where and when can I get the FAQs for this group?"

Mail Lists often store their FAQ files on a Web site and also send it to you as your first message after you subscribe to the list. Save the message as a text or document file for future reference.

An online forum, such as CompuServe's Roots Forum, might have a series of messages or notices that discuss the rules of the forum. When you first join, these are usually shown to you, as in Figure 3-2.

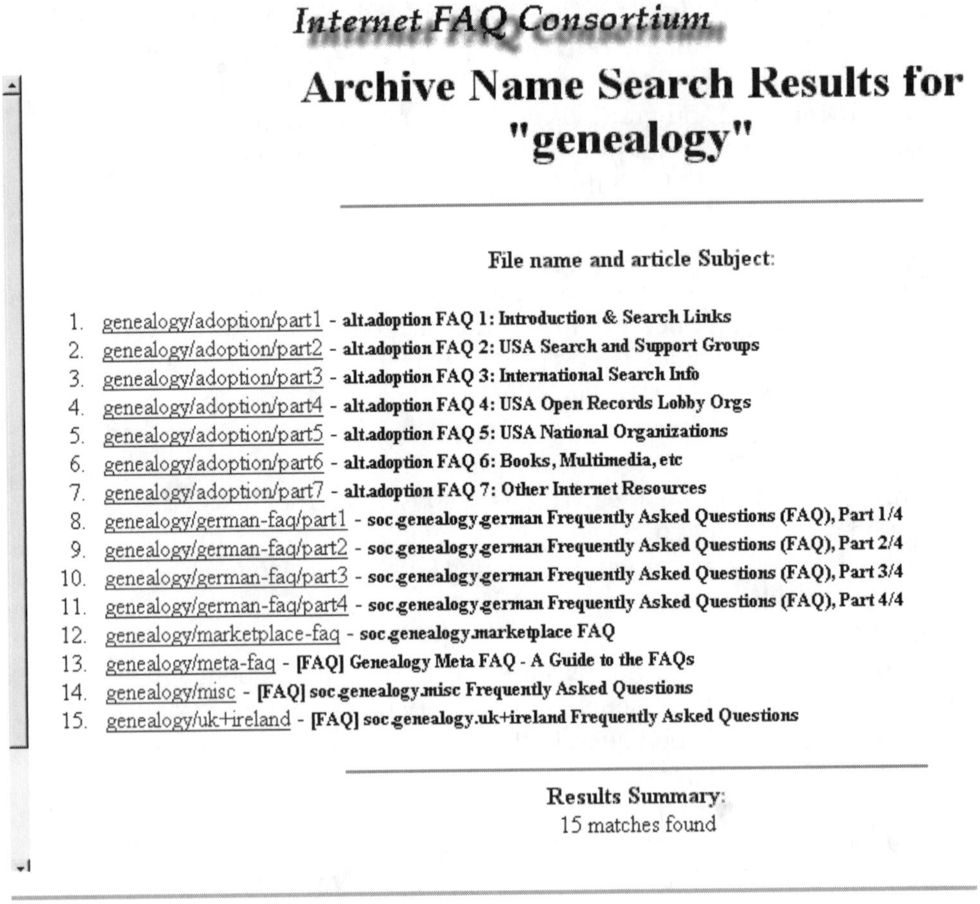

Internet FAQ Consortium

Archive Name Search Results for "genealogy"

File name and article Subject:

1. genealogy/adoption/part1 - **alt.adoption FAQ 1: Introduction & Search Links**
2. genealogy/adoption/part2 - **alt.adoption FAQ 2: USA Search and Support Groups**
3. genealogy/adoption/part3 - **alt.adoption FAQ 3: International Search Info**
4. genealogy/adoption/part4 - **alt.adoption FAQ 4: USA Open Records Lobby Orgs**
5. genealogy/adoption/part5 - **alt.adoption FAQ 5: USA National Organizations**
6. genealogy/adoption/part6 - **alt.adoption FAQ 6: Books, Multimedia, etc**
7. genealogy/adoption/part7 - **alt.adoption FAQ 7: Other Internet Resources**
8. genealogy/german-faq/part1 - **soc.genealogy.german Frequently Asked Questions (FAQ), Part 1/4**
9. genealogy/german-faq/part2 - **soc.genealogy.german Frequently Asked Questions (FAQ), Part 2/4**
10. genealogy/german-faq/part3 - **soc.genealogy.german Frequently Asked Questions (FAQ), Part 3/4**
11. genealogy/german-faq/part4 - **soc.genealogy.german Frequently Asked Questions (FAQ), Part 4/4**
12. genealogy/marketplace-faq - **soc.genealogy.marketplace FAQ**
13. genealogy/meta-faq - **[FAQ] Genealogy Meta FAQ - A Guide to the FAQs**
14. genealogy/misc - **[FAQ] soc.genealogy.misc Frequently Asked Questions**
15. genealogy/uk+ireland - **[FAQ] soc.genealogy.uk+ireland Frequently Asked Questions**

Results Summary:
15 matches found

FIGURE 3-1. *Over a dozen Usenet genealogy groups have posted FAQ files.*

Chat boards might not have formal FAQ, but the following are some general rules for chat.

Getting Along

Try to stick to the topic being discussed in a chat room, newsgroup, mail list, or message list. Again, the FAQ should list the topics a chat will accept.

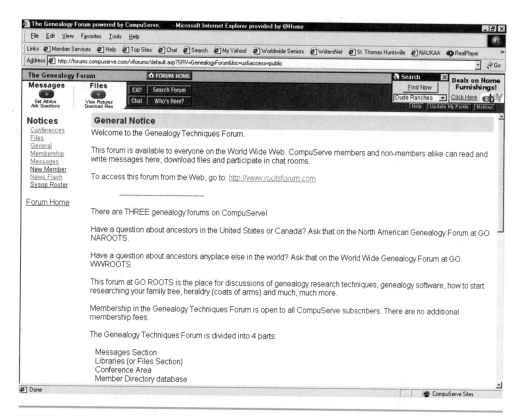

FIGURE 3-2. *CompuServe's Roots Forum has a series of notices containing the rules and guidelines for the site.*

Ads are usually verboten. A product announcement is typically okay, but an outright sales pitch isn't.

Straying off-topic commonly leads to flames. In general, the following topics are welcome in genealogy newsgroups:

- ◆ Your family history information and requests for others to help you find additional sources and material. (Tiny tafels are often posted for this.)

- Information on upcoming genealogical meetings, workshops, symposia, reunions, and so forth.

- Reviews, criticisms, and comments regarding software or hardware you've used in your genealogy/family history efforts.

- Names and addresses of book shops around the world that contain publications or information about genealogy.

- Almost any message about genealogy in general.

Remember, what you send is posted exactly as you send it, unless the site, group, or mail list (such as soc.genealogy.surnames) has a moderator who edits all incoming messages. On chat, when you press ENTER, it's sent off—mistakes and all.

Participants in genealogy groups want the topics of discussion to relate directly to genealogy or family history. In some groups, however, the tacit agreement is that anything a subscriber thinks is appropriate *is appropriate*, as long as it relates to genealogy. To discern these tacit rules at a particular site, lurk for a while to discover if it tends to be more lax about off-topic posting.

Assume an attitude of courtesy among subscribers and readers. Remember, your postings and comments might be seen by as many as 20,000 readers on different networks throughout the world.

Read carefully what you receive to make certain you understand the message before replying. Read what you've written carefully to ensure your message won't be misunderstood. As a matter of fact, routinely let a reply sit overnight, and then read it again before sending. This can prevent that sinking feeling of regret when you realize what you posted wasn't what you meant to say.

Note

A tiny tafel is a compact way of describing a family database so that the information can be scanned visually or by computer. The fields are all fixed length, except name and location. It was first defined in an article called "Tiny-Tafel for Database Scope Indexing" by Paul Andereck in Genealogical Computing (April-May-June 1986, volume 5, number 4).

Avoid sarcasm. If humor seems appropriate, clearly label it as such. A smiley face should indicate humor. It's easy to misunderstand what's being said when no tone of voice, facial expression, or body language can guide you. A corollary: Give others the benefit of the doubt. Perhaps what you understood to be rude was meant to be funny. Communicating online is a fine art!

Know your audience and double-check addresses. Make sure the person or list of people you're sending your message to is the appropriate one(s).

Be tolerant of newcomers, as you expect others to be tolerant of you. No one was born knowing all about the Internet or Usenet. Don't abuse new users of computer networks for their lack of knowledge. As you become more expert, be patient as others first learn to paddle, swim, and then surf the Net, just like you. Be an active participant in teaching newcomers.

Avoid cluttering your messages with excessive emphasis (**, !!, > >, and so on). This can make the message hard to follow.

Also, know how your mail program answers messages. Many mail programs default to copying the entire message over again into the reply. When you respond to a message, either include the relevant part of the original message or explicitly refer to the original's contents, but delete the unimportant parts of the original message. People commonly read your reply to the message before they read the original. (Remember the convention to precede each quoted line of the original message you include with the > character.)

In responses, don't quote more than necessary to make your point clear and, please, never quote the entire message. Learn what happens on your particular system when you reply to messages. Is the message sent to the originator of the message or to the list and when is it sent? When responding to another message, your subject line should be the same, with RE: at the beginning.

Always include a precise subject line, with surname, in your message. This should be something that attracts attention, and the only way to do this is to make sure the subject line describes the main point of your message. Don't put "Looking for..." as the subject line with no surname. People will scroll right past your message and never read it.

If you're seeking information about a family, include the surname in uppercase letters in the message subject. Many readers don't have time to read the contents of all messages.

Example of a bad subject line:

♦   Wondering if anyone is looking for JONES

Examples of good subject lines:

♦   Researching surname ENGLE 1700s

♦   SPENCER: England > MA > NY > OH > IN > MS

♦   Delaware BLIZZARDs pre-1845

♦   ? Civil War Records

In the good examples, note these conventions: surnames are in all caps, but nothing else is. A greater than sign (>) is used as an arrow to denote migration from one place to another. A date is always helpful. If your message is a question, indicate this in the subject line. Although passages in all uppercase are considered shouting, the exception to this rule in genealogy is surnames should be in uppercase, just as in any query.

Limit a message to one subject. This allows readers to quickly decide whether they need to read the message in full. Second subjects within a single message are often missed.

Questions are often the exception to this rule. You might need to post a message that's full of questions on a subject. When you ask a question within such a message, end it with a question mark (?) and press ENTER. This should be the end of that line. This makes it much easier for people to reply, because most newsreaders quote the original message line by line.

Be specific, especially when you ask questions. If you ask about a person, identify when and where the person might have lived. In questions concerning specific genealogical software, make clear what sort of computer (PC/MS-DOS, PC/Windows, Apple Macintosh, and so forth) is involved. The folks reading these newsgroups are helpful, but busy, and are more likely to answer if they don't have to ask what you mean.

A good idea is to put your name in the text of your message, along with your best e-mail address for a reply. You might want to disguise your e-mail address, though, to prevent its being harvested for unsolicited bulk e-mail (see Chapter 2). A good convention is

```
Please reply to libbic "at" prodigy.net.
```

The end of the message is a good place for your name and e-mail address.

Sometimes the message systems get absolutely clogged with messages, such as when, in early 1994, rotten weather, an earthquake, and a national holiday all converged on a certain Monday and many people were at home online because they were unable or not required to go to work. In this case, you must choose what to read based on the subject line or sender because it's impossible to read everything posted to the group that day. This is when a newsreader that lets you filter the messages for the subject headings is invaluable!

Danger: *Scams Ahead!*

For as long as genealogists have been around, those who would try to rip them off have existed, as mentioned in Chapter 1. Back when my mother started her genealogy in the mid '60s, she quickly came up against bogus offers to "find" her heraldic coat of arms, counterfeit "genealogies," which were nothing but phone directory listings, and so on. Most names *don't* have a coat of arms, but that doesn't stop these companies from inventing them. Check out Chapter 1 for a list of sites that track scams and frauds in genealogy. A good source for other scams (false urban legends, fake virus warnings, and so forth) is the Snopes site at www.snopes.com. This site is regularly updated with the reality behind some of the fantasies that go around the Internet.

Chat Etiquette

Chat and instant message programs are discussed in detail in Chapter 6.

Generally, you will find helpful, polite people in genealogy chat rooms in Internet Relay Chat (IRC). Often, if you have one of the instant message programs, you'll be chatting with people you've at least contacted before. And, of course, if you're taking an online course, specific rules are going to be in force as to who can "talk" and when. Nevertheless, in all these scenarios, you must meet certain etiquette standards in chat.

All the etiquette covered earlier in this chapter applies to chat. Using all capital letters, except to mention the surnames you're researching, is considered shouting. Flames are useless and annoying: show respect for everyone. And, make certain you aren't taking offense when none was intended.

IRC servers and the instant message programs track your connection. Many require you to input an e-mail address and select a handle. As a security measure, when you choose a nickname or handle to join a chat or use the Internet presence program, you might want to avoid using one that reveals your real name or gender, where you live, and so forth, unless this is a private chat room. Of course, never use offensive handles or nicknames. Chat is extremely public, so be careful about what you reveal in chat rooms.

Stay on topic or, if you get sidetracked, create a separate room to follow your tangent.

Lurk before you leap into sending messages: check out the room and see if the topic is what you're looking for.

Obscenity, cursing, and the like are forbidden on such systems as AOL. You can report people for using them. You can also use the /IGNORE command in IRC to block all messages from someone who is annoying you. If this becomes persistent, read the MOTD to find the name of the system administrator and report the offender.

You can send your e-mail address by private message, but don't post it in the IRC channel. If someone refuses to give you an address, don't be insulted because it's probably just a security measure.

If you want a particular person's attention (for example, to ask or answer a question), precede your message with his or her handle or its abbreviation.

For example, if my handle is ECWriter, someone with the handle RootsNewbie might send: "ECWriter: where can I buy your book?" I could reply, "RN: it's a mass market paperback, so it should be in most bookstores! :-)".

Smileys will be common, as will all sorts of acronyms. Refer to the Glossary for a list of smileys and acronyms used in online chat.

Many IRC servers and most of the instant message programs, enable you to send sound files, pictures, even programs over the chat room. Be wary of this feature for two reasons: First, it represents a security risk to receive files from someone you don't know well; second, this adds to the traffic on the server and slows down everyone's interaction, not only that of the sender and the receiver.

Chat programs have some limit to the number of characters that can be sent in one chunk. If your thoughts run longer, type the message in parts, each ending in an ellipsis (. . .) until you finish. Don't be surprised to find that, as you do this, other messages are popping up between your lines. Those paying attention can follow your train of thought better if you take advantage of a feature many programs have: the capability to send your text in a specific color and/or typeface.

Don't ignore people asking polite questions (such as "How are you?"). If someone is being rude, you can use the command /ignore < person's handle > .

Note

Several Web sites have tons of information about chat. Check the Cyndi's List page, www.CyndisList.com/chat.html, for the latest!

Wrapping Up

In online discussions, remember these basic rules:

- ♦ Stay on topic.

- ♦ In all queries, include a date, a name, and a place, if at all possible.

- ♦ Capitalize the surnames you're searching for.

- ♦ Ignore those who flame you and don't flame others. Don't be quick to take offense.

- ♦ Those who would scam you are out there. Keep on top of the latest information about scams.

- ♦ Read the FAQ!

Part 2

The Internet

Chapter 4

The World Wide Web

In addition to everything else it can do, the Web is a great resource for online genealogists. As you might imagine, any place on the Internet that combines ease of use regarding genealogical tools, lots of excitement, and lots of new people is a place genealogists want to be.

When most people talk about the Internet these days, they mean the Web. The *Web* is a system that ties together everything the Internet can do in one user interface. That interface is called a *browser*.

In the last chapter of this book, I list specific places on the Web you might find useful. In this chapter, I'll show you how to use the Web.

Ten years ago, the Internet was much harder to use. For each function (or Internet service), you needed to know about a different program, with a different set of commands. Just learning the jargon was a challenge.

Note

Getting a browser is easy. America Online's software comes with a version of Microsoft Internet Explorer as its Web browser, as do CompuServe and Prodigy. Other Internet service providers (ISPs) may supply you with Netscape Navigator, Opera, or some other browser.

Finally, a Swiss research group, CERN, decided to pull all the different services into one interface with a single protocol. At first, their new program, called a *browser,* was also text-based, just as the entire Internet was. Soon, however, graphic interfaces were added, making the browsers even easier to use.

Browser-speak

Even though the Web has made the Internet easier to use, the jargon has not gone away. The Web has its own lexicon, and these terms can be confusing. Here are a few expressions you should know before you get going:

Hypertext Markup Language (HTML) is the language that turns a text document into a Web-browsable one. Many shareware and commercial products have popped up in the past year to help you create HTML documents, but with a good handbook on the subject, you can create HTML code in any word or text processor.

Uniform resource locator (URL) is an address on the Web with the format AccessMethod://MachineName.SiteType/Directory/File.

Access method can be .http, .ftp, gopher, or some other Internet service. The machine name is the computer that holds what you're after. The site type shows what kind of organization is publishing the Web site: a commercial entity uses the suffix .com, a nonprofit organization uses .org, a government site ends in .gov, and an educational institution uses .edu. The directory and file are the location of the object on that computer. If you type something.com, you get a default file called index.html.

To use a URL, you either click a link or you type the URL in your browser's address box. This causes your browser to load the page or, as it's said in Web-speak, "go" to a site.

A *page* is a set of files presented to you in the browser in one display. The basic page itself is written in HTML code and, if you look at the code (using the menu View and the selection Source in your browser), you see simple ASCII text, with embedded commands to tell the browser how things should look to you. Some text is designated as a headline, while other text might tell the browser to show a picture in a certain place.

The most important part of this coding scheme is the link. The *link* instructs the browser to use something called HTTP (Hypertext Transfer Protocol) to show you something. A link is a pointer to another file and the term for linking files is hypertext. *Hypertext* is a system of embedding pointers in text, usually presented to you as underlined colored words or a picture, which prompts the browser to display another file—either on that same site or somewhere else on the Internet. When the cursor changes from an arrow to a hand, you're pointing your mouse at a link.

If you click a link, you're taken to that document, perhaps at another site. Depending on the type of file chosen, the link might take you to a sound bite, if you have a sound card. Or, it might take you to a picture, if you have VGA graphics.

What we love about browsers is they combine many Internet services: sending and receiving e-mail, reading and posting to Usenet, or transferring files with FTP and gopher.

Which Browser Should I Use?

I'm often asked, "Which is the best browser?" In my opinion, this is like asking, "Which is the best car?" It all depends on your taste, habits, and budget.

The current leaders in the browser wars are Netscape Navigator and Microsoft Internet Explorer (IE); entire books are devoted to helping you get the most out of these browsers. The major online services and ISPs have lined up with one or the other for their customers to use and install automatically with their software, so you don't have to do any extra work to use it.

Microsoft IE is free, but it makes major changes to your operating system and, therefore, sometimes causes trouble with other programs. Netscape Navigator can also be obtained free of charge, has a nice user interface, and is easy to use.

Other browsers, such as Opera, Mosaic, and Ariadne are less feature-packed, but they're free, easy to use, and sometimes much faster. Some of these programs are a pain for beginners because they're often harder to learn, have some of compatibility issues, and don't offer much support. They are fun for experienced users, though. For a comprehensive list, visit www.tucows.com and search for browser. My advice is to test-drive a few of them (most let you try before you buy) and see which browser suits you best if you don't like the one that comes with your service's software.

A Guided Tour of a Browser

DearMYRTLE's page is shown in Figure 4-1 in Netscape Navigator Version 6, and in Microsoft IE 5 in Figure 4-2. To see this page in your browser, type **www.dearmyrtle.com** in the address box. You can also use the menu option File | Open and type the URL in the dialog box.

Note the differences in one browser's rendition from the other's. This is something to consider when you start publishing on the Web, as discussed later in this chapter.

Look at the Netscape screen in Figure 4-1. First, you can see the browser's title bar at the top of the screen. This tells you the title of the Web page you're viewing. The title is often the same as the page's first headline, but it can be different. When you save a Web page's address (URL) in your bookmark file, the name associated with the URL is usually taken from the title. Unfortunately, many Web developers don't realize this and name their pages something uninformative such as My Page or Link.

Next is the browser's menu bar. Most browsers have File, Edit, View, Go, Bookmarks (or Hotlist or Favorites), Options, and a few

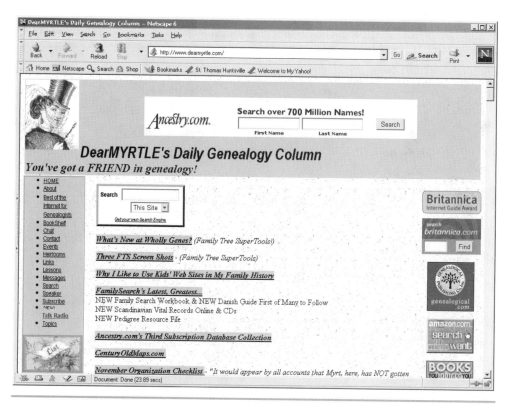

FIGURE 4-1. *This is a typical page in the Netscape Navigator browser.*

others. Usually, under *File* menu options, you can save or open a page, among other commands. *Edit* menu options enable you to search for a word or save something to the clipboard, generally, the same sort of commands in any Edit Windows menu. *View* menu options enable you to reload the page or to see details of the HTML code. *Go* is the navigation command: clicking it gives you a list of the sites you've visited today or a box to input a specific URL. Using *Bookmarks*, you can save the URL of sites that you like. The *Tasks* menu option lets you switch to other Netscape components, such as the Mail program. The *Help* menu option gives you access to online documentation about the program.

Below the menu bar is the toolbar. Most browser *toolbars* let you move backward and forward through Web pages, reload a page, travel

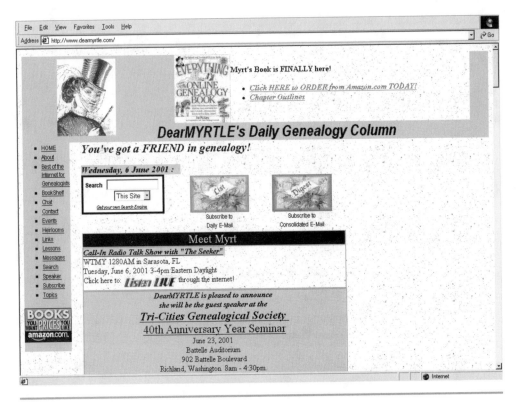

FIGURE 4-2. *This is the same page in Microsoft Internet Explorer.*

to a home page, print a page, stop the current load action, and so on. They are simply one-click shortcuts to the commands in the menu bar.

At the end of this toolbar is the Netscape icon. Whenever you're loading a page, you see an animation of comets raining down on the poor little Netscape planet. If you double click the *N,* you're taken immediately to Netscape's home page at home.netscape.com.

On this URL box, and on its far left, is the Bookmark icon. Click this and a menu pops up enabling you to save the location's address, so you can return to it later. Afterward, you can create different folders to sort and organize your bookmarks. Next to this is a small bookmark icon. Click-and-drag this to your desktop and a bookmark is created at the spot where you released the mouse button. This creates what's called a *shortcut* to that site (at least in Windows 95 and 98). Double-click that shortcut and your browser automatically takes you to the page. Microsoft Internet Explorer has a similar icon that does the same thing.

Take special note of the *Location box,* where you enter a Web site's address. If you need to copy a URL to your clipboard, you can double-click, press CTRL at the same time you press the *C* key (expressed as CTRL-C, the shortcut command for Copy), and it's ready to paste elsewhere. Are your fingers tired of typing www? Just type the unique part of the URL (such as genealogy.com) and the browser will fill in the first part. Type in an .ftp site, such as ftp.symantec.com, and the browser inserts the necessary ftp://. If you click the down arrow on the right side of the Location box, you can see a list of the last 15 or so URLs typed in this way. This feature is handy if you can't remember that neat place you visited yesterday. Place the pointer in the Location box and press the DOWN ARROW key. You'll hop to the next URL in the list.

The next toolbar is your Personal toolbar. You can click and drag bookmarks to your *Personal* toolbar for ready reference. The toolbar also comes with pages Netscape thinks are cool, worthwhile sites. For example, NetSearch takes you to a page of Web search engines. The *People* button, meanwhile, transports you to a form for searching online white pages, while the *Software* button takes you to the Navigator software site, where a new version of the program is posted almost weekly! (Microsoft IE has similar buttons.) If you want to change any of the buttons, you can always delete the buttons on this toolbar that came with the program and add your own.

Below this toolbar and taking up most of the screen, is Netscape's active window, where the current Web page is displayed.

Finally, let's go to the bottom of the screen. In the far right at the bottom of the screen is a little open lock. In Navigator, this means the page you're viewing has no built-in security. That's not a problem in this case because you're not filling out a form or providing any information. If the page had a form, the little open lock would indicate that someone else could see your answers. When a secure site is being viewed, you'll see a solid blue line at the top of the screen and a closed lock. Every browser notes security in different ways. Get to know yours well.

Below the display part, you'll find the status line. The *status line* tells you how much of a page the browser has loaded. Move your mouse pointer over links on a page and you'll see the associated URLs displayed here, too. If the site's developer is versed in Java, a message might even scroll across this box like a ticker tape. Next to the status line is a *thermometer* bar, another visual cue that shows how long you have to wait for an operation to finish.

Over to the far left at the bottom of the screen are icons that take you to other parts of Netscape Communicator like the mail program, HTML editor, and so on.

Browser Tips and Tricks

You can use your browser to surf the Web in several ways. The following are a few helpful tips:

- Versions of Microsoft IE and Netscape Navigator above 3.0 input the http:// prefix if you type in the unique part of the address. For example, type **www.genhomepage.com** and the browser changes it to http://www.genhomepage.com for you.

- Microsoft IE and Netscape Navigator versions 4 and above can also run a search for you. When you input your search terms, place a question mark before it in the address box and the program will try to find related pages for you.

- Type in an address that begins with the letters ftp— ftp.symantec.com for example—and the browser inserts the necessary ftp://. An *FTP site* is a collection of files for public download (covered later in this chapter).

- If you need to copy a URL to your clipboard, you can click the Address box, press CTRL-C, and you'll have a copy of the URL, ready to paste elsewhere. This is useful if you want to reference it in another program.

- You can change your browser's opening page. To do this in Microsoft IE, choose View | Internet Options. On the General tab, in the Home Page section of the tab, click Use Current. This makes IE treat the current page as your home page. You can click Use Default on the same tabbed sheet to restore Microsoft's home page as your browser home page. In Netscape Navigator, use Edit | Preferences and click Use Current to set it to the current page. In both browsers, you can browse your disk and set your bookmark.htm file as your home page.

- Click the down arrow in the address box to see a list of the URLs you've visited recently. This comes in handy if you can't remember how to get back to a particularly neat site.

- If you forgot to bookmark a site and the URL list in the Address box doesn't help, you can look in your History folder. Netscape Navigator and Microsoft IE both keep a history of all the sites and pages you visited recently. You can go to the History folder and rummage around if you think seeing the name of the Web site might get you on the right track. Here's how you do it in Microsoft IE:

    1. Using Windows Explorer, find the History folder in the Windows directory.

    2. Double-click the History folder. You'll see a collection of Calendar folders.

    3. Double-click a Calendar folder. Inside the folder, you see Site folders.

    4. Double-click a Site folder to see links to all the pages you visited recently at that Web site.

    5. Double-click a link to go to that Web page.

    In Netscape Navigator, it's much easier. With Netscape Navigator running, press CTRL-H . You can then search that list by depressing CTRL-F and typing in the word or words you're looking for. See Figure 4-3.

- All browsers save copies of the text, pictures, and other files you see in your Web browser window. They use these stored files the next time you visit the site for a faster display, loading the ones on your disk that are identical to those at the remote site. If you're running low on disk space on your PC, however, you can delete these files. Web pages might take a little longer to load, but you can free a ton of space on your hard drive. On Microsoft IE, in the View | Internet Options window, on the General tab, click Delete Files. In Netscape Navigator, in the Edit | Preferences window, under Advances, click the button that says Clear Disk Cache.

♦ If the server you want to access is too busy, try repeatedly until you hit that moment when someone has just logged off. Another trick: Determine which time zone the remote site is in and access it during local mealtimes, rush hours, or times when users are sleeping. A server in the United Kingdom, for instance, is easier to access at 4 P.M. United Kingdom time when school children are on their way home and many businesses are winding up for the day. Granted, the Internet is international in nature, but a computer tied to a given university or organization has peak use at predictable times. Use this to your advantage.

FTP

File Transfer Protocol (FTP) is a way of getting files from here to there—from another computer to yours or from yours to another computer—via the Internet.

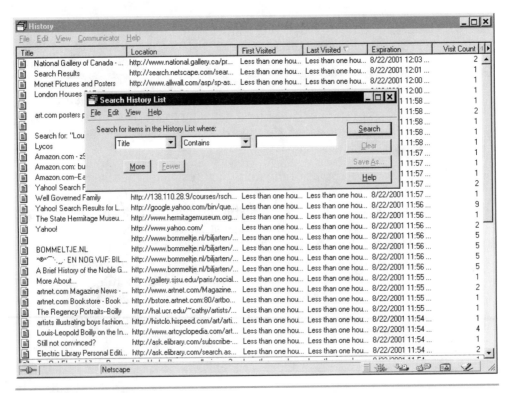

FIGURE 4-3. *Your browsing history can be searched in Netscape Navigator.*

FTP is automatically handled by browsers such as Internet Explorer through pop-up windows so you might not even have to think twice about getting or sending an FTP file.

Browsers can receive files with FTP and, in versions 5 of Microsoft IE and Netscape Navigator, can also send files. Furthermore, many HTML editors now have a built-in FTP engine to submit your finished product to the server, so if you have a Web page and want to share it with the world, FTP can transmit your files to the Internet server. If you want to retrieve a shareware program or a large text file, FTP is your best choice.

The FTP programs WS_FTP32 for PCs and Fetch for Macintosh are good choices and relatively cheap. Both have features I enjoy: the capability to read text files, save the addresses of FTP sites you visit, and batch send and receive. Every FTP program is different, so when you get one, poke around its Help file or manual to discover its particular tricks. Some let you store the settings for several different FTP sites or let you set a default FTP site. Many programs that store sites also let you set the initial directory to search, such as /PUB.

Note

If you're using FTP to get files from a public site, you log in with the username "anonymous" and give your e-mail address as your password. If "anonymous" doesn't work as a login name, try "ftp".

Using the command CD to change directories and LIST to look at filenames, you can send and receive files, usually by clicking an arrow (as in WS_FTP), but if you have a text-based browser, you simply use GET and SEND.

In FTP, case, spelling, and punctuation count. If you try to get to a site with the address FOOBAR.some.edu by typing foobar.some.edu, it probably won't work. If you try to get a file called FAMILY.LOCLIST. README.html, you must follow that punctuation and capitalization exactly or you get a "file not found" error message.

Many Web browsers have a built-in FTP program. If you want to jump to an FTP site, enter the address by prefacing it with FTP://. Be prepared for some unsuccessful attempts to connect to an FTP site, however. Addresses and links are always changing. The Internet is dynamic, so expect a few detours along the way.

FTP Conventions

Before using FTP, you need to know some conventions. Files that end in .zip, lzh, .exe, .arj, .arc, and .com are binary and should be transferred in binary mode. Files that end in anything else are probably text files and should be transferred in *ASCII* mode. If you're transferring files to a UNIX system, *binary* mode is generally the best for all transfers. The programs for uncompressing files can be downloaded from several software sites such as www.shareware. coma and www.tucows.com. Binaries are usually in Zip format with a file extension of .zip. A self-extracting copy of PKware's shareware programs is in the DOS file pkz204g.exe. ZIP files can also be read with the DOS program unz50p1.exe.

Some files are also compressed with lharc, having the ending .lzh. The software to unpack those files can be found in the self-extracting DOS archive lha213.exe. Files that end with .arj can be uncompressed with unarj.exe, which is in the Zip file unarj230.zip. .arc files can be decompressed with a program in pk361.exe. There are also several files that end with .exe. These are generally either self-extracting DOS archives or DOS programs.

Files ending in .Z have been compressed with UNIX compress. Files ending in .gz have been compressed with gzip.

Wrapping Up

- ♦ The Web is a way to combine services of the Internet into one user interface called a browser.

- ♦ The two most popular browsers are Microsoft Internet Explorer and Netscape Navigator.

- ♦ The last chapter of this book has specific Web sites for you to visit.

Chapter 5

Search Engines

Throughout this book, I will try to point you to the best genealogy newsgroups and Web sites. Nevertheless, plenty of reasons exist to search the Internet for other sources. First, things change incredibly fast on the Internet: Web sites disappear or move to a new server, which changes a site's Uniform Resource Locator (URL). Also, new sources of genealogical information appear daily on the Internet, so you might miss an important new resource if you don't do your own searches once in a while. Finally, as a genealogist, you've experienced the thrill of discovering things for yourself—it can be quite a kick to find a Web site or newsgroup none of your friends know about.

So, what you need is a way to find genealogical resources on the Internet on your own. That's where search sites come in.

Defining Terms

Search engine is an all-purpose label used to describe anything that will let you search for terms in a group of data. That data could be on a single site, such as DearMYRTLE.com, or on the entire Internet, or some subset in between the two. Just about anything that lets you search gets called a search engine, but some other terms are more accurate for specific sites.

A *spider* is a program that looks for information on the Internet, creates a database of what it finds, and lets you use a Web browser to run a search engine on that database for specific information. As noted, this can mean millions of pages or only the pages on one site. A *search site* might have one or more search engines and can claim to search "the whole Web," but, in reality, it probably covers about 15 percent of the Web at any given time. This is because pages quickly appear and disappear on the Web. That's why you might want to use several different search sites if you go this route. Or, you might want to try one of the many metasearch engines that try several search sites at one time.

A search site called a *directory* or a *catalog* uses a search engine to let you hunt through an edited list of Internet sites for specific information. The value of these sites is that in a directory or catalog, the newsgroups and Web sites are sorted, categorized, and sometimes rated.

Yahoo! (www.yahoo.com), shown in Figure 5-1, is one of the first catalogs or directories established online; it is also a good example of

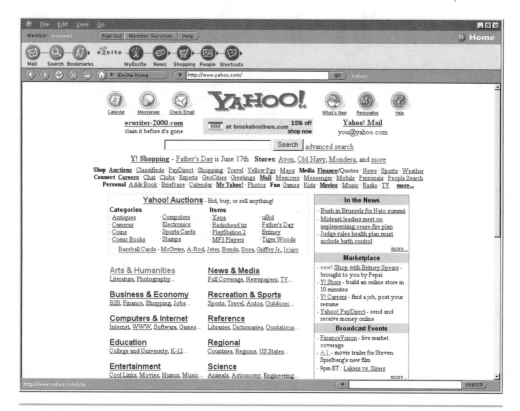

FIGURE 5-1.   *Yahoo! is a portal that can help you find genealogy sites
and information.*

a portal, which offers other services. When a search site offers chat,
news, forums, and other services, it becomes a *portal.* A portal is a little
bit of everything: a search engine for the Web at large, a catalog of sites
the owners recommend, and usually a group of other features, including
stock prices, Web-based e-mail, shopping, and so on.

A *metasearch engine* submits your query to several different search
sites, portals, and catalogs at the same time. You might get more results
and you will usually be able to compare how each one responded to the
query. These searches may take longer, however.

Searching with Savoir Faire

The following sections describe various search engines, portals, and directories. While the content in them overlaps a great deal, each one uses slightly different methods to search Web sites and rate how well your terms were matched. This means you might find what you're looking for with one search engine or directory that you won't find using another.

First, some general search tips:

♦ Use phrases instead of single words in your searches. Type several words that are relevant to your search. Typing **Spencer genealogy Ohio** will narrow a search well.

♦ Enclose phrases in quotes. Searching with the phrase **Spencer family history** without quotation marks will match all pages that have any of those three words included somewhere on the page, in any order, and not necessarily adjacent. Searching with the phrase "**Spencer family history**" (with quotation marks) will return only those pages that have those three words together. The order of the words, however, may or may not be flexible, depending on the specific search engine.

♦ The more specific you are, the better. Searching for **Irish genealogy databases** will give you fewer, but closer matches than searching for **Irish genealogy**.

♦ Use plus (+) and minus (-) in your searches. A word preceded by a plus sign must appear on the page to be considered a match. A word preceded by a minus sign must not appear on the page to be considered a match. No spaces can be between the plus or minus signs and the words they apply to. For example: entering **+Spencer -royal genealogy** would ask the search engine to find pages that definitely used the word "Spencer", but don't use the word "royal", with "genealogy" preferred, but optional. Most search engines would get some Spencer genealogy pages, but leave out those that include Lady Diana, Princess of Wales. More about this type of search is in the sidebar about Boolean searches.

♦ Narrow your searches if you get too many matches. Sometimes the page with your search results will have an input box to narrow or broaden the search. This might mean adding terms or deleting terms, and then running the search again only on the results from the first search. You can also run searches within search results to help narrow choices. This is the easiest way.

Using Boolean Terms

Searching the Internet is no simple matter. With literally hundreds of thousands of sites, millions of documents, and more words than you can imagine, finding exactly the right needle in all that hay can be daunting. The key, of course, is crafting a precise query.

Handy tools for honing searches are Boolean operators. Coined for George Boole, the nineteenth century mathematician who dreamed up symbolic logic, *Boolean* operators represent the relationships among things using terms such as AND, OR, and NOT. When applied to information retrieval, they can expand or narrow a search to uncover as many citations or *hits* as you want.

The Boolean OR

When you search for two or more terms joined with an OR operator, you get back hits that contain any one of your terms. Thus, the query **Powell OR genealogy** will retrieve documents holding "Powell" or "genealogy," but not necessarily both. Note, nearly all search pages default to OR, that is, they assume you want any page with any one or more of your terms in it.

You can see it makes good sense to use OR when you search for synonyms or closely related terms. For example, if you're looking for variations on a name search for **SPENCER SPENCE SPENSER.** The average search engine will assume the OR operator and find any page with any one or more of those terms.

The Boolean AND

In the Boolean boogie, joining search terms with AND means all terms must be found in a document, but not necessarily together. The query **George AND Washington** will result in a list of documents that have both the names "George" and "Washington" somewhere within. Use AND when you have dissimilar terms and need to

narrow a search. Usually to get AND in a search, you type a +
mark or put the term AND between the words, and enclose it all
within parentheses: **(Spencer AND genealogy)**.

Remember, a simple AND doesn't guarantee the words will be
next to each other. Your search for George Washington could turn
up documents about George Benson and Grover Washington.

The Boolean NOT

When you use NOT, search results must exclude certain terms.
Many search engines don't have this. Often, when you can use it,
the syntax is to put a hyphen in front of the unwanted term.

The query **Powell NOT Colin** will return all citations containing
the name "Powell," but none including the word "Colin," whether
or not "Powell" is there. Use NOT when you want to exclude
possible second meanings. "Banks" can be found on genealogy
surname pages, or on pages associated with finance or with rivers.
Searching for **banks AND genealogy NOT river** increases the
chances of finding documents relating to Banks, who are people,
and not riversides. In some search engines, the minus sign often
takes the place of NOT.

The fun part is combining Boolean operators to create a precise
search. Let's say you want to find documents about the city of Dallas.
If you simply search for **Dallas**, you could get irrelevant hits about
Dallas County in Alabama (county seat: Selma), which might not
be the Dallas you want. To avoid that, you would use AND, NOT,
and OR in this fashion:

> **(Dallas AND Texas) NOT (Selma OR Alabama)**
> **(Powell AND genealogy) NOT (Colin AND "SECRETARY OF STATE")**

Note that parentheses group the search terms together.

Beyond AND/OR/NOT

In most Web search engines, unless a phrase option is specifically
offered, the capitalization or order of the terms isn't important: a
Venetian blind is the same as a blind Venetian. However, some
search engines enable you to fine-tune a search further. The WITH
operator, for example, searches for terms much nearer each other.

How "near" is defined depends on the engine. Some would look at "George WITH Washington" and deliver documents only containing the words "George Washington" next to each other. Others might consider words in the same sentence or paragraph to be near enough.

Check the search engine's help files to see if it uses wildcards or word stemming (for finding all variations of a word such as ancestry, ancestral, ancestor, ancestors).

Using these techniques, you can search the Web much more efficiently, finding just the right document on George Washington Carver or a genealogy site on the right set of Powells. Learn the steps to the Boolean boogie and you'll soon be Web dancing wherever you please!

Search Sites

Lots of search sites are out there, some of which are more useful to genealogists than others. The following is a list of genealogy-related catalogs, portals, and search engines in alphabetical order.

Access Genealogy   At this site, www.accessgenealogy.com, you can read and search free of charge for many different types of records for genealogy research, including newspapers and periodicals, emigration and immigration forms, census reports, voting records, and archives from libraries, cemeteries, churches, and courts.

Ancestry-GenPage Finder   A free service from Ancestry.com, GenPage Finder (www.ancestry.com/search /rectype/directories/gpf/main.htm) looks at 2,000,000 genealogical sites and is updated every week. It can use the Boolean WITH. Select the proximity from the drop-down box beneath the query space.

Enter your keywords, choose the Boolean limiters, and click Search. Adding or deleting keywords will fine-tune the number of search results. The more keywords you enter, the more specific your search will be and the fewer search results will return. Some of the pages GenPageFinder will turn up are quite large. If your keywords aren't immediately visible on the page GenPageFinder finds for you, try pressing CTRL-F and entering your keywords again. This should take you to the spot on the page where your keywords appear. Whatever your research interests and whatever searching you've already done, chances are a search on GenPageFinder will yield fruitful new sources.

Biography Guide   Was any ancestor of yours a member of Congress? Search for biographies of members by last name, first name, position, and state at this site, bioguide.congress.gov/biosearch/biosearch.asp. If your ancestors are in the database, this fascinating site can add a new dimension to your family history.

Cyndi's List   The site www.cyndislist.com catalogs over 98,000 genealogy Web sites. You will find links to the genealogy sites and sites that simply would help a genealogist, worldwide. This is the first place many new online genealogists visit. The links are categorized and organized, and there's also a search box for finding the subjects you want quickly. As shown in Figure 5-2, this is a very popular site.

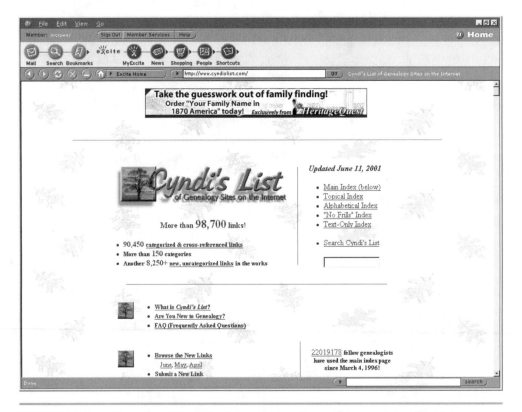

FIGURE 5-2.   *More than 22 million hits attest to the usefulness of Cyndi's List.*

Cyndi Howells works on the list every day, updating, deleting, and adding sites. To keep up, you can frequently check the pages on the list that interest you. Each new or updated link will have a small "new" or "updated" graphic next to it for 30 days.

The main index is updated each time activity occurs on Cyndi's List. Check the date under each category heading to determine when the last update was made for that category. The date is also updated at the bottom of each category page.

But the easiest way to keep on top of the changes is to subscribe to the CyndisList Mailing List. This is a free, announcements-only, e-mail mailing list detailing the updates and news regarding the Web site. You will usually get an update once a day during the work week. To subscribe, send an e-mail message to CyndisList-request@rootsweb.com and, in the body, type only the word **subscribe**.

Similarly, to unsubscribe, send an e-mail message to CyndisList-request@rootsweb.com. In the body type only the word **unsubscribe**.

Be sure not to include your automatic signature when sending either of the previous commands to the RootsWeb mailing list server.

Genealogy Pages   A collected catalog of genealogy sites, the site www.genealogypages.com also offers you a free e-mail box and a browser-based chat site, so it qualifies as a portal.

You can browse the collection of links by category or search the entire collection. Because it's all about genealogy, you don't have to put that term in the search box. A search for "South Carolina Powell" in the regular search box turned up nothing. Even though, in the Advanced Search I could choose between AND (the default) and OR, and even if it was recognized as a phrase, I couldn't get a match on all three. Searching on "South Carolina" got good results, however, as did searching on "Powell".

GeneaSearch.com   This portal, www.geneasearch.com, is along the lines of Genealogy Page. Several search options exist, but searching by surname is your best bet. GeneaSearch gives results similar to those of Genealogy Page. They will both return submitted GEDCOMs from users that will be secondary sources for genealogy.

GenealogyPortal.com   A joint venture of Steve Wood, who founded the original Genealogy Home Page, and Matthew Helm, of Genealogy

Tool Box, www.genealogyportal.com is a site that uses one form for eight separate search engines to help you efficiently search the Web.

The GenealogyPortal.com search engines provide you with five options when conducting searches. Three of the options are under the MATCH drop-down box and two options are under the FORMAT drop-down box.

Under the MATCH drop-down box, you can choose the ALL option (Boolean AND), the ANY option (Boolean OR), or the BOOLEAN option, which lets you insert the operators AND, OR, and NOT into the search terms yourself, using parentheses for nesting to refine your search further by creating sets. For example, a search for (A or B) and (C or D) finds all pages that contain either A or B AND either C or D.

The FORMAT drop-down box contains two options: DETAIL, which will include a brief description of the Web page, and SHORT, which will only show a link to the Web page (no description).

The site also includes a short, edited catalog of sites under headings such as Archives and Libraries, Primary Records, and Guides to Research. You can browse the catalog by clicking the links to these categories from the front page of the site.

GenGateway   Another version of a catalog of Web sites organized into categories for genealogists, www.gengateway.com by Steve Lacy, indexes thousands of Web pages and sources. Choose the category you want to search, such as surname or obituary, and you'll get well-sorted results.

To navigate the site, use one of the many useful gateways listed in the navigation bar to the left of the opening page. If you're new to the site, first try the Beginners Gateway or the Search Pages.

For example, the *Beginner's Gateway* link will give you links to general guides, such as "20 Ways to Avoid Genealogical Grief" (www .smartlink .net/ ~ leverich/20ways.html). The *Search Pages* link is a metasearch engine that uses several sites, such as Infoseek, Magellan, Excite, and Yahoo!, with limiters. It also searches specialized sites, such as Irish on the Net, for surnames.

You might also notice the search field at the top. With the drop-down box, you can select to search only surname listings, site listings, or the entire database. If your main interest is surnames, use the search field or the A-Z search to help you find what you want. The online Guides to the left will also lead you to their interactive message boards where you can ask and answer questions. A search for "Powell" on this box turned up six good pages.

GenServ   An all-volunteer effort, GenServ at www.genserv.com, is a collection of donated GEDCOMS with a sophisticated set of search commands (see Figure 5-3). (Remember, this is all secondary source material. When you seem to have a match, you need to contact the submitter to determine what primary source material he or she might have.) The database has over 19,000,000 individuals in more than 14,000 databases. All this family history data is online and available by search and reports to subscribers.

GenServ has been online since 1991 and on the Web since early 1994. To access the system, you have to at least submit your own GEDCOM. If you pay the optional yearly fees, you can perform many more searches per day than the free access allows.

The capability to do complex searches on the databases means a real learning curve exists. Furthermore, only the "surname count"

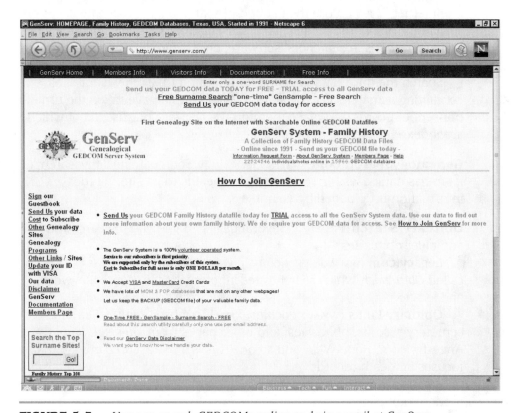

FIGURE 5-3.   *You can search GEDCOMs online and via e-mail at GenServ.*

search can be done from the Web; all the rest are done via e-mail messages. This has the advantage of letting you input your terms, and then surf on to other sites. The results, meanwhile, come back by e-mail (and quickly, too!).

Uploading your data and learning how to query this set of databases is worth your time.

GenSource   The specialized genealogy directory site www.gensource .com provides the online genealogist with three databases to assist with research online.

The first database is called Search Common Threads. You use Search Common Threads to find other genealogists researching your family name. If you're at a "dead end" finding information on an ancestor, add an entry to Common Threads, so other family members can find you.

Search the second database, I Found It!, to locate genealogy sites on the Internet. You can use the I Found It! search engine to locate pages on surnames, one-name studies, ship passenger lists, genealogical societies and associations, researchers, software, books, family mailing lists, online records of churches, census data, cemeteries, and more.

Search the third database, the IFI (I Found It!) Archives for sites containing actual historical records. Many people have taken the time to transcribe records and place them on the Net for your use, all of which are indexed for research purposes.

GenealogySearch.com   Like Genealogy Source, genealogysearch .com has databases for you to search, specific to its site. All the information is uploaded by volunteers.

Obituary Search Pages   Several pages enable you to search recent and older obituaries:

Legacy.com (www.legacy.com/NewspaperMap.asp)   Has a page called *ObitFinder,* which searches recent obituaries by name, keyword, and location.

Obituary Links (www.geocities.com/ ~ cribbswh/obit)   Searches cemetery records, obituaries, and other pages from sites such as Ancestry.com, RootsWeb, and so on. This is a metasearch engine that focuses on death records.

4Obituaries (4obituaries.4anything.com)   Has a list of links to modern obit pages.

Several other sites are worth a brief mention, although they differ from those previously noted only in what they search, not in how.

Surname Web   Located online at www.surnameweb.org, Surname Web has a database of names submitted by users, as well as pages from other Web sites. Simply input the surname.

SurnameSite   SurnameSite.org lets you search an ancestor archive with over 45 pages of wills, obituaries, birth records, and other documents posted by visitors. You can also search a directory of over 1,000 genealogy and historical sites with ancestor names, or post and view queries about your ancestors on the message board.

World Connect   World Connect (worldconnect.rootsweb.com) is a division of RootsWeb. RootWeb's motto is "Connecting the world, one GEDCOM at a time." People are free to upload to and search in this collection of GEDCOM databases. All you need to do is fill out the form with name, place of birth and death, and dates of birth and death. You can choose an exact search if you're sure of your facts, or a range of 2 to 20 years for dates and SOUNDEX searches for names and places. It's fast, but the results depend entirely on the uploaded GEDCOMS. If you have no hits, consider uploading your information for others. If you already uploaded your information, you can exclude your own database from future searches.

   Like GenServ, World Connect is all volunteer, amateur information. You must contact the submitter of a database to find out the sources for the data and, unlike GenServ, you can do the searches via the Web.

Yourfamily.com   Yourfamily.com is a database of genealogy pages by individuals, submitted by the users themselves. To use the search function, click the Family Homepages button. The resulting page gives you a search box to input the surname you need. The site presents you with a list of pages by genealogists, amateur and professional, who are searching that surname.

General Search Sites   Many Web-wide search engines and portals can help you find genealogy resources. Using the search techniques previously mentioned, you'll probably have good results trying these general search engines. Some of them have catalogs of genealogy sites. For those that do, how to browse there is listed with the following entry.

On all of them, though, searches as described in the beginning of this chapter will work.

Alta Vista (www.altavista.com)   Browse through the catalog to Home | Lifestyle | Hobbies | Hobbies/Interests A-Z | Interests G | Genealogy & Heraldry.

AOL NetFind (search.aol.com)   Browse to Main | Society | Genealogy.

AskJeeves (www.ask.com)   Click Browse By Subject | Society | Genealogy.

C|Net Search (www.search.com)   Type **genealogy** and/or the surname and/or the location you need in the search box.

Excite (www.excite.com)   Click the Family link in the Explore Excite box.

FastSearch (www.alltheweb.com)   Type **genealogy** and/or the surname and/or the location you need in the search box.

Go.com (www.go.com)   Type **genealogy** and/or the surname and/or the location you need in the search box.

Google (www.google.com)   Simply type **genealogy** and/or the surname and/or the location you need in the search box.

Hot Bot (www.hotbot.lycos.com)   From the home page, click Society | Genealogy.

MetaCrawler (www.metacrawler.com)   Browse to Lifestyles | Hobbies | Genealogy & Heraldry.

Northern Light (www.northernlight.com)   At this site, you can search Web sites as well as magazines, newspapers, and wire services. Simply type **genealogy** and/or the surname and/or the location you need in the search box.

NBCi (www.nbci.com)   Click the Search and Find tab, and click the Genealogy link under the Living subheadline, or browse through to Society & Politics | Culture and Heritage, and choose your country (see Figure 5-4). You will also find a link to NBCi's Genealogy channel, with news and articles about genealogy.

Yahoo! (www.yahoo.com)   Search the whole Yahoo! catalog by typing **genealogy** and/or the surname and/or the location in the search box, or browse to Arts | Humanities | History | Genealogy.

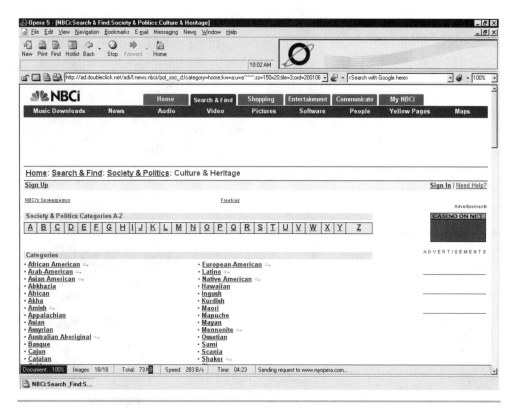

FIGURE 5-4. *General search sites, such as NBCi, often have edited lists of genealogy pages and resources.*

White Page Directories

So far, you've looked at search engines and directories for finding a Web site. But, what if you need to find lost, living relatives? Or, you want to write to people with the same surnames you're researching?

In that case, you need people search engines, called White Page directories. Like the White Pages of your phone book, these specialize in finding people, not pages. In fact, all the search engine sites mentioned previously have White Page directories.

The AT&T site (www.att.com/directory) has an excellent set of directories for people and businesses, with a reverse phone number lookup (put in the phone number, get the name). See Figure 5-5.

Switchboard (www.switchboard.com) is one of many White Pages services on the Web. It's free, and it lists the e-mail and telephone numbers of millions of people and businesses taken from public records, as well as a Web site catalog. If you register as a user (it's free), you can ensure that your listing is not only accurate, but has only the information you want it to reveal.

BigFoot (www.bigfoot.com) is another such effort to catalog people, with the same general rules: Input your information and you get searches

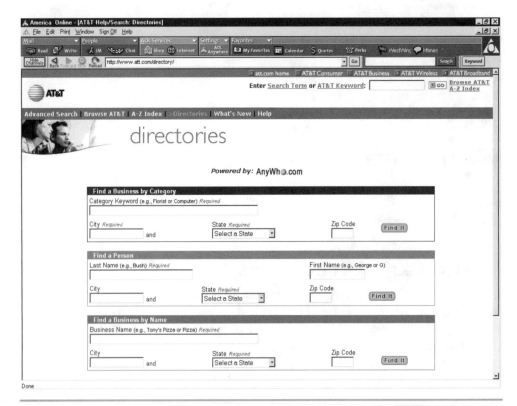

FIGURE 5-5. *White Page directories are a good way to find living people.*

that are more specific. BigFoot also has surface mail addresses in addition to e-mail and telephone information.

Wrapping Up

- ♦ Learn to use Boolean search terms to target your Web searches.

- ♦ Use genealogy-specific sites to search for your surnames and localities.

- ♦ Use general search sites and catalogs that gather news and links about genealogy.

- ♦ Use White Pages sites to find living people.

Chapter 6

Chat: Hail Thy Fellow on the Net!

Sometimes you might want to talk to another person to resolve problems you're encountering in your research. The online world can help you there, too, with chat.

Can We Talk?

Online chat has been around for a long time. From the earliest days of The Source and CompuServe to the era of America Online (AOL) and the Web, *chat* has been a staple of online communication. Chat is useful whether you're collaborating on a genealogy project, sending digital reunion memos to your extended family, or discussing your hobby with a large crowd.

> **Note**
>
> *Throughout this chapter, you'll find references to newsgroups, mail lists, and Web sites. This is just an example of how interconnected the genealogy resources on the Internet can be. You'll learn everything you need to know about newsgroups and Web sites in other chapters.*

Internet Relay Chat, better known as IRC, is the most popular form of chat. Although IRC can support one-to-one, one-to-many, and many-to-many messages, usually IRC is a lot of people on a "channel" typing messages back and forth in a many-to-many format. IRC uses a system of clients and servers that enables people all over the world to communicate in real time by typing on their computers. So, for example, folks in Australia, France, Hong Kong, Kenya, British Columbia, and Vermont can all sit at their computers at the same time, log in to the same server, connect to the same channel, and type messages interactively, each seeing what all the others are saying.

A group of people chatting on a channel at the same time are said to be in a *chat room.* You can create private, invitation-only chat rooms or join in on a public one.

> **Note**
>
> *A chat channel and a chat room are the same thing. It's a connection to a chat server where several people are seeing each other's messages on a topic.*

If you just wander into any old chat room, you may be dismayed at the level and tone of the conversation. Everyday chat conversations tend to be either mundane or racy. You need to search the chat server for rooms devoted to the subjects of family history and/or genealogy.

Even when you do get into a genealogy chat, the conversations overlap. This makes it hard to keep track of who's saying what. Unmoderated, general chat rooms (sometimes called *drop-ins*) are like strolling by the corner coffee shop. You don't know whom you'll find there or whether anyone inside will be of help to you. Typically, a lot of what's going on will be totally irrelevant to your search.

A moderated or hosted chat, however, is more like attending a class or a genealogy club meeting. There's usually a specific topic being discussed, an expert or two available, and a system for asking and answering questions, so the conversations are at least a little easier to follow. A one-on-one chat between yourself and a buddy can be even more productive. If you can set up a specific time and channel to discuss a problem or a great find, you can get a lot done this way.

Another, more controlled type of chat is called *instant messaging* or *instant message,* which grows in popularity daily, thanks in large part to America Online's Instant Messenger program. In this form of chat, a select, invited list of people (from two to a whole "room"), exchange typed messages in real time. This feature has become so popular that instant messaging is used 180 million times a day, according to AOL. Another example: ICQ (I-seek-you), a different instant messaging program, gets hundreds of new users a day. And newer programs exist, such as *Microsoft Meeting,* which can be used as an intranet/Internet collaboration tool.

Note

An intranet is a system that uses Internet protocols and technology, but isn't publicly accessible. AOL is an example of an intranet: you must use the AOL connection number or line to get on to get to the proprietary content, such as the weekly genealogy chats.

Web-based chat uses Java or ActiveX in your browser to present the conversations. This is slow and I've found few rewarding Web-based genealogy chats. However, searching for "Web genealogy chat" in a search engine might turn up some links. In general, the best genealogy chats are on IRC, voice chat, or instant message systems.

Note

You might ask, why not just use e-mail instead? Live chat can be more efficient, especially if you're collaborating on a project. You can create a channel where the only people allowed to participate are the ones you invite. Instant messaging programs can tell you who's online now and hook you up for a conversation on the spot. Best of all, many chat clients discussed here are free. And, so far, most aren't bombarding you with ads or asking for much demographic data.

Important Warnings About Chat

In Chapter 2, I discussed unsolicited bulk e-mail (UCE) in detail. Those who send UCE, especially the pornographic kind, have special programs that spy on chat rooms and report the e-mail addresses of everyone who logs on, regardless of the topic of the chat room. They are especially vigilant about chat rooms on AOL. Within minutes of participating in a typical AOL chat, you'll be bombarded by unsolicited e-mail about porn sites.

How do you prevent this? Simple: You wear a disguise.

On AOL, CompuServe, and Prodigy, you can create screen names under your primary account. You should create one just for chat and encourage everyone in the family to use this screen name only for chat purposes. Then, on AOL, you can block all e-mail sent to that screen name. However, on a system that provided you with POP e-mail, such as Mindspring, Earthlink, or Prodigy, at press time, you need only set up mail filters (see Chapter 2) that delete any messages sent to the chat account.

If you use AOL Instant Messenger, ICQ, or a similar program, you're protected from the unsolicited bulk e-mailers because these programs use secure, private chat servers. So, thankfully, you can use your real e-mail address here. These programs use their own private, secure servers, and everyone on them has agreed to a Terms Of Service statement that forbids sending unsolicited e-mail to members. Furthermore, these e-mail programs give you the capability to filter out specific people. Thus, you don't have to worry that your chats will result in a flood of UCE.

If you avail yourself of other chat clients who use open, public chat servers (such as mIRC), you could enter false information in the e-mail address portion of the setup screens to hide from unsolicited bulk e-mail. You could also enter your e-mail address as something like libbic@nospam.prodigy.net. Most people will know to take out the "nospam" part to get your real e-mail address, but the unsolicited bulk e-mailer's automatic programs won't.

All the clients mentioned here have security features: You can block others from adding you to their buddy list until you permit them to; you can block people from sending you messages until you give permission; and so forth. Each program has its own way of handling "twit" filters and all are constantly trying to improve their privacy features. You'll have to try each out to see what's new with them.

Some chat is based on Java, meaning you don't need a chat client to use them. Several personal and commercial genealogy sites have Java-based chats that require only a browser capable of dealing with Java (Microsoft Internet Explorer or Netscape Navigator 4.0 or newer are examples). If your e-mail address is recorded in your browser's settings, however, UCE senders might get hold of it.

How It Works

How do chat services and programs work? You use the client program to log on to a chat server. Where to find servers is covered at the end of this chapter.

If it's an open, public chat server, such as Internet Relay Chat (IRC), you can use a program like mIRC. You log on and search for a channel that suits your interests. If there isn't one at the moment, you can create one (calling it #genealogy, perhaps) and wait for interested people to come chat with you. Once the chat gets going, it's a lot like citizens' band radio, but in print.

Other programs like AOL Instant Messenger are set up so that only people using the same program can contact you. With such a program, you can usually indicate your status (gone, accepting calls, connected but away from your desk, and so on) and keep a list of people you want to contact (often called a *buddy list* or *address book*), as well as those who are allowed to contact *you.* (Alas, you can't import a buddy list from your e-mail address book—you usually have to ask permission to add someone to your list!) To find people to add to your list, you can look them up by e-mail address, or e-mail them an invitation to use the same program you are using, and then exchange ID names.

When someone hails you, a sound or small message window (or both) will alert you. Chatting typically takes place in two panes of one window: one for your outgoing messages and one for incoming ones.

If you're worried about security or just want to be left alone, fret not. Most of these programs let you shield your presence from specific people or from the world at large, as suits your mood. You can also let yourself be "seen," but not heard, with an online "I'm-busy-now" indicator.

You can choose a *handle* or nickname for your login ID. This is the name by which people will know you on IRC (everyone in a channel must have a unique nickname). Remember, hundreds of thousands of people are on IRC, so it's possible someone might already be using the nickname you've chosen. If that's the case, simply choose another one. Some programs record your preferred nickname in the setup screen and let you choose an alternative if someone is using your first choice in a certain channel.

Also, be sure to make use of the chat program's help files. They'll help you get the most out of your chat time.

Security Risks In *IRC*

When you use the IRC type of chat, you're open to some security risks.

For example, while you're logged on to an IRC server, bad guys can look up your dynamic IP settings and bombard you with packets, clogging your TCP/IP connection until you disconnect and reconnect.

Microsoft's security page at www.microsoft.com/security contains information on these security threats, as well as links to fixes.

Another important caution: If someone you don't know tells you to type an unfamiliar key sequence, phrase, or command in chat, don't do it! You might be opening the chat room, or even your own computer, to hackers.

Finally: Never, ever give out any credit card information or login passwords in a chat. Report anyone who asks for such information to the chat server or online service you're using.

Chat Flavors

Different programs enable you to have one-on-one and multiperson conversations with people. Some require you to sign on to a chat server, where the program you use doesn't matter. Others only let you chat with people using the same program, who have allowed you to put them on their buddy list. The former lets you connect with more people; the latter gives you more security. A few, as noted, will let you do both.

AOL Instant Messenger

You can find AOL Instant Messenger (known as AIM) at www.aim.com. It's free and it's a proprietary type of service, unlike IRC, which is open. AOL's Instant Messenger (AIM) program, which is separate from the instant message facility on the AOL service, but coordinates with it, is the most widely used instant messaging program. The Instant Messenger software gives Internet users the capability to send instant messages and create chat rooms with other AIM users, whether or not they use AOL (see Figure 6-1). While easy to use, AIM doesn't have all the features of ICQ (covered in the following). The program is available as a Navigator or Eudora plug-in and comes in the Windows 9*x*, NT, and CE versions, as well as with Macintosh. There is also an all-Java version called *Quick Buddy* that runs in your browser, but it's very slow. The newest edition of AIM also supports voice chat, which is discussed later in the chapter.

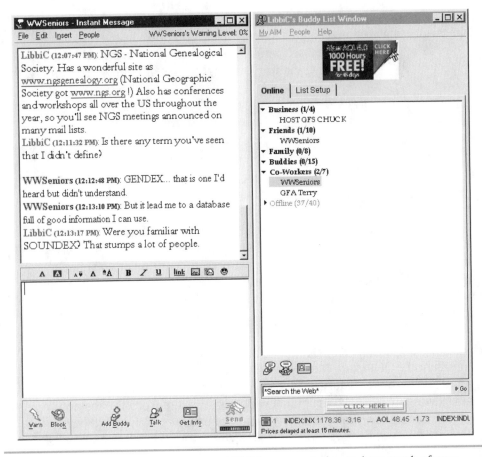

FIGURE 6-1. *AOL Instant Messenger (AIM) has one window to keep track of your buddies and another to carry on your chats.*

ICQ

ICQ (available at www.icq.com) is a system similar to AIM that's free of charge. *ICQ* is a one-to-one or multiple person chat in the instant messaging model. When you're online, it registers your presence with the secure ICQ server, so other ICQ users can "see" you. You can keep a buddy list and be informed when your buddies log on. You can send messages and files, even talk by voice or send live video. All the while, the program runs in the background, taking up a minimum amount of memory and Net resources, so you can continue to surf the Web or run your genealogy program. You can start ICQ, and then look for ongoing genealogy chats, as in Figure 6-2.

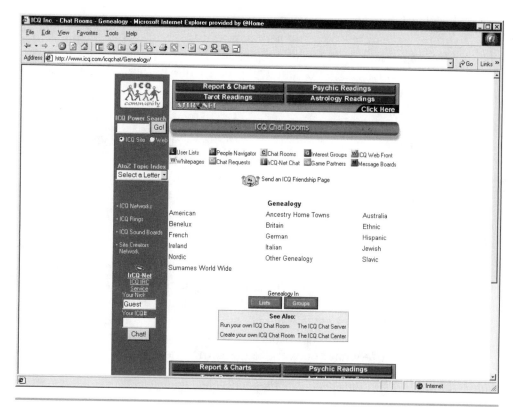

FIGURE 6-2. *To join a genealogy group or chat, visit the ICQ Web page and look for "genealogy."*

Avatar Chat

This is just like other chat programs, but everyone is represented by an *avatar,* which is a graphic, and might be a cartoon, a photograph, or a symbol. Excite's chat program uses avatars and a genealogy chat is usually going about any time of day. This takes a lot of bandwidth (meaning it'll be very slow on telephone-line, dial-up connections).

Other sites that use avatar chat are About.com and WWSeniors.com, both of which have genealogy chats on a regular basis.

mIRC

You can buy mIRC at www.mirc.co.uk/get.html for $20. With it, you can talk to others on IRC channels whether they are using mIRC or some other IRC program. mIRC is an excellent—and popular—program with many features. You can set favorite IRC servers, change the colors of messages sent by different people, and more. A popular IRC program, mIRC is shareware, so you can try it for a while before you send the author the money for it.

Voice Chat Clients

With a microphone, a sound card, and the right software you can participate in voice chats on many Web sites. This usually involves downloading a free software program, such as Wonderhorse, to use Lycos Radio. More about this later in the chapter.

How to Chat

IRC and instant messaging programs work in different ways, but have many of the same functions. Let me urge you again to read the Help file of your program. Most of the time, the Help file is a mini manual that will tell you how to best use the client.

Many modern IRC chat programs type your commands for you. You just choose what you want to do from a menu. Still, you should learn a few commands (see the following box if you want to type commands directly).

> *Note*
>
> *Check the help file of your chosen chat client to learn the commands for IRC. Most chat clients have toolbar buttons and menu items for these commands, but it's fun to know you can enter commands, such as /MOTD, to get the message of the day, and so on.*

When you join an IRC chat room, the server will send you the Message of the Day (MOTD). Some IRC programs show you this in a side window, some in the main window. If the MOTD flies by too fast for you to see it, send the command /MOTD. Just type that into the same place you would type a message. (Anything preceded by a / is a command in an IRC chat room.) The MOTD usually has a greeting, some statistics about how many people are on the server right now, and, sometimes, the rules for this particular server.

Most IRC clients will log you in to the default channel, usually called *Lobby,* while you search for a channel or room you want. You must choose a handle, or nickname, to log on. Once you find a good channel and log on, lurk for a moment, reading the messages. If this is a room you want to join, send a polite greeting (like "Hello, everyone!"). You might find some rooms so friendly that the moment you log on, someone sends you a greeting. Politely acknowledge it.

Besides /JOIN and /MOTD, the most important IRC command for you to know is /IGNORE (or whatever is the equivalent for that server). When someone is offending, bothering, or flaming you, typing **/IGNORE < badguy's handle >** will keep that person's messages from appearing on your screen.

If the chat is moderated, you often have to send a line with a question mark, wait for the moderator to recognize you, and then send your question or comment.

Instant messaging programs, such as AOL Instant Messenger, enable you to block people from paging you or chatting with you.

Chat can be a useful Internet tool, especially when moderated and when a specific subject is chosen. But it can also be addictive and, if you're not careful, you might find yourself doing more chatting than researching. Just remember, I warned you!

A Voice Chat with DearMYRTLE

An up-and-coming format for chat is *voice chat.* DearMYRTLE is hosting regular chats on *Lycos Radio,* a voice chat program. Excite, Yahoo!, Genealogy.com, and other portals are also jumping on the voice-chat bandwagon. Search for "voice genealogy chat" in any search engine to find such sites.

To voice chat, you need to download a program, have a microphone and a sound card, and usually sign on at a certain time.

Unlike text chat, everyone cannot talk at once on voice chat. In the Lycos system, the host controls who is allowed to speak when. You have to speak slowly and say "Over" when you are done for the next person to speak. Unless you have a high-speed connection, such as a cable modem or ISDN, the sound quality will be poor to mediocre.

In Figure 6-3, you can see the screen presented when you are a guest on a Lycos Radio chat. To use Lycos Radio, you download a program called Wonderhorse, go through a setup routine, and then sign on to the program you want. The Wonderhorse window is usually presented to you when you first try to enter a voice chat area on Lycos.

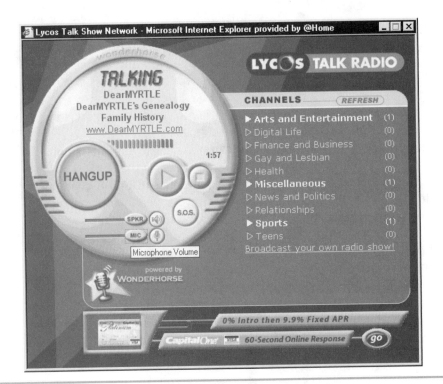

FIGURE 6-3. *Voice chat involves special software, a microphone, and a sound card.*

When you're ready to speak, you can press the TALK button on the screen. The host will receive a message and tell you when it's your turn. If you don't have a microphone set up, you can type in messages. The host will receive the messages and read them aloud.

On a recent chat, I was DearMYRTLE's guest speaker in a session on how to get started in genealogy. Several participants sent DearMYRTLE questions and comments. She received text messages on who wanted to speak next and she gave the go-ahead, when appropriate. As we mentioned specific sites, she could post the URL in the window for all to see. The URL is a live link, and participants can click the link while listening to see the site. The listener's browser opens to the site while the chat continues. (For a schedule of DearMYRTLE's chats, go to www.dearmyrtle.com.)

Because this method of chat requires special software and equipment, and it works best if it's conducted over high-speed connections, it isn't as prevalent as the text versions of chat, but you'll see more of it in the future.

Where to Chat

Okay, let's say you have mIRC, or some other text-based program that uses public, open chat servers. Where do you go to chat?

Several Genealogy sites have both scheduled and impromptu chats. RootsWeb, (point your chat client to irc.rootsweb.com, port 6667, alternative 7000) is just about the best place for genealogy chats.

The chat server is hosted in conjunction with the International Internet Genealogical Society (IIGS) at www.iigs.org. If you point your IRC chat client to irc.IIGS.org, it'll send you on to irc.rootsweb.com in a couple of seconds. There's usually an impromptu open chat going on among the people who manage genealogy Web sites. However, among the most wonderful resources on the whole Net are the moderated, as opposed to the impromptu, RootsWeb/IIGS chats. The scheduled ones are listed at www.iigs.org/cgi/ircthemes/ircthemes. The topics range from very general, such as the Diana Hansen's question-and-answer sessions to discuss all aspects of genealogy research and methodology, to very specific, such as Estill County, Kentucky genealogy.

Besides the wonderful experts and helpful people, the niftiest thing about this IRC server is the translation bot. The *translation bot* is a program on the server that enables you to log on to a chat channel and have the conversations translated to another language. DearMYRTLE told me of a recent chat where people speaking German, Spanish, and Norwegian were all able to ask her questions (which were translated into English for her) and receive her answers (translated back to their respective languages).

Note

If you want to keep on top of the genealogy IRC scene, subscribe to GEN-IRC-L (GEN-IRC-D-digest mode). Send an e-mail message to GEN-IRC-L-request@rootsweb.com (or -D if you want Digest mode) with the single word subscribe *in the body of the message. This mailing list covers mainly the IRC genealogy channels on NewNet, but other networks are also discussed. The main purposes of this list are to enable a genealogist to communicate and set times for live discussions on IRC with other genealogists, post problems, or ask questions relating to genealogy and IRC, and to announce new channels or topics of channels in genealogy and IRC. See Chapter 7 for a discussion of mail lists.*

Another good source of scheduled chats is the About.com set of pages, specifically, About.Genealogy. The page genealogy.about.com/hobbies/genealogy/mpchat.htm has a list of the scheduled genealogy chats.

Note

Often, IRC programs come with a list of chat servers. Just let your IRC client connect to one and look for rooms with the word "genealogy" in them.

In particular, look for the channels on the servers listed in the following table:

Server	Channels
irc.chat.org:6667	#FTMCC (Family Tree Maker Chat), #genealogy
irc.IIGS.org:6667 or irc.IIGS.org:7000	Australia, #Benelux, #Canadian-Gen, #cert, #Cogenweb, #CZER-Group, #DEUgen, #genealogie.fr, #Ger-Rus, #htmlhelp, #IIGS-Ontario, #IIGS-Ukgen, #IIGS-UK-IRE, #IIGS-UnivHelp, #Ireland-gen, #KY-Estill, #NewEngland, #SE-USA, #SHANNON
irc.dal.net:7000	#Canadian GEN #Fianna (Irish Genealogy), #genealogy-events, #genealogy-help, #Genealogy_IRC, #Gen_Family_Tree, #Gentrace, #lunie-links (Lunenburg Co., NS, Canada)
irc.another.net:6667	#genealogy
irc.afternet.org	#GenealogyForum, #Genealogy-n-UK
irc.rootsweb.com	#DearMYRTLE, #IIGS-UnivHelp, #htmlhelp
irc.newnet.net:6667	#family_history, #genealogy, #genealogy101
irc.rootsweb.com:6667 or irc.rootsweb.com:7000	#MSGenWeb
irc.scscorp.net:6667	#genealogy
irc.superchat.org:6660	#Genealogy
irc.webmaster.com	#TMG (The Master Genealogist software discussion)

Wrapping Up

- Chat is the real-time exchange of typed messages over an online connection.

- You can have a private chat with one other person through an instant message program or use an Internet Relay Chat (IRC) server.

- You can talk with many people at one time with either an instant message program or an IRC server.

- Voice chat is an emerging trend and resembles a radio call-in show.

- Many sites have Web-based chats. Such programs run more slowly than IRC or instant message programs.

- Genealogy chat rooms abound. Be careful not to get addicted!

Chapter 7

Genealogy Mailing Lists and Newsletters

Electronic mailing lists are electronic discussion groups based on e-mail messages. All subscribers can send e-mail to the list and receive e-mail from the list. Messages sent to the mailing list get forwarded to everyone who subscribes to it. Replies to messages from the list get sent to the list, where they get forwarded to all participants. And so it goes.

Mailing lists can be completely automated, with a program taking care of subscribing people to the list, forwarding messages, and removing people from the list. Or, people can get into the loop, handling any and all of the mailing list functions that programs can do. Such *moderated mailing lists* can take two forms: They might have restricted memberships where you need to be approved to subscribe or moderator(s) might let anyone join, but would review each incoming message before it gets distributed, preventing inappropriate material from getting on to the list.

Many mailing lists focus specifically on genealogy. In addition, many more lists, while not specifically for genealogists, cover topics of interest to genealogists, such as ethnic groups or historic events.

With a decent mail program (see Chapter 2), participating in mailing lists is easy.

Note

Throughout this chapter, you'll find references to newsgroups and Web sites. This is just an example of how interconnected the genealogy resources on the Internet can be. You'll learn everything you need to know about newsgroups and Web sites in other chapters.

Proper Addressing

Most mail lists have two e-mail addresses. You use one address to subscribe or change how you use the mail list and another to post messages to the other people on the mail list. Some other mail lists might have a third address to use for certain administrative chores, such as reporting some violation of the list's rules to the moderator. Later in this chapter, you'll find plenty of mailing lists to subscribe to. The next few paragraphs will tell you how to do it.

General Subscribing Tips

Say you want to subscribe to the Kent, England, Genealogy mailing list and you know you need to send e-mail to kentgene-subscribe@ egroups.com with the message `subscribe` to join the list. Here's how you do it:

1. Click the Compose Mail icon in your mail program.

2. In the To: box, type **kentgene-subscribe@@egroups.com**.

3. In the Message box, type **subscribe**. Don't add anything else. If your mail program is set to append a signature file automatically, disable it for this message.

4. Click the Send button.

Note

When you subscribe, you usually receive a message in reply that has the commands to unsubscribe and the rules of the list. Save this message to a text or document file for future reference.

This is the general procedure. For some lists, you might also have to add your full real name. For other lists, you might have to add the actual name of the list here. For Roots-L, all you need is `subscribe`. Don't put any signature at the bottom.

An In-Depth Visit to ROOTS-L

Imagine a worldwide, never-ending conversation about genealogy, where novices and experts exchange help, information, ideas, and gossip. Now imagine this conversation is conducted by electronic mail (e-mail), so you needn't worry about missing anything. You've just imagined *ROOTS-L,* the grandparent of genealogy mailing lists on the Internet.

ROOTS-L has spawned entire generations of newer genealogy mailing lists—some large, some small—but this is the original. The mail list page at lists.rootsweb.com hosts thousands of mailing lists about genealogy and history (see Figure 7-1).

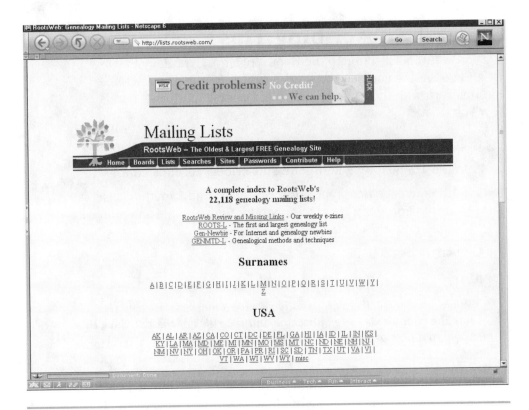

FIGURE 7-1. *The RootsWeb site has thousands of mail lists and Roots-L is the oldest.*

To subscribe, you need to do two things:

1. Make sure your e-mail in-box is large enough to hold the volume of messages you'll receive.

2. Send an e-mail message to roots-l-request@rootsweb.org, with the message `subscribe`. You don't need to include anything else in the message: no signature block, no name or address.

Note

If you decide you want to leave the list, unsubscribe by sending an e-mail message to roots-l-request@rootsweb.org, with the message unsubscribe.

Some ROOTS-L Rules

Roots-L clearly states its rules in its welcome message. It would be wise to apply these rules to every mail list you join, whether or not they're explicitly stated.

- Memorize this rule: messages to people go to roots-l@rootsweb.org. Commands to programs go to roots-l-request@rootsweb.org. I use this trick: I save the "request" address in my e-mail's address book under the name ROOTS-L REQUEST and the posting address under ROOTS-L POST. When I'm ready to send a message to one or the other, I choose it from the address list, just as I would a person's address.

- The list isn't a place to bring up wars of the past, or to discuss religion or politics.

- Advertising or selling a product is not, in general, acceptable. You can, however, post a new-product announcement.

- Make sure you spell the word "genealogy" correctly in all your messages.

- Don't post messages longer than about 150 lines unless you're sure they'll be of very general interest.

- Don't include a "surname signature" in your messages. These are lists of surnames that appear at the end of every message some people send. The surnames play havoc with the list's archive searches, so don't use them.

- Don't post copyrighted material like newspaper articles or e-mail messages sent to you by other people.

- Requote *only* enough of previous messages to be clear about what the discussion is about. Never quote previous messages in their entirety because this bogs down the list.

Communicating with People and Programs

I mentioned this rule earlier in the chapter, but people tend to get confused about it, so here are more details. If you're already sure you know where to send messages to people subscribed to ROOTS-L, as opposed to sending commands to the software at ROOTS-L, you can skip the rest of this section.

It can be hard to remember the distinction between the list server that runs a mailing list and the list itself. This problem is common to most mailing lists. The *list server* gets all the commands: subscribe, unsubscribe, send message digests, and so forth. The *list* gets messages you want to send to other people. For ROOTS-L, messages addressed to roots-l@rootsweb.org go to the mailing list. Messages addressed to roots-l@rootsweb.org get posted on the list for all to see.

So, if you want to request help finding information about your Aunt Tilly, send your message to roots-l@rootsweb.org. If you want to request a copy of the Roots Surname List (described in the next section), send your message to roots-l-request@rootsweb.org.

Available Files and Databases

ROOTS-L has tons of files and databases, which you can get by e-mailing the appropriate commands to the list server that runs ROOTS-L. You can search the ROOTS-L Library for everything from a fabulous collection devoted to obtaining vital records, to useful tips for beginners, to book lists from the Library of Congress, and more. Some of the available files are

- **The Roots Surname List (RSL)** A list of over 350,000 surnames and contact information for the 50,000 people researching those surnames.

- **The Roots Location List (RLL)** Lists locations of special interest to individual researchers, along with contact information for those researchers.

- **U.S. Civil War Units** A file containing information about the military units that served in the United States Civil War.

- **The Irish-Canadian List** A list of Irish immigrants who settled in Canada, including (where available) dates and locations.

- **Books We Own** Books and other genealogical resources owned by Internet genealogists, in which, under certain conditions, the owners are willing to look up information.

When you subscribe to ROOTS-L, you receive a long welcome message that tells you everything you need to know to get started with ROOTS-L, including how to ask the list server to e-mail files to you.

Note

You can also retrieve files yourself by going to the RootsWeb site and browsing for them.

Putting ROOTS-L to Work

Now that you've subscribed to ROOTS-L and you know all the rules, it's time to learn how to put the list server to work. You can control your subscription from your e-mail program. But, you must remember this: you can only control your subscription from the same e-mail account with which you subscribed in the first place. The commands you send will be processed automatically by the list processor—if you remember to send them to roots-l-request@rootsweb.org. If you send your commands to roots-l@rootsweb.org, you'll only succeed in irritating the people running the list.

When you first subscribe to ROOTS-L, you're subscribed in *digest* mode. This means, once or twice a day, you'll receive a large message from ROOTS-L containing a list of all the messages that have been posted to the list since the last digest message. For each topic, there's a topic number, a subject, and the name of the person who posted it. Figure 7-2 shows a piece of a typical digest message.

Digests from ROOTS-L tend to be larger than many e-mail programs —including AOL—can view. Instead of showing the whole message, you might get a display of only the first part of the message or even a blank message with an icon noting an attachment. A copy of the entire message is converted into a text file and stored as an attachment which, on AOL, you have to download (most e-mail programs such as Eudora will download the attachment automatically unless you have set the default not to). From there, it's up to you to open the file with a word processor or text editor and read the messages.

You can get around this by telling the list server to give you each message separately by switching to *mail* mode or index mode. Instructions on how to switch modes are included in the files rootsl.welcome2 and

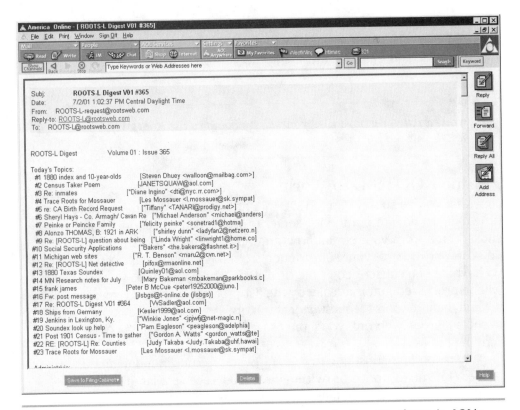

FIGURE 7-2. *ROOTS-L normally delivers in digest mode. Here it's shown in AOL's mail reader.*

rootsl.welcome3. To get them, send e-mail to ROOTS- L-request@ rootsweb.org, put the word "archive" (without the quotation marks) in the subject line and, as the message, include the commands

```
get roots-l.welcome2
get roots-l.welcome3
```

Note, an *l* (ell) is after the dash, not the number 1. Don't include your name, tagline, signature, or anything else besides the commands.

If you just like to browse the messages, go to www.rootsweb.com/ roots-l and scroll down to link to the Archives, and then click the date you want to see (see Figure 7-3). The *Daily Indexes* are where a separate page for each digest is posted in HTML form, with associated message

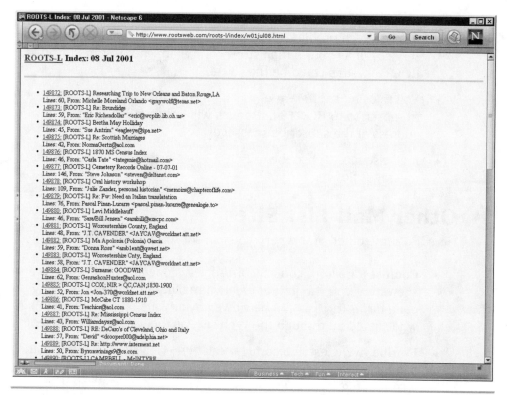

FIGURE 7-3. *Daily Indexes list the Roots-L messages in an HTML format.*

numbers. The searchable archive is where you can select one year, search for a string of letters, such as SPENCER or POWELL, and get the corresponding messages.

Losing Contact with a Mailing List

It's possible you'll stop receiving messages from a mail list, even though you didn't unsubscribe. If this happens, there are two likely causes:

♦ Your Internet service provider (ISP) could be having trouble with its e-mail service. Any service can have intermittent service problems. Sometimes, a whole section of the Internet might be out of order for a few minutes or even for hours. In fact, AOL has had such problems in the past, as have many other online services. If all your e-mail stops coming in—not just mail from ROOTS-L—this could be the cause.

♦ You're using a different e-mail address than the one you used to subscribe to ROOTS-L. Roots-L will only send to the return address of the subscribe message.

♦ If all else fails, subscribe to ROOTS-L again. That should get the messages flowing for you.

Other Mail List Sites

Here are some other sites where you can subscribe to mail lists:

♦ **Coollist** (directory.coollist.com/society/genealogy) *Coollist* is a site where you can join or create a mailing list by simply filling out a form. The lists can be viewed by anyone or only by members who signed up through the Web site, as the list owner chooses.

♦ **Escribe** (www.escribe.com/genealogy) This site has a few lists: some general, some surname specific, and some about history of a certain region. *eScribe* provides a free, Web-based set of tools for list management: a completely searchable Web-based archive of messages, bulletin boards, polls, classifieds, chat rooms, and so forth. eScribe offers personalized service and support.

♦ **JewishGen** (www.jewishgen.org) The *Jewish Genealogy site* hosts two or three dozen groups based on geography, projects of the site, and other interests. Go to the home page and scroll down to Discussion Groups, and then click the link for Special Interest Groups (SIGS) for a current listing. See Figure 7-4.

♦ **Prodigy Genealogy News** (goodstuff.prodigy. com/Mailing_ Lists/index.html) *Prodigy* offers free mailing lists. Go to the Prodigy mailing lists' page, click Hobbies, and then click Genealogy to see the offerings. A worthwhile one is *The Genealogy Newsletter,* a weekly genealogy newsletter with information about discussions on Prodigy's Genealogy bulletin board (message board), schedules for the Genealogy Chat Area's regular sessions and special events, news of interest to all Prodigy members concerning software upgrades and new features, genealogy tips from expert Myra Venderpool Gormley, and other special features as time and space allow.

♦ **USRoots/Rootsquest** (www.rootsquest.com)   This site has surname-based mailists. You can e-mail the site owners to start your own mailing list. Of course, before you start one, check Roots-L, FamilySearch, and other sites to be certain you aren't replicating an existing list.

♦ **Yahoo!** (groups.yahoo.com or www.egroups.com)   Yahoo! and Egroups have merged to provide thousands of discussion groups based on surnames, geography, and ethnicity. Some are public, which means anyone can post to them, and some require you to sign up before you can post to them. Go to the groups.yahoo.com page and search for "genealogy" and/or the surnames you need.

FIGURE 7-4. *JewishGen offers a range of discussion groups by electronic mail.*

Read-Only Lists

Another category of lists is the "read-only" or "announcement-only" list. These are compiled, sometimes by staff and sometimes by an individual, with news and announcements on genealogy. You don't post to them but, instead, you simply receive them like a newsletter or a magazine. Some worth your attention include the following:

Ancestry Daily News   *Ancestry Daily News* is a daily news service from the Ancestry site with free family history tips, news, and updates. Subscribe at www.ancestry.com/library/view/news/articles/dailynews.asp.

DearMYRTLE   *DearMYRTLE*'s daily column can be delivered to your mailbox if you don't remember to visit her site. Simply go to www.dearmyrtle.com and click Subscribe in the navigation bar to the left. Click the "list" (every column individually, as it's posted) or "digest" (consolidated columns, once or twice a week) button. A message will be generated in your e-mail program. Take out any automatic signatures and send.

Eastman's Genealogy Newsletter   Dick Eastman is one of the most respected online genealogists and his weekly newsletter, *Eastman's Genealogy Newsletter,* covers "A Weekly Summary of Events and Topics of Interest to Online Genealogists." Always worth reading! You can subscribe at www.rootsforum.com/newsletter.

Everton's Family History Newsletter   A newsletter of short genealogy tips by Frank Beacon, *Everton's Family History Newsletter,* will give you clues about history and genealogy you'd never have thought about. To subscribe, send a message to history-request@everton.com with the message: subscribe. To unsubscribe, send a message to history-request@everton.com with the message: unsubscribe.

Missing Links and Rootsweb Review   *Missing Links* contains articles on all aspects of genealogical research worldwide, research success stories, book reviews, "Somebody's Links" notices (genealogical treasures such as Bibles, diaries, old letters, and photos), announcements of genealogical conferences, seminars, workshops, family reunions, and humor. *Rootsweb Review* provides news about RootsWeb, its new databases, mailing lists, home pages, and Web sites. Both are weekly. Subscribe by sending a blank e-mail to rootsweb-review-subscribe@ rootsweb.com.

Paper Roots   *Paper Roots* is a "Weekly Round-Up of Genealogy in the News" by Hobson Woodward, a professional genealogist. He searches the news sites for stories that involve genealogy, family history and heritage, and then summarizes them in pithy paragraphs. Subscribe at people.ne.mediaone.net/ehwoodward/paperroots.html.

What's New on Cyndi's List   This is a daily update of new sites added to Cyndi's List. To subscribe, send an e-mail message to: CyndisList-request@rootsweb.com. In the body, include only one word: subscribe. To unsubscribe, send an e-mail message to: CyndisList-request @rootsweb.com and, in the body, include only one word: unsubscribe. Be sure to turn *off* your automatic signature file when sending either of the previous commands to the RootsWeb mailing list server.

Emazing's Genealogy Tip of the Day   *Emazing's Genealogy Tip of the Day* is a once-a-day message with a tip on genealogy online. Go to www.emazing.com/genealogy.jsp (you must have a Java-enabled browser) and click the Options. Enter your e-mail and the tip of the day will be delivered to your mailbox.

Finding More Mailing Lists

Even though that may seem like more mail lists than you can shake a stick at, many more exist. To find more mail lists, first check out RootsWeb's Web site for their ever-growing list. If you point your Web browser to www.rootsweb.org/~maillist, you'll have access to the hundreds of mailing lists hosted by Rootsweb.

John Fuller and Christine Gaunt maintain a categorized directory of genealogy mail lists at www.rootsweb.org/~jfuller/gen_mail.html (see Figure 7-5).

Cyndi's List (www.CyndisList.com/magazine.htm) is a good site to visit to keep up on the latest in mail lists and newsletters.

Finally, you can search a database of publicly accessible mailing lists at the Publicly Accessible Mailing List site, paml.net. You can search this database by keyword or browse the index of hundreds of mailing lists.

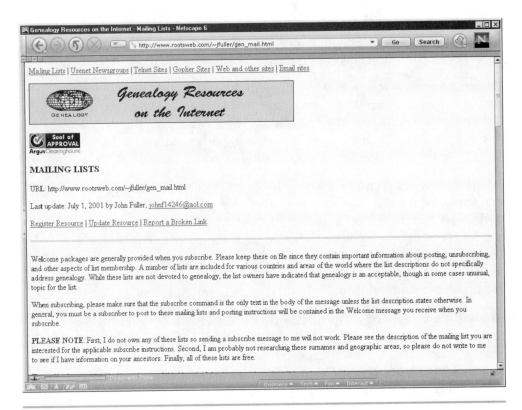

FIGURE 7-5. *Fuller and Gaunt's page on genealogy mail lists categorizes by topic.*

Wrapping Up

♦ E-mail discussion lists bring other genealogists right to your electronic mail box.

♦ When you subscribe to a mail list, always save the reply message, which usually has the unsubscribe instructions, as well as the rules of the list.

♦ Most mail lists are interactive and have one address for subscribing and another for posting messages.

♦ Some e-mail lists are "announce-only," that is, you subscribe to them, but you don't submit to them.

Chapter 8

Usenet

Over the years, Usenet has been called an "Internet bulletin board," an "Internet news service," and many other things. My personal definition of it is this: *Usenet* is an Internet service where messages to the world are posted. E-mail messages might give you the ear of a specific person or group, and forums and bulletin boards might open you to an even wider audience, but when you post to Usenet, you post your messages to the whole world.

Usenet is neither an organization per se nor is it in any one place. Lots of machines carry the messages, receiving them and sending them on down the line. In the end, your Usenet feed comes from your Internet service provider (ISP).

Note

Throughout this chapter, you'll find references to mailing lists and Web sites; an example of just how interconnected genealogy resources on the Internet can be. Stay tuned. In other chapters, you'll learn everything you need to know about mail lists and Web sites to make your research efforts that much easier.

Like so many things concerning the online world, Usenet has its own frequently asked questions (FAQ) file. This file is updated about once a month and, thereafter, posted to the newsgroups news.announce.newusers, news.admin.misc, and news.answers, as well as the Web site www.faqs.org/faqs (see Figure 8-1). Much of what those sites say is contained in this chapter, but reading them won't hurt!

Complicated, but *Useful*

The first thing to understand about Usenet is that it's hard to understand. Don't be discouraged. Some say many Usenet flame wars arise because the users themselves don't comprehend the nature of the network. And these flames, by necessity, come from people who are actually using Usenet. Imagine, then, how hard it is for those unfamiliar with Usenet to understand it! On the other hand, novices should find comfort in knowing that so many people are using Usenet successfully without fully understanding it.

One reason for the confusion is that Usenet is part of the Internet and, for some people, it's the only part they use. Yet, Usenet isn't the whole Internet, any more than Boston constitutes all of Massachusetts.

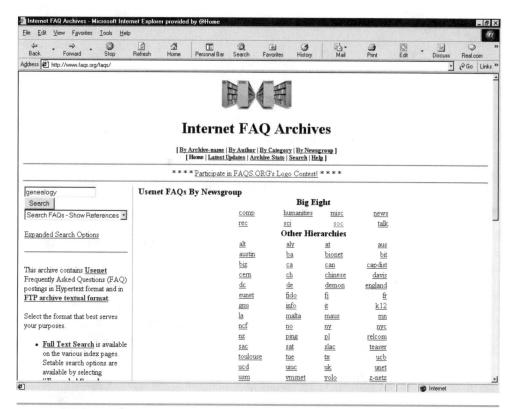

FIGURE 8-1. *Frequently Asked Questions and answers are at www.faqs.org/faqs.*

Usenet's Structure

Usenet's messages are sorted into thousands of *newsgroups,* which are a bit like magazines (because you subscribe to them), in some ways like late-night dorm discussions, and, in other ways, like symposia. A newsgroup is supposed to be a set of messages restricted to a certain subject, but abuses abound. Usenet's flavor depends on the newsgroups you subscribe to. Some newsgroups are wild, some are dull and most in-between.

A *moderated* newsgroup has a referee, who decides what messages get to go on that newsgroup. An *unmoderated* newsgroup (the most popular kind) isn't edited in any way, except you'll get flamed (insulted) if you post a message off the proper topic.

Eight major categories of newsgroups exist:

- COMP for computer-science-related topics
- HUMANITIES for the discussion of philosophy and the classics
- MISC for miscellaneous items
- NEWS for topics about Usenet itself
- REC for recreation, hobbies, and interests
- SCI for science not related to computers
- SOC for social interaction and hobbies (most genealogy topics are in SOC)
- TALK for general conversation

Tom Czarnik, who is a Usenet guru from way back, says, "Let's make a distinction between the Internet and Usenet. The Internet has come to mean the sum of the regional nets, while Usenet is a system for the exchange of newsgroups." Despite this clear separation, you'll often hear of "pictures sent over the Internet" or "messages on the Internet," as if Usenet *were* the Internet, instead of just a part of it.

No person or group has control of Usenet as a whole. No one person authorizes who gets news feeds, which articles are propagated where, who can post articles, or anything else. These things are handled one newsgroup at a time. You won't find a Usenet Incorporated or even a Usenet User's Group. This means, although the freedoms of expression and association are almost absolute, Usenet isn't a democracy. The Usenet is anarchy, to put it frankly, something with little or no control placed on it except that exerted by the social pressures of those participating.

Therefore, sometimes Usenet isn't fair—in part because getting everyone to agree to what's fair is difficult and, in part, because stopping people from proving themselves foolish is also hard.

Although many people are connected through their workplace, Usenet isn't meant as a billboard for advertising. The commercials that *are* tolerated are infrequent, informative, low-key, and preferably in direct response to a specific question. The only exception to this policy occurs in the .biz groups, where advertisements are accepted.

Remember, too, that Usenet isn't restricted to the United States. Many correspondents from around the globe are in places like Europe, Australia, and Japan—so be polite about grammar and spelling.

The Software

To read a Usenet newsgroup, you need a *newsreader client*. Many mail readers, such as Microsoft Outlook, include a newsreader. America Online, Netcom, CompuServe, Delphi, Microsoft Network, Portal, PSI, The Well, and many other high-speed Internet services offer their clients Usenet connections, as well as an appropriate newsreader. A list of publicly accessible Usenet servers (that is, you needn't be a subscriber to sign on to the news server) is at Publicly Accessible UseNet News Servers freenews.maxbaud.net.

You can get to Usenet without a newsreader: several sites have the most recent postings available for search. One of these is Google Groups (formerly Deja.com) at http://groups.google.com. On the opening page, click Advanced Groups Search, and then on the next page, input your terms. A search for Powell genealogy, dates March 1, 2001 to June 17, 2001 is illustrated in Figure 8-2.

You can also search Usenet postings at HotBot and other search engine sites. For most people, however, the most convenient way is to use a newsreader.

Newsreaders

In the "old days" (the first edition of this book!), we had to learn disagreeable, arcane UNIX commands and use unfriendly UNIX newsreaders to obtain the wonders of the Usenet. But, happily, times have changed. We now have a plethora of graphical newsreaders for any platform, be it Windows, Mac, UNIX, X Windows, or whatever. The online commercial services have all integrated newsreaders into their front-end software, too.

You might want to use a dedicated newsreader, however. Outlook Express, a free e-mail and newsreader client from Microsoft, is a popular choice, and it's probably already on your computer system if you have Microsoft Internet Explorer. You can see an illustration of Outlook Express in Figure 8-3.

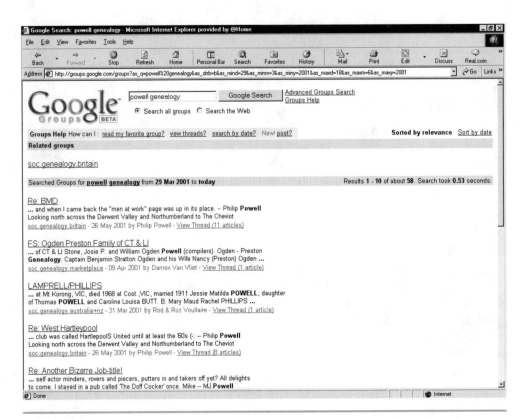

FIGURE 8-2. *At Google Groups, you can read and post to Usenet from the Web. This page is the result of searching Usenet for Powell genealogy.*

The first time you use Outlook Express to read Usenet, you need to tell the newsreader the name of your news server. Your ISP tech support people should tell you what the name is (it will be something like news.yourISP.com). For example, the news server at CompuServe is news.compuserve.com; the news server on Prodigy is news.prodigy.com. Generally, you must be a signed-in customer to use an ISP's news server. For example, you can't get into CompuServe's news server if your connection is through Prodigy.

The layout of Outlook Express is typical. The default is three panes of the window that show you information from your Usenet site. The left pane shows the names of the newsgroups. The upper-right pane shows the message headers of a selected newsgroup. The lower-right

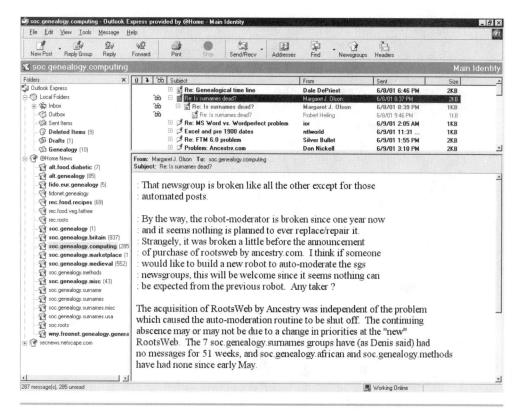

FIGURE 8-3. *Outlook Express has a typical three-pane layout.*

pane shows the body of the selected message. Other newsreaders give you the option of changing this to a different layout (for example, stacking all three panes vertically).

The newsgroups pane will show you the newsgroups to which you have "subscribed" (that is, told the program you want to read regularly). You can set Outlook Express to hide the message headers of the postings you've already read or to show them.

In the newsreader display, the upper-right pane is where information is given about current newsgroup messages (messages are called *articles* in Usenet parlance). Double-clicking one of these lines opens the message in the lower pane. Subject lines in boldface denote unread messages, while previously viewed messages are displayed in regular text.

One nice component of this reader is the search feature. By using Edit | Find on the menu, or the Find button on the toolbar, you can search the whole list of newsgroup articles in alt.genealogy for surnames or place names of interest. Place your cursor in the body of a specific message and you can search the text of that message alone. A newsreader with a search function can save you tons of time and online charges.

Furthermore, you can set filters for the messages, just as you can for e-mail. In Outlook Express, you can click Message in the menu bar and choose Create New Rule for Message. Then you can choose to have subsequent messages (matching that sender, topic, or message text) deleted, marked as read, highlighted with color, marked for following replies, or ignored all together. You can even have them downloaded as text files to your disk.

Replying and posting are accomplished by simply clicking icons on the toolbar at the top. You can reply by e-mail to just the person who posted the message or to the whole Usenet group.

Browsers

Reading Newsgroups with a Web browser (see Chapter 2) is another way to go. Microsoft Internet Explorer uses Outlook Express. Netscape Navigator has a news-reading window.

In Netscape Navigator 6, this means first opening Mail from the menu item Task, clicking Edit | Mail/News Account Settings, and then choosing the Newsgroup Servers, as shown in Figure 8-4. Click Add and put in the information for your news server (for example, news.prodigy.net). Now, Netscape Navigator is ready to read news for you.

In some other browsers, you might have to find the helper programs dialog box, and add the news server and newsreader information.

Internet Service Providers

Microsoft Network, CompuServe, America Online, and the other major online services also have ways for you to read Usenet. Most of them involve reading online, while the meter is ticking (or your phone line is tied up, if you have an "all you can eat," fixed rate, unlimited use plan).

AOL, however, has an option that lets you fetch newsgroup articles when you retrieve e-mail for offline reading. First, you use the keyword USENET to choose your newsgroups. Simply click the search newsgroup button, search for the genealogy groups you want, and click the subscribe

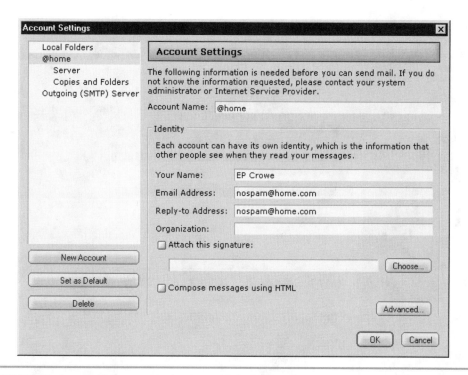

FIGURE 8-4.   *In Netscape Navigator, add the name of your ISP's news server in the Mail/News Account Settings screen.*

button. Then close the window. When you go back to the AOL Usenet window, click the Read Offline button in the upper-right corner of the window. Put articles you want to read offline in the right-hand pane of the window (see Figure 8-5).

Note

Ever since AOL bought CompuServe, the two services' software have become more and more alike. The offline reading function and many other functions on AOL usually work just the same on CompuServe. On AOL, you can also read and write to a newsgroup without formally subscribing to it.

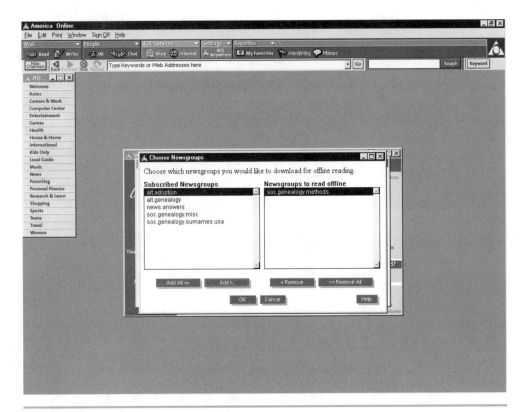

FIGURE 8-5. *On AOL, use KEYWORD Usenet, choose Read Offline, and then choose those you want to read offline.*

Close that window and click the menu Mail/Set Up Automatic AOL. Put check marks in the boxes about sending and receiving newsgroup messages. Now, whenever you run Automatic AOL to retrieve your AOL mail, you'll also get the genealogy newsgroups you chose. This makes the sessions longer, but it takes less online time than reading the newsgroups "live."

On CompuServe, the process works the same way. On MSN, you'll have to read Usenet online (this was true at press time, anyway).

Newsgroups of Interest to Online Genealogists

Once upon a time, only one online genealogy Usenet newsgroup for genealogists was available: soc.roots. As more genealogy researchers came onboard, more messages were posted. Trying to deal with an overwhelming array of genealogical topics—ranging from beginners' questions to historical epochs—soon became unwieldy. Thankfully, after much discussion and soul-searching, we now have an embarrassment of riches in genealogical newsgroups.

However, the ebb and flow of genealogy newsgroups is as constant as it is bewildering. To find genealogy newsgroups, sign on to your ISP and search the list for the word "genealogy." For example, in Outlook Express, I would click the news server, click the Newsgroups button in the toolbar, and then, in the box under "Display newsgroups which contain:", type **Genealogy**.

Some newsgroups you might find particularly interesting are the following:

- **alt.adoption**   A newsgroup that discusses adoption issues, including the search for birth parents.

- **alt.genealogy**   A genealogy group that discusses more general topics. Copied to the ALT-GENEALOGY mailing list.

- **alt.culture.cajun**   A newsgroup devoted to discussions of Cajun history, genealogy, culture, and events.

- **fido.eur.genealogy**   For those researching European genealogy. FidoNet is a message network for dial-up bulletin board systems; some FidoNet discussion groups are copied to Usenet, as this one is.

- **fido.ger.genealogy**   The same as fido.eur.genealogy, but intended for German genealogy research (with most messages posted in German).

- **fr.rec.genealogie**   Copied to the GEN-FF-L mailing list for the discussion of Francophone genealogy, the genealogy of French-speaking people (with messages posted in French).

♦ **soc.genealogy** These original RootsWeb newsgroups have been inactive for most of the first half of 2001. They may be revived later but, at press time, they have little or, in some cases, no traffic.

♦ **soc.genealogy.African** When active, about African genealogy but, at press time, the last post was in March 2001.

♦ **soc.genealogy.computing** An exception to the previous, it remains popular. It has information about various genealogical programs and their corresponding bugs (including how-to instructions). Topics mostly concern software (with some hardware discussions). Copied to the SOFTWARE.GENCMP-L mailing list.

♦ **soc.genealogy.french** Genealogy of French-speaking peoples (with most messages posted in French). Copied to the GEN-FR-L mailing list.

♦ **soc.genealogy.german** Discussions of family history for those with Germanic backgrounds (messages are mainly in German). Copied to the GEN-DE-L mailing list.

♦ **soc.genealogy.hispanic** Genealogical discussions as related to Hispanics (some centering around Central and South American family lines), with many messages in Spanish.

♦ **soc.genealogy.jewish** A moderated discussion of Judaic genealogy. Copied to the JEWISHGEN mailing list.

♦ **soc.genealogy.marketplace** Buy, sell, and trade books; read about programs, seminars, and so forth related to genealogy.

♦ **soc.genealogy.medieval** Copied to the GEN-MEDIEVAL mailing list for genealogy and family history discussions among people researching individuals living during medieval times. Medieval times are loosely defined as the period from the breakup of the Western Roman Empire until the time public records relating to the general population began to be kept, roughly from A.D. 500 to A.D. 1600.

♦ **soc.genealogy.methods** A general discussion of genealogy and methods of genealogical research. Copied to the GENMTD-L mailing list, but inactive lately.

- **soc.genealogy.misc**   This is what became of soc.roots. It's essentially a general discussion of genealogy. Copies to the GENMSC-L mailing list. This is a catch-all for topics that don't fit into other soc.genealogy.* categories.

- **soc.genealogy.nordic**   Genealogical products and services pertaining to Northern Europe.

- **soc.genealogy.slavic**   Slavic genealogy, with some messages in Slavic languages.

- **soc.genealogy.surnames.global**   A central database for sending queries about surnames from around the world. This newsgroup is moderated.

- **soc.genealogy.uk + ireland**   Copied to the GENUKI-L mailing list for the discussion of genealogy and family history. Also used for discussions among people researching ancestors, family members, or others who have a genealogical connection to people in any part of the British Isles (England, Wales, Ireland, Scotland, the Channel Isles, and the Isle of Man).

- **soc.genealogy.west-indies**   Covers Caribbean genealogy and most, but not all, of the messages are in English.

In addition to this list are several groups in the soc.history hierarchies that discuss issues genealogists typically face, such as records, sources, and so on.

Binary Files on Usenet

Some newsgroups carry binary files (recognizable because they usually have binaries in their names). This isn't seen so much on Usenet any more because the Web is far superior for trading sounds, pictures, and

Caution

Viruses have been propagated on Usenet because of binary messages pretending to be pictures, sounds, movies, or other binary file types. Be careful about downloading a binary file from Usenet.

programs. Still, sometimes people do encode a binary file, which has nontext characters, into ASCII codes that can transfer on Usenet.

Some newsreaders automatically take care of this for you. On AOL, you have to jump through a few hoops, however.

When you first join AOL, your account is set to the default to block all binary files in Usenet because most of the groups that send binaries are pornographic. To turn this off, go to Keyword Parental Controls | Set Parental Controls Now | Custom Controls | Newsgroups. Then click Newsgroups Controls | Edit. Choose the Screen Name, and then uncheck the box Block binary downloads.

Encoded binary files are often broken up across several different messages. Gathering the pieces, putting them together, and converting them to their original form used to be a real hassle. America Online's FileGrabber feature makes it simple now.

To get the most out of it, set the Complete Binaries Only preference. To do this, go to the Usenet window and click Read My Newsgroups. Click a newsgroup name in your list that contains the word "binary" or "binaries" to select it, and then click the Preferences button and select the Complete Binaries Only preference. Note, you'll unfortunately have to perform this operation newsgroup by newsgroup because the setting isn't available in the Global Newsgroups Preferences window.

AOL's newsreader alerts you when you're viewing encoded data and gives you three choices: download the file (the AOL software will automatically decode it for you), download the article that contains the code or piece of it (you will then have to decode the pieces yourself), or Cancel. (Remember, CompuServe is running basically the same software as AOL now, so all this works there, too.)

Again, I caution you: don't download and decode binaries on Usenet unless you know and trust the sender.

Newsgroup Frequently Asked Questions (FAQs) Files

Many newsgroups post files of information called FAQs. About once a month, these get posted to their own newsgroup and to the newsgroup soc.answers. Look for a message called the Meta Genealogy FAQ, posted about the 22nd of each month to most of the soc.genealogy newsgroups. This message will show you how to get the FAQ files for the individual genealogy newsgroups.

Net Etiquette and Tips on Usenet

Usenet is a fast-paced way of messaging. It's not quite so "instant" as chat (see Chapter 7), but you will find new postings and responses appear more quickly than on a mail list (see Chapter 5). Sometimes you can get caught up in these almost real-time discussions and forget the conventions. All the rules of conduct covered in previous chapters also apply to Usenet. The most important ones in this area are to try to stay on topic in a newsgroup or you might receive insulting messages, called *flames*.

In general, the following topics are welcomed in genealogy newsgroups:

♦   Your family history information and requests for others to help you find additional sources and material. (Tiny tafels are often posted for this. See Chapter 3 for more information about tiny tafels.)

♦   Information on upcoming genealogical meetings, workshops, symposia, reunions, and so forth.

♦   Reviews, criticisms, and comments regarding software or hardware you've used in your genealogy/family history efforts.

♦   Telling others about bookshops around the world that contain publications or information about this subject.

♦   Almost any message about genealogy in general.

Remember, what you send is posted just as you sent it—almost instantly—unless the newsgroup (such as soc.genealogy.surnames) has a moderator who edits all incoming messages. Think before you click that Send button!

Participants in any genealogy newsgroup want the topics of discussion to relate directly to genealogy or family history. In some groups, however, the tacit agreement is that anything a subscriber thinks is appropriate is appropriate, as long as it relates to genealogy. To discern the lay of the land at a particular site, *lurk* (read without posting) for a while to discover if it tends to be more lax about off-topic posting.

Whenever any newsgroup posts an FAQ, read it. If you can't find an FAQ message or file, make one of your first questions on the group, "Where and when can I get the Frequently Asked Questions for this group?"

Wrapping Up

- Usenet is a message exchange system that's worldwide and ever-changing.

- To read Usenet, you need a newsreader.

- Stand-alone newsreaders are available.

- Microsoft Internet Explorer, Netscape Navigator, AOL, and other browsers have built-in capabilities.

- Web-based Usenet readers also exist.

- Some Usenet groups are copied to mail list groups.

- Read the FAQs!

Part 3

Specific Online Resources

Chapter 9

The Library of Congress and the NARA

Among the best of the online sites maintained by the United States federal government are the Library of Congress (LOC) and the National Archives and Records Administration (NARA). The LOC site is slightly more navigable than the NARA and also has more original source material available. Still, you'll find the NARA site useful to help you decide what to ask for by mail or if you should visit in person.

You'll eventually want to visit a NARA site or the LOC in person because, although many resources are online, not every book or document is available that way.

This chapter gives you a short overview of what's there and how to access the resources of these two sites.

Library of Congress

The mission of the Library of Congress at www.loc.gov is to "make its resources available and useful to the Congress and the American people and to sustain and preserve a universal collection of knowledge and creativity for future generations." To that end, the LOC, since its founding in 1800, has amassed more than 100 million items and become one of the world's leading cultural institutions. The LOC Web site (Figure 9-1) makes a small portion of the LOC's contents available to the world through the Internet.

Three sections of the Web site are of particular use to genealogists. The American Memory section contains documents, photographs, movies, and sound recordings that tell some of America's story. The Research Tools section of the site offers many online databases and connections to resources at other sites. The American Treasures section of the site is of interest more for the wonderful historical artifacts found there than for any specific genealogy information.

American Memory

Click the American Memory link to begin your exploration of the LOC site. The subtitle for this page is "Historical Collections for the National Digital Library." This project is a public-private partnership designed to create a digital library of reproductions of primary source material to support research into the history and culture of the United States of America. Because this is an ongoing project, you can expect the resources here will continue to grow for the foreseeable future.

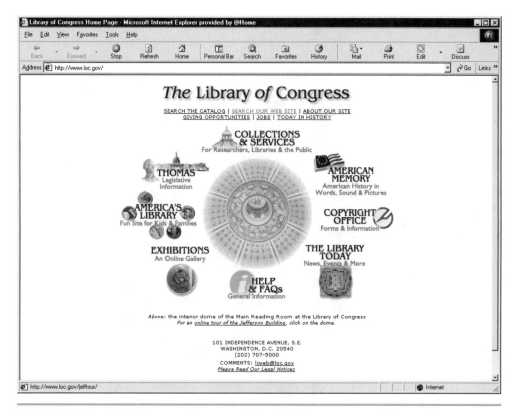

FIGURE 9-1.   *The Library of Congress Web site is a vast general information source, with some significant genealogical resources.*

If you're researching African American roots, you want to look at the African American Odyssey page at memory.loc.gov/ammem/ aaohtml/aohome.html. This exhibition examines the African American quest for full citizenship and contains primary source material, as well as links to other African American materials at the LOC.

Going back to the American Memory Home Page, you can click Collection Finder to explore other primary source material. The best way to find specific things in American Memory is often to find collections first that interest you the most. Each collection has its own distinct character and subject matter, as well as narrative information to describe the content of the collection. While searching all the collections at once could leave items of interest to you "buried" in a long list, visiting a collection's home page and reading the descriptive information about the collection can give you more direction in finding what you want.

The drawbacks to the Collection Finder are that it's a catalog you browse—not an index you search—and it doesn't always list every single item in a collection but, instead, gives an overview of the topic. For instance, if only a few items in a collection pertain to the Broad Topic of "Agriculture," the collection might not appear under that topic. Clicking a category is like saying "I want to see a collection mainly about a certain subject." The list of subjects is at memory.loc.gov/ammem/collections/collsubjindex1.html. Say you know an ancestor owned a hotel in the early twentieth century. In that case, the collection "Hotels 1870–1930" might help you research that ancestor.

Searching the American Memory

You can search for phrases or keywords across all collections and look at essays, images, and primary source material, but do realize you'll get a lot of hits. Searching for the word "genealogy" across all collections gave me 52 hits, which included a genealogy of Pocahontas, letters written to Abraham Lincoln about genealogy (see Figure 9-2), and Memoirs of a Southern Woman Within the Lines (Civil War).

Some of the items you can find in the American Memory include:

♦ Almost 200 books describing the personal experiences of individuals in and on the way to California during and after the Gold Rush

♦ Hundreds of objects dealing with the Women's Suffrage movement

♦ Significant and interesting documents from Americans obscure to famous, as collected in the first 100 years of the Library of Congress Manuscript Division

♦ American Life Histories: Manuscripts from the Federal Writer's Project, 1936–1940

A third area of the American Memory section of the LOC for you to explore is the Maps section. On the Subject page mentioned previously, click "Geography." Then you can search collections containing hundreds

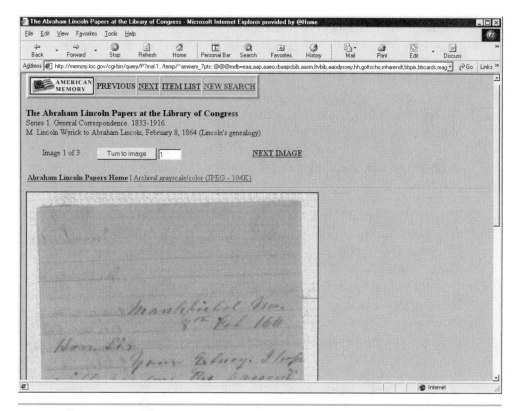

FIGURE 9-2. *Oliver Phelps wrote to Abraham Lincoln about a genealogy he was working on. The letter is in the American Memory collection, The Abraham Lincoln Papers.*

of digitized maps from 1639–1988. You can find city maps, conservation maps, exploration maps, immigration and settlement maps, military maps, and transportation maps, to name a few. And the amazing thing is this wealth of maps is only a tiny part of the LOC's full 4.5 million item Geography and Map Division holdings.

Using the Library of Congress

Click Using the Library of Congress on the home page, and you can click your way through an excellent tutorial on the ins and outs of researching the library in person. Specifically, pay attention to the Local History and Genealogy page in this section, lcweb.loc.gov/rr/genealogy. This tells you about tours, how to prepare for a visit to the LOC, and links to other Internet genealogy resources.

Remember, not everything is available online. If you need to make a trip to the LOC, reading this section first can save you some time and frustration.

The Library Today

This link from the home page tells you about new exhibits, collections, and events at the LOC and its Web site. Visit it at least once a week because anything new posted to the Web site will be announced here.

Research Tools

The Research Tools page at lcweb.loc.gov/rr/tools.html takes you to a large set of useful links of interest for researchers, both on the LOC site and on other World Wide Web sites. These include desk references you can use on the Web, the LOC card catalog of all materials, including those not online, and special databases.

One of these is the Vietnam Era Prisoner of War/Missing in Action and Task Force Russia Databases at lcweb2.loc.gov/pow/powhome.html. This takes you to a page that gives you access to a massive database of over 137,000 records pertaining to United States military personnel listed as unaccounted for as of December 1991. At the bottom of this page is a link to Task Force Russia at lcweb2.loc.gov/frd/tfrquery.html, a set of documents dealing with Americans who are believed to have been held in the former Soviet Union.

Exhibitions

Finally, under the Exhibitions heading on the LOC Home Page, check out the Featured Attractions. You'll find reproductions of dozens of the most treasured objects in the Library's collection. Each one of the objects featured—from the *Whole Booke of Psalmes Faithfully Translated into English Metre, 1640* to an image of the New York *Herald*'s story on the sinking of the Titanic, to a game program from a baseball game between the Kansas City Monarchs vs. Indianapolis Clowns in 1954—has some special historical significance. You might not find any long-lost ancestors when browsing this collection, but such artifacts can fill in the details of the times of our ancestors' lives.

National Archives and Records Administration

While the Web site of the National Archives and Records Administration (NARA) at www.nara.gov is neither as user-friendly nor as professional-looking as the LOC site, it still has some useful features. Specifically, a genealogist would be interested in the NARA Web databases. One of these is the NARA Archival Information Locator (NAIL) system. You can use this to search the catalogs of NARA holdings; the genealogy column of the NARA quarterly, *Prologue*; and the Genealogy Page, which is an outline of how to research genealogy with NARA resources.

The opening page of NARA is a bit of a mishmash, but the navigation bar at the top has a tab called Research Room. This is the place to start. On the Research Room page, you can find links to articles containing general information, such as "How to do Research at NARA." All of these links are worth exploring. However, the quick link to "Genealogy & Family History" is the place for the beginner.

The Genealogy Page

This is a general outline of the finding aids, guides, and research tools to help you prepare before you visit one of NARA facilities or for requesting records from NARA, or for using the Web to look for information. Divided into six parts, it links you to various documents and sites for specific genealogy tasks.

Part 1 notes the different NARA facilities across the country and links you to pages with hours, location, and directions. Part 2 links you to essays and data on how to do genealogical and biographical research, especially with specific topics, such as Census records, women, and African American research. Part 3 explains NARA's polices and plans as they affect genealogists. Part 4 directs you to free and for-fee publications of NARA that can help you with specific topics, such as military service records and how to order them. Part 5 links you to workshops and courses being offered by NARA in Washington, D.C., and around the country at regional facilities. Part 6 directs you to other genealogical resources on the Web, with links to the National Genealogical Society, Association of Professional Genealogists, and Ancestry, to name a few.

Although NARA isn't updated at regular intervals (at press time, the site says it was updated in April 5, 2001) it still has useful information for the beginning genealogist and even for the experienced one who has hit a brick wall.

After touring this general help, you're ready to tackle the specific resources on NARA.

NARA Web Databases

You can search various subsets of the NARA holdings from their Web databases, starting at search.nara.gov. Click Search in the navigation bar at the top of every page in the NARA site to get there.

On the Search page, you can input any term and search the NARA Web site (see Figure 9-3). You can also search individual databases, which find items that could be on other Web sites, on the NARA Web site, or might be at some regional NARA site.

To search the main site, simply put in a term or two in the box at the top. Entering **Powell genealogy** got over 900 hits—obviously an embarrassment of riches! Note, however, you can search the results to narrow them down, you can exclude the Presidential Libraries, and so on. So, instead, you might want to choose Advanced Search.

On the Advanced Search page, you can uncheck the boxes by the sites to search: Main: Full text of all Web pages; Presidential Libraries: Full text of all Web pages on Presidential Library Web sites; and a prototype collection of selected federal agency records' schedules and manuals called ARDOR. You can also define search words in Boolean terms: must (AND), must not (NOT), and should (OR). You can limit the date of the results and how many hits to display on a page.

Using genealogy as a "should" term and Powell as a "must" term, got 266 hits. When I unchecked the boxes on ARDOR and the Presidential Libraries, that was more than cut in half, to 177 hits. Making both terms "must" cut it down to five. You can see how the advanced search can be a powerful tool.

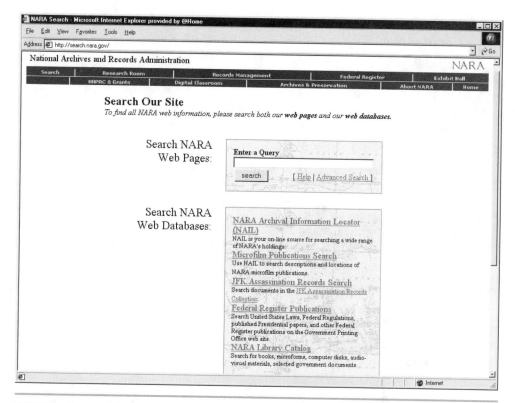

FIGURE 9-3. *The Search page is a good place to start using the NARA Web site.*

NAIL

NAIL is an experimental version of what is hoped to be the future online catalog for NARA. In final form, NAIL should catalog the holdings in Washington, D.C., the regional records services facilities, and the Presidential libraries.

In its present form, NAIL contains more than 3,000 microfilm publications descriptions, 400,446 archival holdings descriptions, and 124,000 digital copies. However, it represents only a fraction of NARA's vast holdings. For example, not even all images on the NARA Web site are described in NAIL. To find other images, you can go to the Digital

Classroom, the Online Exhibit Hall, and the individual Presidential Libraries' Web sites, all linked from the NARA Research Room page.

From the NAIL main page at www.nara.gov/nara/nail.html, you can choose to search microfilms or archival holdings. If you choose the archival holdings, you can choose the following:

- **NAIL Standard Search**   This is a basic search by keyword, media type, and/or NARA unit.

- **NAIL Expert Search**   An advanced search that enables you to limit for keyword, title, media type, NARA unit, description level, control number, and/or specific description level identifiers.

- **NAIL Digital Copies Search**   This page searches only for archival descriptions that link to digital copies. You can limit the searches by keyword, media type, and/or NARA unit.

- **NAIL Physical Holdings Search**   In this, you search only the physical holdings information for motion picture films and sound and video recordings of NARA's Motion Picture, Sound, and Video Branch. Media type, specific titles or title keywords, control number, and/or specific description level might limit search terms.

Choosing Digital Copies search, for example, turned up the record shown in Figure 9-4, a draft registration from World War II.

Microfilm Publications Search

The NAIL microfilm publications search is a basic search of up to two terms (using AND, OR, or NOT), the Microfilm ID, or the Record Group Number. You can also choose all NARA units or limit the search to one. The results for each individual hit tell you what NARA locations have the microfilm for viewing and how to order a copy from NARA.

JFK Assassination Records Collection

As the name states, this is every document the NARA has on the assassination of John F. Kennedy. A disclaimer on the site says, "Users should be aware, this database is a compilation of entries input by the originating agencies. Although the National Archives and Records Administration provided guidelines for data entry, the master database is inconsistent in the terms used to describe records. Please keep this in mind when planning your database searches."

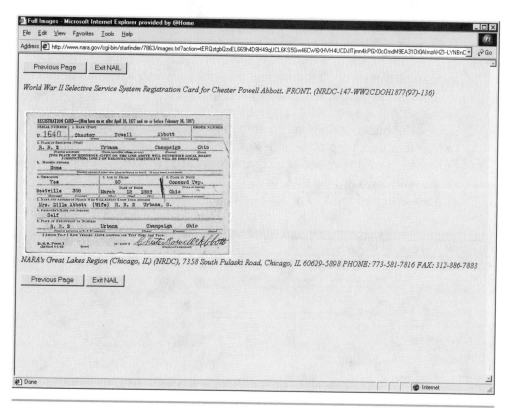

FIGURE 9-4.   *This draft registration is one of the images available from the NAIL search of NARA databases.*

Federal Register Publications

The main attraction for family historians here would be the public papers of the presidents, if you have a president in your genealogy.

NARA Library Catalog

If you click the link for the NARA Library Catalog from the search page, you get another page that directs you to www.nara.gov/alic. Some of this is available only to the archivists at NARA, which means you must go to a NARA facility and ask the staff to do the search for you to get the actual record or document.

Other parts of it, however, are available from the Web. As explained in Chapter 12, looking at a card catalog before you go can save you a lot of time and frustration during your visit. If what you need is available by loan or can be copied for a fee, it might save you a trip altogether.

You simply fill out the form shown in Figure 9-5 with the desired terms. The page comes back just the same as before, except the number of hits is shown in red at the top. You then have to click the button that says Display Search Results. From that page, you can sort by Subject or Author, and see complete records for the items you select.

As with any card catalog, you get the call number, details on the size of the work, and links to related items on the same subject.

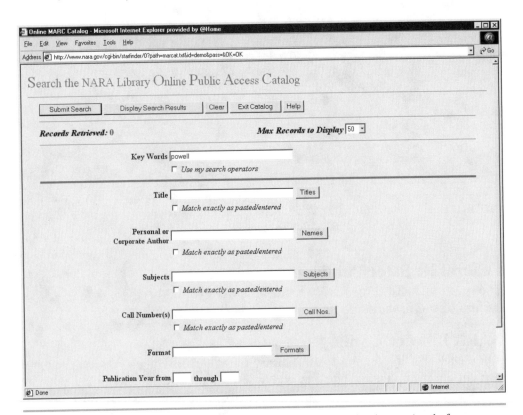

FIGURE 9-5. *The NARA Library Online Public Access Catalog has a simple form to complete.*

Prologue

The quarterly NARA magazine, *Prologue,* has a Web page you can link to from the NARA home page or go to directly at www.nara.gov/ publications/ prologue/prologue.html. Special issues, such as the recent *Federal Records in African-American Research*, may be posted almost in entirety, but usually a regular issue has one or two features on the Web site, plus the regular column, Genealogy Notes. A list of previous columns is at www.nara.gov/publications/prologue/artlist.html#genea. This site is worth bookmarking.

Some Experience Helpful

Much of what is available at the LOC and NARA sites would be most helpful for intermediate-to-advanced genealogists: The best way to use these sites is to know what you're looking for to start, such as a specific military record or a particular WPA oral history. The beginner can find the schedules of workshops on NARA and the how-to articles on the LOC helpful, as well.

Wrapping Up

♦ The Library of Congress (LOC) and the National Archives and Records Administration (NARA) have online guides to genealogy, as well as some full-text and scanned image resources.

♦ Both the LOC and NARA have several search functions to help you find records and materials.

♦ Using the online versions can help you before you visit the physical location and visiting the physical location might be necessary.

Chapter 10

The Church of Jesus Christ of Latter-day Saints

What we've all been hoping and praying for finally came true in 1999: The Church of Jesus Christ of Latter-day Saints (often abbreviated as LDS) put up a searchable Web site of their millions of names in May 1999. Access to the Web site is free.

> ### Note
> *The information in this chapter is accurate at press time. Refinements, additions, and deletions are sure to be introduced as users give the Webmasters feedback. Consider this chapter a general guide to the site.*

FamilySearch Internet

FamilySearch Internet at www.FamilySearch.org searches these records:

- Ancestral File

- International Genealogical Index

- FamilySearch Internet Pedigree Resource File

- Family History Library Catalog

- Family History SourceGuide

- Non-LDS Genealogical Web sites from a list compiled by LDS editors, some of which have original source records

All except the last are from LDS records. FamilySearch Internet is designed to be a first step in searching for family history information. When you're searching LDS proprietary sources, the first screen doesn't give you the information itself. The search results simply tell you if the information you need is available, with links to the Web site, Family History Library Catalog citation, International Genealogical Index (IGI), Ancestral File (AF) reference, or citation in one of the CD-ROMS the LDS has for sale.

This is more helpful than it sounds, however. Just finding a match in the Family History Library Catalog can save you hours of research. Some FHCs are so busy, patrons are only allowed one hour a week at the computer! Searching the catalog before you go can make your trip much more productive. Finding a reference in the CD-ROMs might tell you if it's worth the price for you to order it. Finding a reference in the IGI or AF can tell you if someone else has already found the primary record or source you're looking for, and sometimes how to contact the person who found it. In short, this can save you a lot of time and travel. Only rarely, though, can you use this resource to get to primary (original record) sources.

Most of the records in FamilySearch Internet are abstracts of original records. If you find a reference to a record you want in the LDS sources, you usually can get a complete copy of it from a Family History Center (FHC). FHCs are located throughout the world and have many of the records found in FamilySearch Internet. You learn more about FHCs later in the chapter.

Another big advantage to this site is it has more international data than most online sources. While the greatest part of the data is from English-speaking countries, you can find some information from every continent. Asian sources are the most limited, while North American and European are the most abundant.

A Run-Through

Many days, the site is so popular, I find getting through to the server is difficult. The record so far is 11 million hits in one day, according to some newspaper reports. Even after I get on the site, I sometimes find maintaining contact with the server is hard. Don't give up! Keep pressing ENTER once you have www.familysearch.org entered in the address box.

The opening page of FamilySearch Internet is shown in Figure 10-1. To the left is a navigation bar with links to information on the Mormon church and genealogy in general. On the top is a navigation bar to the most-often used features of the site. It's worth your while to click "Why Family History?" and "Where Do I Begin?" on this page. These take you to basic how-to files.

In Search for Ancestors (the tab Search in the navigation bar takes you to the same page), you can search the AF, IGI, the Pedigree Resource File, and Web sites. The Web sites are from a catalog gathered by FamilySearch editors and submitted by FamilySearch users. You can click any one of these on the left to limit your search to just one; the default is all four. The link above the input form, "Tips on How to Search for Your Ancestors," is worth exploring. This tells you in plain language what can work and what won't work on the search page (you can't search for just a given name, for example), and how to narrow your search.

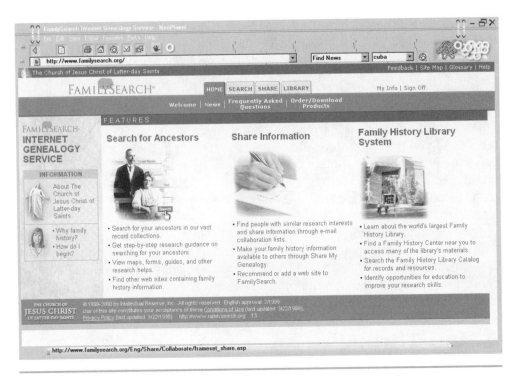

FIGURE 10-1. *FamilySearch's opening page gives you several choices.*

Using a pedigree chart form on this screen, you can input only a last name, or both first and last names, and even the names of a spouse and parents if you know them. Of course, the more information you put in, the fewer matches you get. The less specific you are, the more matches you get.

I searched for my family's most elusive ancestor, Abraham Spencer. After 20 years of searching, Mother and I still cannot find his parents. We know he was born in New York in 1792, so I limited my search to that year and to the United States. The results were the two records from IGI and one from Ancestral File shown in Figure 10-2.

Clicking the one that seemed the closest match, I can see no one has yet recorded parents for Abraham. Still, if I needed what information is there, I could click Prepare records for download at the bottom of the page and save it to my disk.

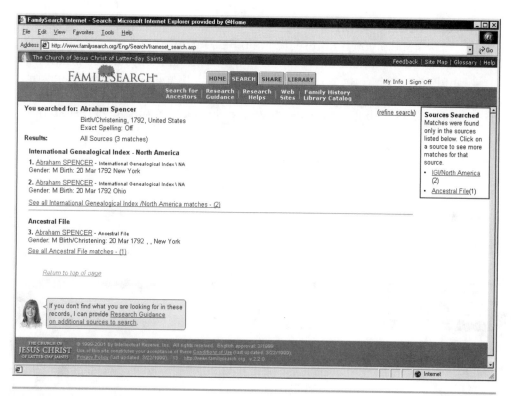

FIGURE 10-2.   *Three records matched my Abraham Spencer.*

Research Guidance

Research Guidance is a tool that helps you decide what records are most likely to have information about your ancestor. It lists the best records to use, recommends the order in which to search them, provides step-by-step instructions for finding information in the records, and tells you where the copies of the records may be located. Select a place where your ancestor was born, christened, married, or died. If you aren't sure of the country, click Determining the Country Where Your Ancestor Lived for some ways to determine it. Only places for which research guides have been created are listed on the page. As more are added, they'll appear. So, for example, you can find guidance for Baden, Germany, but not for Zaire.

Research Helps

This can help you find research outlines, forms, maps, historical backgrounds, and information on how to find a map, name variations, and so forth. You can sort the list of links by place, title, subject, or document type. As in Figure 10-3, you can sort by document type and choose helps that are forms, government publications, LDS research guides (excellent resources and they're all available online!), maps, and word lists.

Note

Word Lists help you spot key genealogy words in foreign languages.

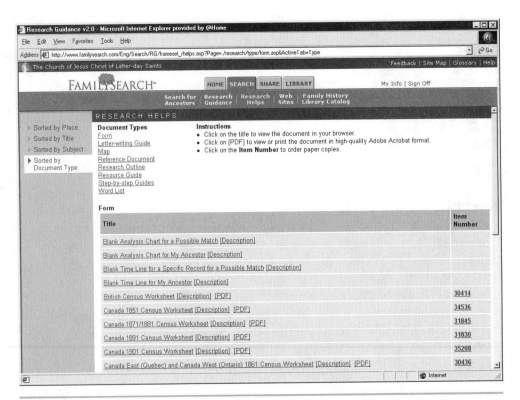

FIGURE 10-3. *You can find research helps by document type.*

Other Cool Stuff

Just as with any Web site worth its salt, FamilySearch Internet has interactive elements. You find this under Share on the navigation bar tabs. Before you can enter this area, you need to register as a user. Enter your name and address, e-mail address, and then choose a user name and password. When I registered as a user and accepted the terms of service, I searched the mail lists, such as those shown in Figure 10-4.

One click on Join and I was a member of one of the lists. Lists exist for specific persons, as well as for general surnames.

Another interactive area enables you to share your research with others on FamilySearch Internet. By clicking Share Your Genealogy, you get instructions on how to upload a GEDCOM for the LDS church to store in its granite vaults in Utah.

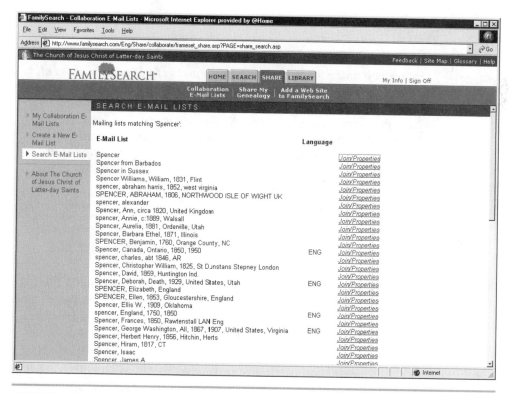

FIGURE 10-4. *You can search for e-mail lists of interest on FamilySearch.*

> **Note**
>
> *Be sure of the accuracy of your data before you submit it. Preserving mistakes and miscalculations for all time would be a shame! Also, be aware that when you submit, you must verify you have the right to submit the information and allow it to be used. You also accept legal responsibility for any permitted use made of the information, by LDS or anyone using the site.*

GEDCOMS submitted to FamilySearch Internet will be preserved at the Granite Mountain Records Vault, near Salt Lake City, Utah. They also become part of the FamilySearch Internet databases. The information then becomes publicly available on compact disc or at the FamilySearch Internet site. Although your genealogy may later be added to Ancestral File, if you want to be sure this happens, follow the normal process for contributing information to it.

> **Note**
>
> *As with any online service, you must carefully read the conditions before you upload! For example, you must get permission from all living persons named in your GEDCOM to send their information to FamilySearch Internet. By uploading, you give the LDS permission to publish your name and address as the contributor of the information you submitted. Uploading your GECOM gives the LDS permission to use, copy, modify, and distribute any of the information included in your submission without compensation and permission to use information from your submission to create new databases.*

Even though you give LDS certain rights to your information, uploading it to the FamilySearch Internet doesn't limit your right to publish, sell, or give the information you submit to others.

To upload your GEDCOM, have your genealogy program create the file. Click the Share tab and then click Share My Genealogy. Read the information at the links "How do I submit my genealogy?" and "What will be done with my genealogy?" When you're ready, click "I am ready to submit," read the rules, and click "I agree." Fill out the form and click Submit.

In Add A Site, you can register your genealogy site with FamilySearch Internet. The editors of the site then review your information and decide if it will be included in the database of Web pages to be searched from the opening page of the site.

Library

The *Library* tab of the navigation bar leads to information on the Family History Library in Salt Lake City, a search form to find a Family History Center near you, an online version of the card catalog to the Family History Library, and a list of courses and classes on the library and genealogy.

Other Resources

From the Family Search Home Page, the link Order/Download Products leads to a page that lists books, forms, CD-ROMs, and other items you can buy from the LDS store. You can also download the free PAF program using this option. All you have to do is register. The new PAF version has an option to use with Palm computers.

How to Use Information from LDS

The LDS has scores of computerized resources. They willingly share much of the data as a public service through their Family History Centers. Their microfilms, computer programs, and other sources are slowly becoming available to libraries, archives, societies, and the general public. Modern genealogical research owes a great deal to the Mormons and it seems natural to include their publicly available resources, whether or not they're available online.

As of June 2001, Family History Centers were granted Internet access from their computers. Gradually, many centers will add online access—an exciting development.

Information is collected from Temple work that goes into the IGI from both submissions and extractions, and other submissions that may or may not have Temple work go to the Ancestral File. Many nonmembers also submitted to the Ancestral File, so their information would be preserved before the days of the Pedigree Resource Files came about.

If you haven't submitted your ancestors to one of these files and they haven't been extracted as part of some other activity, they won't be in there. Also, if they're in there, you should check out the original documents to make certain they are your ancestors and the submissions are correct. Remember, these files, like books and CDs you can purchase, are only as good as the work of the submitter or author. All of these are wonderful guides that can help you find your ancestors, but you still have to do the work to determine whether they are your ancestors as well as whether the information is accurate. Errors can occur in published work, whether they're published in paper, CD-ROM, or on the Web.

Some Background

Without trying to explain the theology involved, I'll simply say that Mormons consider it a religious duty to research their family history. A detailed explanation can be found at the LDS home site.

The results are archived at the church's headquarters in Salt Lake City and are distributed in microfilm, microfiche, and CD-ROM to their many Family History Centers throughout the world. The data is in several forms, but the most important to the online genealogist are the AF and the IGI. These are updated regularly: new data is inserted in the databases and you can search them at local Family History Centers on CD-ROM.

The Pedigree Resource Files are similar to the Ancestral File and they're growing rapidly. The Pedigree Resource File is a new lineage-linked pedigree file containing genealogical data. Like the well-known AF, it contains pedigrees and family group sheet data in electronic form. Unlike the Ancestral File, it contains notes and source documentation, which varies in thoroughness, and it only contains the data as of that moment. Data isn't updated from CD to CD unless the submitter resubmits it for inclusion on another CD.

One of the LDS church's objectives is to build its copyrighted databases known as the AF and the IGI, and to continually improve their accuracy and the software used to search them. The IGI is a record of the Temple work. The AF offers pedigrees the IGI doesn't.

> **Note**
>
> *According to LDS, the IGI contains "several million names of deceased persons from throughout the world." These are "entries," however, not distinct individuals. Different people descended from the same family duplicate many entries. Furthermore, many individuals are listed with both a birth and a marriage entry.*

The IGI contains two basic kinds of entries: submissions by individual LDS members of data on their ancestors (which may or may not be accurate); and submissions from the extraction program. This is a systematic and well-controlled volunteer program of the church. Members all over the world extract birth or Christening dates, as well as marriage dates and locations from microfilms of original parish and civil records.

The source of the data from information provided for each entry is on the CD-ROM version of the IGI. But, always remember, the IGI is only an index. You should go to the source document to verify the information.

The IGI, and the AF and Pedigree Resource Files are unrelated because data entered in one file doesn't necessarily show up in the other file. Each has a value of its own and all files are worth searching. The advantage of the AF is you can get pedigrees from it. The advantage of the IGI is that it provides more detailed information.

Most non-LDS genealogists see the IGI as the more valuable of the two. While errors turn up in both, the IGI is closer to the original records (data is normally entered into the IGI first) and it has excellent bits and pieces of information, especially its references to where the information originated. Many non-LDS genealogists always go to the IGI first, but the Ancestral File with the new 5.5 GEDCOM format enables you to find out what documentation supports the entry. Considering you can get the submitter's name and address, as well as pedigree or descendant charts, the Ancestral File is also a valuable resource.

While errors do exist, the percentage seems low. Plenty of genealogy books printed in the past 100 years have more errors than these databases.

Treat the AF and IGI the same way you treat a printed book about a surname—with informed caution. Use it as an excellent source of clues, but always crosscheck it with primary records. While the computer increases the amount of data you can scan and makes things much easier, it doesn't necessarily improve accuracy. Human beings are still the source of the data.

The LDS apparently wants to make the AF and IGI available to more people. Originally, you had to visit the Family History Library in Salt Lake City, Utah, to use these databases. Today, that library has CD-ROMs on a LAN that's connected to the Joseph Smith Memorial Building next door and about 200 access terminals scattered about the buildings.

About 15 years ago, the church set up local Family History Centers (FHCs) around the world. In 1988, they started selling the databases on microfiche. In 1991, the church released them on CD-ROM to their local centers, and later to societies and libraries. The New England Historic Genealogical Society has a copy at their library in Boston, as does the California State Sutro Library in San Francisco.

The pattern here is more and more access via more and more means. The Mormons are cautious, though, and they take small steps, one at a time. The church hasn't worked out all the legalities of online access, and it's concerned about presenting a useful, viable program and database for its members and the rest of the world. The main concern of the church is not to turn out a bad product.

A Visit to an FHC

Terry Morgan, Genealogy Forum Staff Member on America Online at terryann2@aol.com is also a volunteer at the two FHCs in Huntsville, Alabama. These setups are typical, Terry says, and she gave me a personal tour of the one closest to our homes.

"The best way to find one near you is to look in the White Pages of the phone book for the nearest Church of Jesus Christ of Latter-day Saints," Terry says. "Call them and find out where the nearest FHC is, and the hours. Honestly, because the hours vary so much from place to place, the best time to call is Sunday morning around 10. Everyone's at church then!" If you call any other time, she says, give the staffers lots of rings to answer the phones, which might be on the other side of the church from the FHC. Or, Terry says, you could write to the LDS main library at the address listed in the last section and ask for the latest list of FHCs. An excellent list of FHCs is maintained by Cyndi Howells at www.cyndislist.com/lds.htm and a list of the larger FHCs at the LDS home site at www.familysearch.org/Eng/Library/FHC/frameset_fhc.asp.

All FHCs are branches of the main LDS Family History Library in Salt Lake City. The typical FHC is a few rooms at the local Mormon church, with anywhere from one to ten computers; a similar number of microfilm and microfiche readers; and a collection of books (usually atlases), manuals, and how-to genealogy books.

The FHC I was visiting had two IBM-compatibles that shared a printer in a room with a small library of about 25 reference books. In a room close by were two film readers and two fiche readers. Users are asked to sign in and out, and a cork bulletin board holds the latest genealogical technique brochures from the Salt Lake City Family History Library.

In some FHCs, Terry told me, the computers are networked, so patrons can use the CD-ROMs in a shared environment. The FHCs are going on the Internet and can access FamilySearch.org. Meanwhile, FamilySearch Internet and IGI are available at most FHCs, and usually only one person at a time can use them.

"Some centers offer training on the programs, some insist they train you before you start using the computers, and some only help if you ask," Terry says. "We offer help if you ask. We've not had much trouble installing ours here. The only tricks were it has to have expanded memory, and you can have some TSRs [terminate-and-stay-resident programs, which sometimes cause conflicts] running, but few enough to have low memory and expanded memory as well." The FHC computers usually are on Windows platforms.

In the typical FHC setup, you must reserve a computer and you're given a certain block of time to use it. Printouts of what you find usually cost nickel a page. Some centers allow you to bring your own disk to record the information, but others insist that you buy certified virus-free disks from the FHC at a nominal fee.

Before you make a trip to the FHC near you, check out FamilySearch and determine which resources you need. You can save lots of time!

Wrapping Up

♦   The LDS Church has a searchable index online.

♦   The site also includes mail lists and a catalog of genealogy sites.

♦   Family History Centers are where you can view microfiches and films of actual records or order copies of records.

Chapter 11

Ellis Island Online: The American Family Immigration History Center

Are you one of the 40 percent of Americans who can trace an ancestor to the immigration center at Ellis Island? If so, you definitely want to check out Ellis Island Records Online at www.ellisislandrecords.com. This site is the best thing to happen to online genealogy since the launch of FamilySearch. The interface is a little cluttered, but still easy to navigate. The response to search input is fast and the results are understandable.

The Family History Center is available on the Internet, or on a first-come, first-served basis or by appointment at the Ellis Island Immigration Museum. It features an electronic database on immigrants, passengers, and crew members who entered the United States through the Port of New York between 1892 and 1924, the peak years of Ellis Island's processing. The data, taken directly from microfilms of the ships' passenger manifests provided by the National Archives and Records Administration, has never before been available electronically. It was extracted and transcribed through the phenomenal efforts of 12,000 volunteers from The Church of Jesus Christ of Latter-day Saints, spending 5.6 million hours on the project. With over 22 million records, the countries with the highest representation in the database are Italy, Austria, Hungary, Russia, Finland, England, Ireland, Scotland, Germany, and Poland.

The Grand Opening

On April 17, 2001, The Statue of Liberty-Ellis Island Foundation (the Foundation), National Park Service (NPS), Ellis Island immigrants and their families, dignitaries, and other guests gathered at the Ellis Island Immigration Museum to celebrate the opening of the American Family Immigration History Center. The Web site went online at 6 A.M. Eastern time that day.

The grand opening included appearances by Tom Brokaw, Charles Grodin, and Joel Grey; a search for Irving Berlin's immigration records involving his daughters and great grandson; an overview of the Family History Center's Family Scrapbook activity; and a presentation by Foundation Founding Chairman Lee A. Iacocca.

It was also the first annual Ellis Island Family History Day, an event that's cosponsored by the Foundation, the National Genealogical Society, and America's governors. That date in 1907 saw the largest number of immigrants ever processed on one day at Ellis Island—11,747 people, more than twice the usual number. That record-breaker will be honored every year.

The American Family Immigration History Center (not to be confused with a regular LDS Family History Center) provides easy access to information such as an immigrant's given name and surname, ethnicity, last town and country of residence, date of arrival, age, gender, marital status, ship of travel, port of departure, and line number on the manifest. The database is free-of-charge on the Internet or can be accessed at the Center for an entrance fee of $5 that includes a printout of an immigrant's arrival data. A scanned reproduction of the original ship's manifest, as well as a photo of the ship of passage, in the near future, will be available either on CD-ROM or on archival paper for an additional fee.

The Center, designed by Edwin Schlossberg Incorporated, also offers the Family History Scrapbook, which is discussed later in this chapter. As with previous Ellis Island projects, funding has come from the private sector, with no government funds employed.

The original ships' manifests show the passenger names, ages, and associated passengers, which is useful for clues to relationships. The ship information, often with a picture, gives the history and background of each ship that brought the immigrants.

If you register as a regular user, which is free, you can keep copies of the passenger records, manifests, and ship images in Your Ellis Island File. This can be opened on the computers at Ellis Island or on this Web site. You can purchase copies of these documents at the online Gift Shop (more about this follows) or at the Interpretive Shop on Ellis Island.

If you join as a Foundation member at $45 per year, you can

- Annotate passenger records in the Ellis Island Archives

- Create and maintain your Family History Scrapbook

- Order one free copy of your initial Scrapbook (print or CD-ROM)

- Receive a 10 percent discount at the online Gift Shop or at the Center

- Support the ongoing work of the Foundation at Ellis Island

- Possibly get a tax deduction (check with your accountant)

A Guided Tour

The site has two parts: free services and services available only to Foundation members.

Even without the free registration, you can have access to "The Immigrant Experience," two sets of articles on the population of the United States. "Family Histories" give real-life examples of people whose ancestors passed through Ellis Island. "The Peopling of America" is a series of articles showing the timeline of people coming to the United States from all over the world, beginning with those that crossed the Bering Straits 20,000 years ago.

To gain access to the free searches, you must register. This involves choosing a log on name and password, and giving your name and address.

Searches

As a registered (free) user, you can use the Passenger Search. Click Passenger Search from the main page to get to the screen in Figure 11-1.

Simply put in the first and last name, and then click Search Archives. If you want to do a more targeted search, click Passenger Search at the top of the page, and then click New Search. On that search page, you can input a first name and a last name, and then choose Male, Female, or don't use gender.

The results will be presented to you in a table, as shown in Figure 11-2. If the results list is too long, you can refine the search with the choices in the bar at the left of the screen, filtering for year of arrival, ethnicity, age on arrival, port of departure, and/or name of ship. For example, without the exact match, "Abraham" would also return "Ibrahim," "Abraam," and other near matches.

Choosing one of the names gives you the screen in Figure 11-3. The details of the person as they appear on the manifest are listed. You can look at the transcription of the ship's manifest to see who is recorded near the person and click the Ship link to view details about the vessel. Registered members can save the searches and results in an online file for later reference and use.

Community Archives

Only members of the Foundation can create annotations to the records, but all registered users of the Web site can view them. Annotations supplement information in the record, telling more about the passenger's

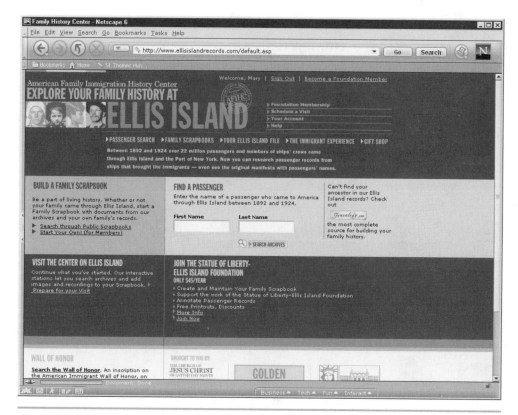

FIGURE 11-1. *Ellis Island Records Passenger Search enables you to look for your needle in the 22 million-immigrant haystack.*

background and life in the United States. This information hasn't been verified as accurate and complete—it's simply what the annotating member believes to be the facts.

Click View Annotations on the passenger record (if no View Annotations button exists, the record hasn't yet been annotated). If you're registered with the site, you'll see a list of annotations. If you haven't yet registered, a screen will appear, enabling you to do so.

Ellis Island Family History Scrapbooks

If you've paid for a membership to The Statue of Liberty-Ellis Island Foundation, you can contribute Family History Scrapbooks on the Web

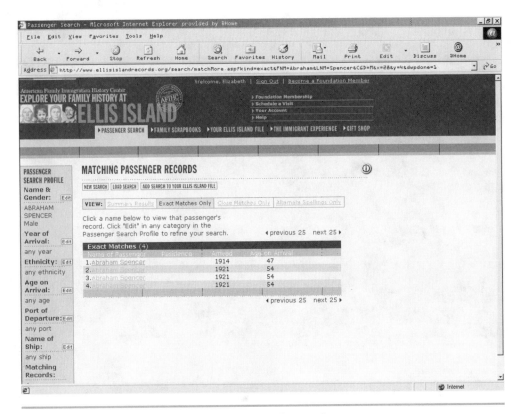

FIGURE 11-2. *A table of results from a simple search*

site or at the American Family Immigration History Center itself on Ellis Island.

Family Scrapbooks combine member-submitted pictures, images from the Ellis Island archives, written stories and memories, and sound recordings. Members can choose to keep the Scrapbook private or add it to the publicly available Ellis Island Family History Archive. If you visit the Center, you can use a scanner, a camera, and recording equipment to work on Scrapbooks.

When you begin your Scrapbook, you have 16 pages to work on, including a Title Page and an Author Page. Ten of those pages have space for your images and four have space for an image from the Ellis

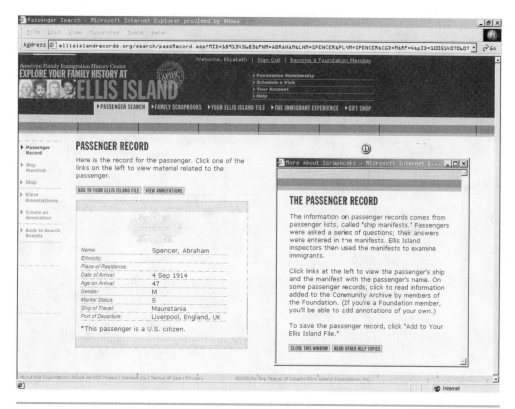

FIGURE 11-3. *A passenger record gives you details on a specific person.*

Island Foundation archives. The site's documentation suggests you decide on a particular story or theme for your scrapbook. Begin with a Passenger Search in the archives to find passenger records, ship images, and ship manifests to save in Your Ellis Island File and add to your Scrapbook, for example.

If you're a paying member, you can click Family Scrapbooks on the main menu, and then click Start New Scrapbook (if this is the first time) or Create New Scrapbook (if previous Scrapbooks exist). You get to choose a style and create a Title Page and an Author Page. Once you complete those steps, you'll see the Scrapbook's Table of Contents. From there, you compose the Scrapbook pages. A page under composition is shown in Figure 11-4.

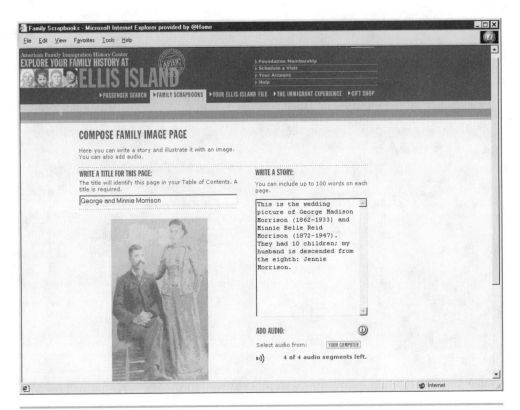

FIGURE 11-4. *You can upload pictures and record stories of your ancestors.*

The Scrapbook pages can accept both pictures and audio recordings. It's recommended that you gather image and audio files in one location on the local computer's hard drive, so they're easy to find. On a Scrapbook page, under Add an Image, click Your Computer. In the Upload Image window, you can browse the local computer for the file or simply enter the filename. The files are uploaded one at a time and they can be 180 kilobytes or smaller. If a file is larger than 210×210 pixels, it will be resized, proportionally. If a file is smaller, it won't be resized. When Use Selected Image is clicked, the image will appear on the page and the window will close.

Members can also add files from the Ellis Island Library by clicking Our Library on a Scrapbook page under Add an Image. Your Ellis Island

File may also contain passenger records, ship images, and ship manifests, which you saved during a Passenger Search. Click the left and right arrows to review the images in Our Library or Your Ellis Island File, and then click Use This Image to add it to the page. A finished page is shown in Figure 11-5.

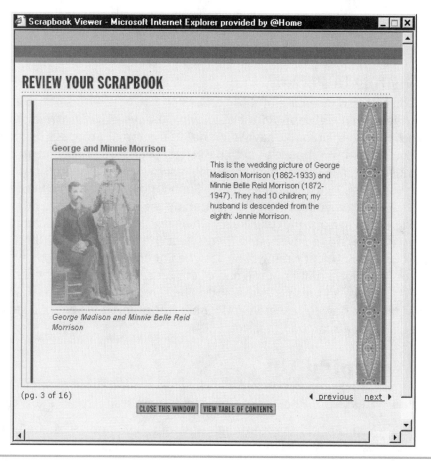

FIGURE 11-5.   *Finished pages in the scrapbook have the elements you've chosen.*

On a Scrapbook page, under Add Audio, click Your Computer and choose an audio file. You can upload up to 1.8 megabytes per file. Then enter a title for the audio file. When you click Use Selected File, the title assigned to the file appears on the page and the window will close. To remove an audio file, under Remove Audio? click Delete This Audio File.

At the online Gift Shop, paid Foundation members can order one free copy of their Scrapbooks, choosing either a high-quality print or a CD-ROM copy. Additional copies are available for purchase. On the Table of Contents, click Purchase Scrapbook.

Visiting In Person

You can also take care of these chores on site at the museum, but you have to make an appointment within 90 days of your arrival. Click Schedule A Visit in the navigation bar at the top of any page on the site. You can simply choose to do a passenger search ($5 entry fee to the museum) or to work on a Scrapbook (as with the online version, you must be an annual member of the Foundation to work on a Scrapbook).

You input your choice of undertaking for the visit, list the number of people in your party (and whether any will need wheelchair assistance) up to seven, and then select the date and check-in time. Your appointment time will be assigned at check-in. You'll be given a confirmation number at the end of the process to present at check-in. Print a copy to present at the desk. The screen also gives you links to articles on how to research and gather information for either a search session or a scrapbook session.

Wrapping Up

- ♦ Ellis Island Records is a wonderful new resource on the Web.

- ♦ You can search for immigrants from 1892 and 1924, the peak years of Ellis Island's processing by name, date, and ship.

- ♦ You can upload pictures, sounds, and text to an online scrapbook if you're a member of the Statue of Liberty Foundation ($45) or if you visit the museum itself in New York.

Chapter 12

Online Library Card Catalogs

Despite all the wonderful things appearing online, many of your genealogical expeditions will still be in libraries. The online world can help you here, too.

One of the wonderful things about the online world is the plethora of libraries now using electronic card catalogs. This greatly speeds up your search while you're at the library. Not only can you perform an instant search of all of a library's holdings (and, sometimes, even place a hold on the material), but also, with many terminals scattered throughout the building, you needn't look up your subject, author, or title on one floor, and then repeatedly run to another floor to find the referenced material. If your local library hasn't computerized its card catalog yet, it probably will soon.

But, oh, the joys of looking in the card catalog before you actually visit the library! You know immediately whether that library owns the title. With a few more keystrokes, you can find out whether the title is on the shelf, on reserve, on loan to someone, or lost without a trace. You can find out whether the book is available by interlibrary loan or found in a nearby branch library.

You can connect to online card catalogs in two main ways. The newest and easiest way is through the World Wide Web. Here, the card catalog appears like any of the Web-based databases you encountered in this book.

With older online library card catalogs, however, the connection could be by telnet. If this is the case, you use a separate program to send commands to, and receive information from, the database. I'll explain this later in the chapter.

A third way to connect to an online card catalog is with a hybrid Web-telnet connection. In this case, the library (or libraries) maintains a Web site with all the relevant information on how to use the card catalog. Then, when it's time to look at the card catalog database, your browser starts a telnet program to work with the database.

Connecting to Card Catalogs by Web Browser

The easiest and most visually appealing way to connect to online card catalogs is via the Web. The mechanics of how this works is irrelevant. What's important is a Web-based interface lets you use the card catalog without having to install and load a telnet program.

A wonderful example is the University of Texas at Austin's UTNetCAT at dpweb1.dp.utexas.edu/lib/utnetcat. You can use the forms that appear at this Web site to search by author, title, subject, or any combination thereof. The results of the search are links to the card catalog. Click one and you get a full display of that item's record, as shown in Figure 12-1.

A Sample OCC Search

Another slightly more complicated example is the Web site at the University of Alabama in Huntsville. To log in, go directly to the card catalog's search page at library.uah.edu and click the I'm a Guest button.

The search screen is shown in Figure 12-2. Once in the system, you can look for items in any field that contain certain words or phrases. Even better, by using Boolean options (AND, OR), you can specify that words, author names, title words, or subject terms must have a particular relationship to each other. If you want something written by a specific

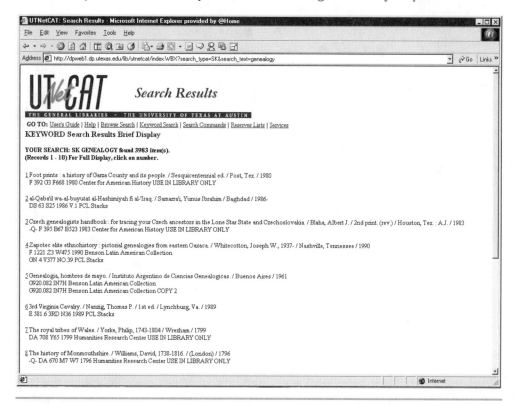

FIGURE 12-1.   *The University of Texas provides a wonderful example of Web-based card catalogs.*

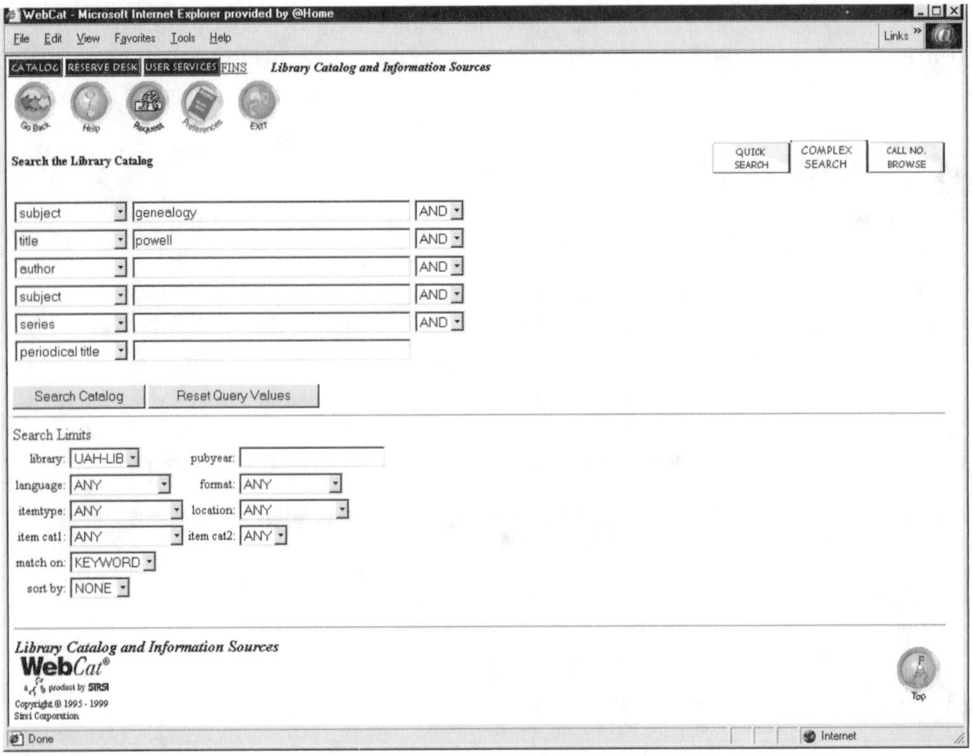

FIGURE 12-2. *The library card catalog at the University of Alabama in Huntsville lets you construct complicated queries if you select Complex Search.*

person, searching by Author makes sense. If you know most of the words in the Title, a Title search can tell you if the library has the item and where it's located. If you don't know an author or title, you can search by Subject.

You can have better luck with your searches if you narrow them as much as possible. You can choose to search on Author and Title, Subject, and Word or Phrase, or any combination of these. You can also search recent issues of magazines using the Periodical Title option.

To show you how this works, I chose a search with "genealogy" in the general keyword field, and "Alabama" in the subject field. Figure 12-3 shows the results of that search, which turned up seven cards matching the search criteria. Each card has a short synopsis that appears on the

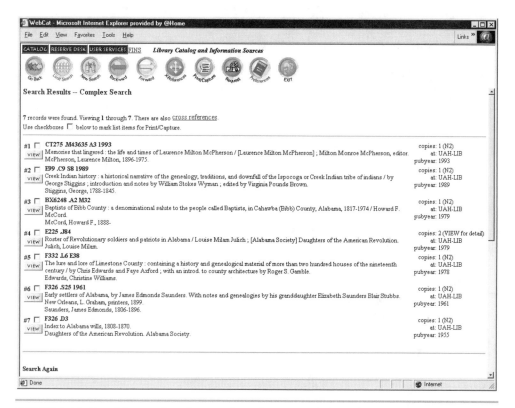

FIGURE 12-3.   *The results of a search at this site include a short synopsis.*

Results page. By clicking the View button next to a synopsis, you can get additional details about the book like the publication date, author, and cross-links to other relevant cards in the catalog. Then, if you like, you can print the results or have a copy of them e-mailed to you.

The Library of Virginia is home to a similarly powerful online card catalog, located at eagle.vsla.edu/catalog.

I ran a test with "genealogy" as the general keyword, and "Powell" as the subject keyword. The results can be seen in Figure 12-4. If I want to refine my search further, I could also use Boolean terms such as AND, NOT, and so on.

Overall, the Library of Virginia's card catalog is easy to understand and read—and, I might add, a pleasure to work with.

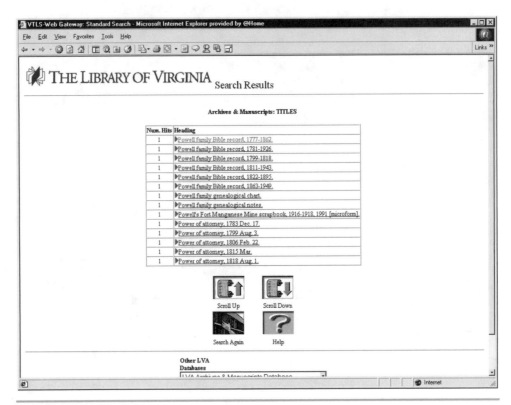

FIGURE 12-4. *Search results at the Library of Virginia show holdings for Powell and genealogy.*

Connecting to Card Catalogs by Telnet

Some card catalogs, while online, haven't been put in Web format yet. This means you have to get at them another way. Enter telnet. *Telnet* is a system that lets you connect to another computer as if your PC were a terminal on that computer. Although telnet is an older Internet service, it's still widely used for online card catalogs.

Windows comes with a basic telnet program that's activated by Microsoft Internet Explorer and Netscape Navigator whenever you try to connect to a telnet address. Just enter the address, for example telnet:// 206.155.86.131, on the browser's Address line and a telnet window pops up, ready to go. (That address, by the way, is for the Wauconda Area Library, Wauconda, IL.)

A typical card catalog you can reach using telnet and the Internet is the South Carolina State Library card catalog (telnet://leo.scsl.state.sc.us). When you type the address in the address box, the Web browser automatically starts the telnet program, establishing a connection to the library. Afterward, enter the password (LION) listed in the first window (type it in where the cursor appears) and press ENTER. You see the library's Main Menu, as shown in Figure 12-5.

I started by typing a 1 to get into the LION card catalog, and then searched by Subject using the term "genealogy." As a result, the catalog returned a list of cards containing my search word. I also received several references to other sections of the card catalog (see Figure 12-6).

If you've ever used the electronic card catalog at your local library,

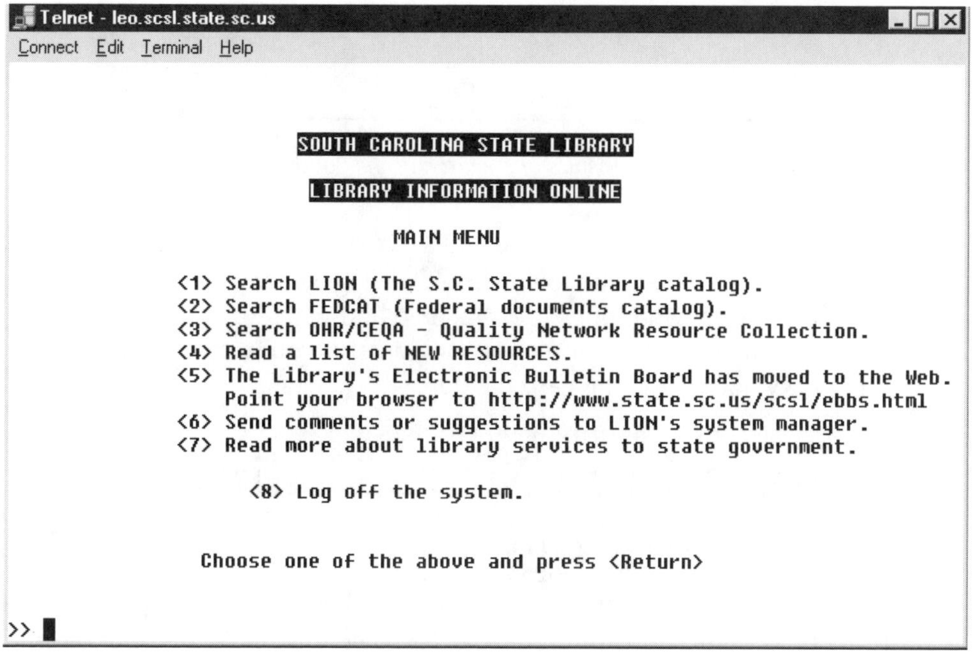

```
Telnet - leo.scsl.state.sc.us                        _ □ X
Connect  Edit  Terminal  Help


                  SOUTH CAROLINA STATE LIBRARY

                  LIBRARY INFORMATION ONLINE

                         MAIN MENU

         <1> Search LION (The S.C. State Library catalog).
         <2> Search FEDCAT (Federal documents catalog).
         <3> Search OHR/CEQA - Quality Network Resource Collection.
         <4> Read a list of NEW RESOURCES.
         <5> The Library's Electronic Bulletin Board has moved to the Web.
             Point your browser to http://www.state.sc.us/scsl/ebbs.html
         <6> Send comments or suggestions to LION's system manager.
         <7> Read more about library services to state government.

             <8> Log off the system.


         Choose one of the above and press <Return>

>> █
```

FIGURE 12-5.   *The telnet LION system menu gives you several choices*

```
 Telnet - leo.scsl.state.sc.us                                    _ ▣ ▲
 Connect  Edit  Terminal  Help
                                                              *LION*
 Your search: S=GENEALOGY

 LINE
   #    --------Author--------   --------------------Title-------------------  Date
   1    America the Beautiful    Old Glory; a pictorial report on the grass   1973
   2    American Society of Ge   Genealogical research: methods and sources   1960
   3                             Ancestors [videorecording] / Brigham Young   1997
   4    Arnold, Jackie Smith.    Kinship: it's all relative / by Jackie Smi   1990
   5    Beard, Timothy F. (Tim   How to find your family roots / by Timothy   1977
   6    Carmack, Sharon DeBart   The genealogy sourcebook / by Sharon DeBar   1997
   7    Carmack, Sharon DeBart   Organizing your family history search : ef   1999
   8    Colket, Meredith B. (M   Guide to genealogical records in the Natio   1964
   9    Colwell, Stella.         Family roots : discovering the past in the   1991
  10    Crandall, Ralph J.       Shaking your family tree : a basic guide t   1986
 (More)

 Enter:  Line #    (1,2,3, etc.) to see more information.
         N         to see Next screen.       P    to see the Previous screen.
         B         to Backup.                ST   to start over.
         You may begin a new search at any time.

 >>
                                             Enter ? for HELP.
```

FIGURE 12-6.   *These are the results of a search of the South Carolina State Library card catalog.*

this should all look familiar to you. By following the onscreen instructions, you can find out what titles are available and where they're located—in short, find all the information you would get if you were physically in the library, looking at the card catalog.

Where to Find More Online Card Catalogs

Once you explore the online card catalogs shown in this chapter, you'll probably want to find some more. One place to look for both the Web and telnet kinds is the Genealogy Resources page at the University of Minnesota. Browse down to the Libraries and Archives section at www.tc.umn.edu/~pmg/libraries.html. Other places to look for online library card catalogs are the following:

- **Gateway to Library Catalogs**   A page by the Library of Congress is at lcweb.loc.gov/z3950/gateway.html. This is a simple alphabetical list of sites.

- **Libdex** (www.libdex.com)   A worldwide directory of library homepages, Web-based OPACs, Friends of the Library pages, and library e-commerce affiliate links.

- **National Union Catalog of Manuscript Collections, or NUCMC**   It can point you not only to library card catalogs, but also to archives and repositories with Web sites. You can find it at lcweb.loc .gov /coll/nucmc/index.html.

- **USGenWeb** (www.usgenweb.com)   When you visit this site, look under the state, and then the county you're researching to see if the library catalog is linked.

- **Yale University Library** (www.library.yale.edu/pubstation/ libcats.html)   The site has a page that includes connections to Yale Library online catalogs, information about card catalogs, and connections to library catalogs from around the world.

Learn to use these systems. Who knows what treasures you can find?

Wrapping Up

- You can search the card catalogs of many libraries across the world from the Internet.

- Some libraries have begun scanning in images and actual text of their genealogical holdings.

- You can search for such libraries at several sites across the Internet.

Chapter 13

International Genealogy Resources

Sooner or later, you'll get "back to the boat"—that is, you'll find your original immigrant in a certain line. The first immigrant in your family might have arrived just a generation ago, or centuries ago.

Of course, the next step is to start researching in "the old country," outside the United States. Can you do this online? Well, that depends on the country. Some countries do, indeed, have online records for you to search, especially those countries where English is spoken. But some countries only have sites with the most general information and you'll be lucky to find the address of the civil records offices. You'll probably wind up doing a combination of online and in-person research and, possibly, some research by mail, too.

You'll find these sources useful in doing this sort of research:

- ◆ **LDS research guides** The Church of Jesus Christ of Latter-day Saints has developed pamphlets on researching immigrants and ancestors around the world. Later in this chapter, I describe how to get these pamphlets online, but you can also order them for a nominal fee from any Family History Center. Look in the Yellow Pages or in the White Pages for "The Church of Jesus Christ of Latter-day Saints" for a Family History Center near you.

- ◆ **Ships' passenger lists** When you have positively identified your immigrant ancestor, you can find a lot of information from the ships' passenger list. The Ellis Island Records site (see Chapter 11) is one such repository. Others are listed at Cyndi's List Ships and Passenger's Lists Page at www.cyndislist.com/ships.htm.

- ◆ **National Archives** A country's National Archives might have a Web page describing genealogy how-tos for that country.

Perhaps you might find the experience of a real-life genealogist helpful. Denzil J. Klippel had quite a bit of success and was kind enough to share his story with me.

A Success Story

It didn't happen overnight. Denzil started with what he knew, researched back to the boat and, finally, found his family's village of origin. How he did this is fascinating.

Denzil only knew his parents, his grandmother on his mother's side, and her brother and sister. "In the beginning, I didn't take advantage of the resources on the Net like DearMYRTLE, and so forth and ask questions.

(See Figure 13-1). But I soon learned everyone in the online genealogy community is willing to help answer questions. We don't need to reinvent the wheel—just ask if anyone has done this or that," Denzil says.

Denzil visited a local Family History Center (FHC) in New York City. There, he found his grandmother's family, but not his grandmother, on one of the microfilms. Requesting the name and address of the submitter, he contacted him with a query, including his e-mail address. Soon, another researcher contacted him by e-mail, and everything began to fall together.

Note

A complete listing of Family History Centers, searchable by state, is at deseretbook.com/browse/family-history/index.html.

Klippel sent for his father's death certificate (New York) and found his place and date of birth (California), his father's place of birth

FIGURE 13-1. *Getting help from people who have done international genealogy is only one way the online world can make your quest easier.*

(Upstate New York), as well as his mother's maiden name (Settle) and place of birth (California). He was able to order some of these records

> *Note*
>
> **You can find where to write for many vital records at The National Center for Health Statistics page www.cdc.gov/nchs/howto/w2w/ w2welcom.htm (see Figure 13-2).**

online through various vital records sites maintained by these states.

"After going back to my great-grandfather and finding he came from Germany, I hit a brick wall. Not knowing what to do, I went to one of the search engines—Yahoo!—and put in the name Klippel. It gave me 6,000 places where the name appeared on the Net, most of them regarding an illness discovered by a Klippel. I captured all of the Klippel

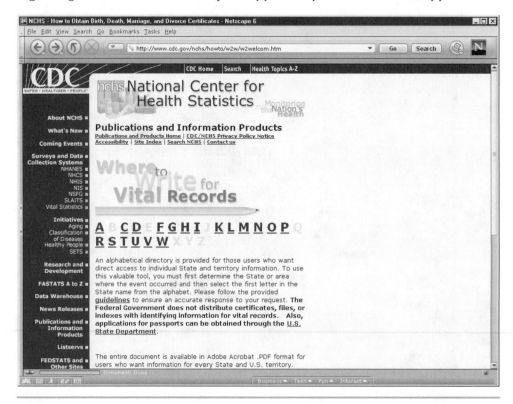

FIGURE 13-2. *Find where to write for vital records from the United States at Where to Write for Vital Records at www.cdc.gov/nchs /howto/w2w/ w2welcom.htm.*

e-mail addresses and sent them a message saying I was researching the Klippel family name and if they were interested in working with me, perhaps we could find some common ancestors, or at least discover where the Klippels originated."

Denzil said he doesn't recommend this approach. "This shotgun approach never works. I still send e-mails to all Klippels I find, but refer them to my Klippel site at www.channel21.com/family/klippel that talks about the origins of the Klippel name and not family lines," he said. What worked was searching for the surname on www.google.com and looking for the genealogy sites.

After e-mailing people with Klippel genealogy sites, as opposed to every Klippel he could find online, Denzil heard from people who had been searching the line. Several were cousins he didn't know he had and, since that time, he now calls all Klippels he comes in contact with "cousin."

"One of these cousins had the name of the town in Germany where my Klippel line came from (Ober-Hilbersheim). I found this village had a

FIGURE 13-3. *Denzil found his ancestors' village online at www.gau-algesheimvg.de.*

Web site (see Figure 13-3) and sent a letter to the mayor. He responded via e-mail and said he knew of my line and told me there were still Klippels living in the village," Denzil said.

"In the meantime, other Klippels in Europe contacted me and, before I knew it, I was planning a trip to visit some of them and Ober-Hilbersheim. When they heard I was going to visit they all said I had to stay with them. I bought my airline tickets online via Priceline.com and my train pass online."

Now Denzil was really into the in-person, offline mode! Through electronic and surface mail, he made appointments at all the archives he planned to visit in Germany. When he arrived, they were ready for him and, in most cases, they'd already done all the lookups. As Denzil gathered the research material, he mailed it home to himself. This was important insurance against losing or misplacing any of the papers during his sojourn.

"My trip started in Ober-Hilbersheim and I stayed with the mayor. He took me to all the archives and helped me get all the Klippel family history back to 1650! My distant cousins in the village welcomed me with open arms. I then went to the Netherlands and stayed with the Klippels there and they took me to the Island of Tholen where the first Klippel came from in the 1400s. Then on to Hamburg to visit Helmut Klippel and the archive there," Denzil said.

Note

Denzil was also able to discover some family history, along with the names and dates. His great-great-grandfather Johann Klippel was the baker in Ober-Hilbersheim, having moved there from Bubenheim, and the Klippels there are still bakers and work in the same building. Johann Klippel was married four times and had 22 children. Johann was a member of the village council. Be sure to look for such details in your research.

"And last, but not least, on to Sweden to stay with Alf Klippel, who had given me a wealth of information about the origins of the Klippel name via e-mail and done most of the translating of the Old German documents I had been receiving over the Net."

It took some footwork and perseverance but, after seven years, Denzil feels he accomplished a lot in his international search and the online resources made it possible (see Table 13-1 for some good sites to start your international search).

Site Name	URL
DearMYRTLE	www.DearMYRTLE.com
Everton's World Resources	www.everton.com/reference/world-resource.php
Go.com Translator	translator.go.com
International Internet Genealogical Society (IIGS)	www.iigs.org
Internet Family History Association of Australia (IFHAA)	www.shoalhaven.net.au/~cathyd/austmenu.html
RootsWeb lists	rootsweb.com (HESSE-L; PFALZ-L)
Sephardic and Sephardim Genealogy	www.orthohelp.com/geneal/sefardim.htm
Tracing Immigrant Origins Research Outline	Go to www.familysearch.org. Click the Search tab in the navigation bar. Click Research Helps. Sort the list by title (choices on left.) Click *T.* Look for Tracing Immigrant Origins
Tracing Your Immigrant Ancestors from New York State Library	www.nysl.nysed.gov/genealogy/tracimmi.htm
World-Wide Genealogy Resources	www.genhomepage.com/world.html

TABLE 13-1.   *Good sites for international resources*

Where to Look

In many of the places covered in previous chapters, you can find links to sites for genealogy beyond the United States. For online links, I recommend starting at Cyndi's List at www.cyndislist.com and RootsWeb at www.rootsweb.org.

You need to learn how to research in those countries. Each place has its own method of recording vital statistics, history, and other information. Before you start looking for records, you need to know what those records are called and who keeps them.

LDS Research Guides

The place to begin before you start looking for records beyond the United States is the Church of Jesus Christ of Latter-day Saints (LDS) site

FamilySearch (see Chapter 10). The Research Guides are indispensable for these tasks. The first one to read is the guide "Tracing Immigrant Origins," a 49-page outline of tips, procedures, and strategies. (See Figure 13-4.)

Other Research Outlines give you step-by-step pointers on the best way to pursue historical records in a particular state, province, or country. The letter-writing guides tell you what you need to know before you write the letter, where to write, how to address the envelope, how to enclose return postage, and an example letter in the appropriate language.

Arm yourself with the research outlines and, if available, a letter-writing guide for the appropriate country, before you begin. Also, look at the LDS "word lists" for various languages: this can help you recognize the words for "birth," "marriage," "death," and so on in the records even if you can't read the language.

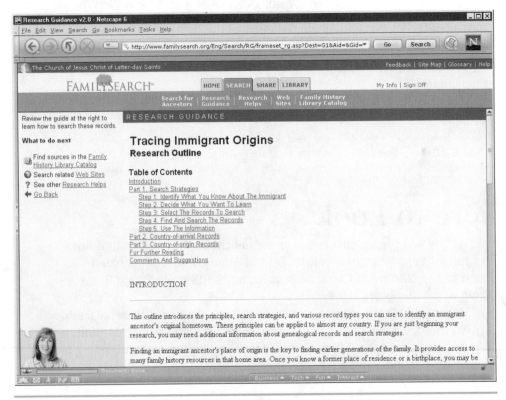

FIGURE 13-4. *You can find and print the Tracing Immigrant Origins or you can get a printed copy at a local Family History Center for a small fee.*

WorldGenWeb

The WorldGenWeb Project was created in 1996 by Dale Schneider to help folks researching in countries around the world. The goal is to have every country in the world represented by an online Web site and hosted by researchers who either live in that country or are familiar with that country's resources. The site is at www.worldgenweb.org (see Figure 13-5).

When the WorldGenWeb Project opened on the Internet in October 1996, volunteers were recruited to host country Web sites. By coordinating with the USGenWeb Project, soon the major countries in the world had Web sites online. Throughout the next year, WorldGenWeb continued to grow. On September 13, 1997, the WorldGenWeb Project decided

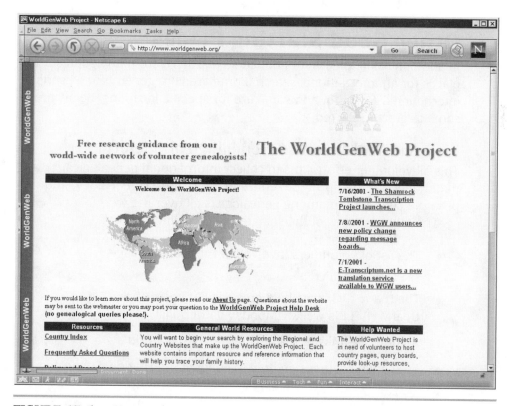

FIGURE 13-5.   *You can begin any international genealogy search at WorldGenWeb.*

to move to RootsWeb. The support of the RootsWeb staff helped WorldGenWeb to expand to its present size.

Divided into 11 regions (Africa, Asia, British Isles, Central Europe, Caribbean, Eastern Europe, Mediterranean, Middle East, North America, Pacific, and South America), WorldGenWeb gives links to local sites with local resource addresses of county/country public records offices, cemetery locations, maps, library addresses, archive addresses, and association addresses, including Family History Centers or other genealogical or historical societies, and some history and culture of the region. Other resources may include query pages or message boards, mail lists, historical data including census records, cemetery records, biographies, bibliographies, and family/surname registration Web sites.

Between RootsWeb and WorldGenWeb, you should be able to find something about the country you need to search.

Other Good Starting Places

In addition to the places mentioned so far, there are many good starting places for an international search. Some are very general for all sorts of international research, and some are for specific locations. Below are some to get you started.

International Internet Genealogical Society

This all-volunteer effort aims to collect international genealogical material to one site, promote ethics in international genealogy, and promote cooperation among genealogists all over the world.

The main features of the site are the following:

- The list of volunteers involved at the Global Village Representatives page

- The many IRC chats held on a regular basis (including DearMYRTLE's weekly Monday gatherings)

- A library of links to resources all over the world

- Free online courses on how to conduct international genealogy

- A newsletter

Once a lively and active group, at press time, the pages hadn't been updated in over six months. The chats still occur regularly and the how-to lessons are still applicable, but the last newsletter was posted in March 2000.

Sites that can provide a translation of a Web page into English include the following:

♦ Alta Vista Babel Fish at babelfish.altavista.digital.com/translate.dyn.

♦ GO Translator at translator.go.com.

♦ Netscape 6 has Gist-In-Time translation service integrated in it. Simply get the page into Netscape 6, and then choose View | Translate.

Asia

Chinese Immigrant Files (Catalogs of holdings in Regional Archives and in Washington, D.C.) can be searched at www.ins.usdoj.gov/graphics/aboutins/history/CHINESE.html. This collection of United States government records on immigrants is full of good information.

Chineseroots.com at www.chineseroots.com is a site for searching Chinese genealogy. Chineseroots.com has an alliance with Shanghai Library, which has the world's largest collection of Chinese ancestry records. Through this site, you can look at a catalog of 90,000 volumes of family details dating back to the tenth century. Other partnerships include various world renowned genealogy organizations, such as the Taiwan Surnames Association and the Shanxi Genealogy Centre in China. The Web sites are in English, Chinese Big 5, and Chinese GB. The site has articles, a calendar of events, and message boards.

AsianGenNet at www.rootsweb.org/~asiagw, is part of WorldGenWeb and has some sites, but needs hosts for many more.

Chinese Surnames at 206.184.157.220/names, is a fascinating page with the most common Chinese surnames and their history.

Europe

There are many sites where you can research your European roots. I recommend you start with the following.

Benelux   At Digital Resources Netherlands and Belgium at geneaknowhow.net/digi/resources.html, you can find resources from the Netherlands and Belgium, including over 350 Internet links to online resources (including more than 150 passenger lists), nearly 900 online resources on Dutch and Belgian bulletin board systems, and hundreds of digital resources.

Note ⁔⁔⁔⁔⁔⁔⁔⁔⁔⁔⁔⁔⁔⁔⁔⁔⁔⁔⁔⁔⁔⁔

Most European countries have a page on WorldGenWeb. Also, always check Cyndi's List for links. Cyndi updates her list daily!

Eastern Europe   Yahoo! has a category for Czech genealogy discussion and research at dir.yahoo.com/Regiona l/Countries/Czech_Republic/ Arts_and_Humanities/Humanities/History.

The Ukranian Roots genealogy Web Ring begins at ukrcommunities. 8k.com/ukrroots.html.

Eastern Slovakia, Slovak, and Carpatho-Rusyn Genealogy Research www.iarelative.com/slovakia.htm.

France   Besides the usual sites, such as Cyndi's List and WorldGenWeb, check out FrancoGene at www.francogene.com. Links to genealogy sites in former French colonies around the world, such as Quebec and Haiti, as well as to genealogy societies and institutions, can be found there.

Germany   Genealogy.net at www.genealogienetz.de/genealogy.html, has how-tos, sample request letters, databases, translations of common terms, and many more tools for researching genealogy in Germany.

GermanRoots at http://www.germanroots.com/, has tips, links, and research helps.

The Telephone Book for Germany at www.teleauskunft.de/NSAPI/ &BUAB = BUNDESWEIT.

Deutsche Bahn at www.bahn.de.

Germany Genealogy Net at www.genealogienetz .de/gene/misc/ geoserv.html.

Italy   The Italian Genealogy Homepage at www.italgen.com is the place to start. This includes links to how-to articles, discussion groups, and history.

Spain   A personal site, Spanish Genealogy at www.geocities.com/ CapitolHill/Senate/4593/geneal.html, has tips, data, and links about Spain, and more.

Portugal   LusaWeb is a site for Portuguese Ancestry at www.lusaweb. com/genealogy and the Portuguese-American Historical & Research Foundation has a page for genealogy questions and answers at www. portuguesefoundation.org/genealogy.htm.

Scandinavia   Census records of Norway are being transcribed and posted by volunteers at Norwegian Census and Bergen Emigration Information at digitalarkivet.uib.no/index-eng.htm.

National Archives of Norway at www.riksarkivet.no/national.html covers the central administrative institutions and the eight regional state archives, covering the local branches of the state administration.

Genealogy Research Denmark at www.ida.net/users/really is a personal page of one woman's collected research, plus links to other resources.

Norwegian Emigration and Genealogy Center offers information for descendants at www.utvandrersenteret.no/index.htm.

Martin's Norwegian Genealogy Dictionary at www.geocities.com/ Heartland/Estates/5536/eidhalist.html can help you decipher words for relationships, occupations, and so on.

Swedish Genealogy at sd.datatorget.educ.goteborg.se has queries, data, and a few things translated into English.

United Kingdom   The United Kingdom (U.K.) and Ireland Genealogy site at www.genuki.org.uk is the best starting point. This site has transcribed data, such as parish records, plus links to individuals' pages where genealogy research (secondary material) is posted. Look at the Index Page at www.genuki.org.uk/mindex.html for specific counties, surnames, and so forth.

The Free BMD (Free Birth, Marriage, and Death records) project at freebmd.rootsweb.com provides free Internet access to the Civil Registration index information for England and Wales from 1837. The transcriptions are ongoing and the updates are posted once or twice a month. You can volunteer to help!

AncestorSuperSearch at www.ancestorsupersearch.com has 1.46 million English birth, marriage, and census events 1355–1891, searchable online.

The National Archives of Ireland at www.nationalarchives.ie has a genealogy how-to page.

The U.K. National Digital Archive of Datasets at ndad.ulcc.ac.uk has archived digital data from UK government departments and agencies. The system has been available since March 1998 and provides open access to the catalogues of all its holdings, and free access to open datasets following a simple registration process.

The National Archives of Scotland has records from the twelfth century. The family history fact sheet at www.nas.gov.uk /family_history_factsheet.htm has good how-to information.

South America

Genealogy.com has a good list of South American genealogy links at www.genealogy.com/links/c/c-places-geographic.south-america.html.

H. R. Henly's site, Genealogical Research in Latin America, at www.saqnet.co.uk/users/hrhenly/latinaml.html, has gathered the links that helped him the most in his searches.

Created by Rebecca R. Horne and maintained by Salena B. Ashton at www.hfhr.com/websites.html is another good collection of links.

Australia

Australia is rich with genealogy Web sites. Start with Yahoo!'s category, dir.yahoo.com/Regional/Countries/Australia/Arts_and_Humanities/Humanities/History/Genealogy, but don't miss the following pages:

The Society of Australian Genealogists at www.sag.org.au has materials, meetings, and special interest groups.

Dead Person's Society, a site for genealogy in Melbourne, Australia, has a graphic of dancing skeletons at home.vicnet.net.au / ~ dpsoc/welcome.htm (see Figure 13–6).

Convicts to Australia, a guide to researching ancestry during the time Australia was used as a large prison, is at www.convictcentral.com/index.html.

KiwiGen Web Ring has links to New Zealand genealogy at nav.webring.yahoo.com/hub?ring = kiwigen&list.

First Families of Australia 2001 is at sites.netscape.net/mgswebaus/firstfam.

National Archives of Australia, at www.naa.gov.au, has an entire section on Family History and what records to look for.

Africa

Conrod Mercer's page at home.global.co.za/ ~ mercon is a personal collection of tips on doing South African (white) genealogy.

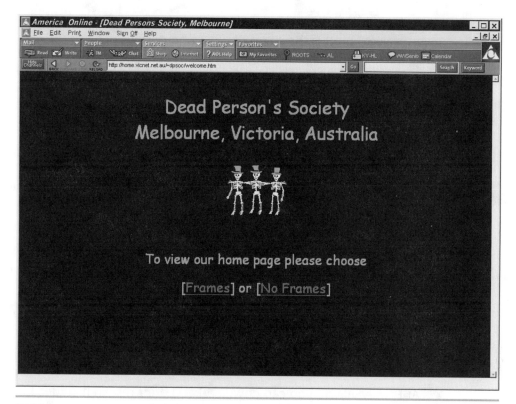

FIGURE 13-6.   *Dancing skeletons on the Dead Person's Society site, a site for genealogy in Melbourne, Australia*

North America

The following sites are good places to start to search for information on ancestors from Canada and Mexico.

Canada   Canadian Genealogy and History at www.islandnet.com/ ~ jveinot/cghl/cghl.html lists online sites for vital records, genealogies, and general history, sorted by province.

Immigrants to Canada at www.dcs.uwaterloo.ca/ ~ marj/genealogy/ thevoyage.html.

The genealogy page of the National Archives of Canada is at www. archives.ca/02/020202_e.html. The National Archives of Canada publishes the free booklet, *Tracing your Ancestors in Canada*, which describes the major genealogical sources available at the National Archives and makes reference to sources in other Canadian repositories. You can order a hard copy or access a PDF version online.

Mexico Archivo Historico del Agua at www2.h-net.msu.edu/ ~ latam/ archives/project4.html is the site of the national archives of Mexico.

Local Catholic Church History and Ancestors at home.att.net/ ~ Local_Catholic/Catholic-Mexico.htm has addresses to write for parish records in Mexico.

Texas General Land Office has a page at www.glo.state.tx.us/ archives that describes records dating back to Spanish times. The page shows how to write for the information.

The Genealogy of Mexico at members.tripod.com/ ~ GaryFelix/ index1.htm is one genealogists' compilation of starting places.

The Hispanic Genealogical Society of New York at www. hispanicgenealogy.com includes Mexico, Puerto Rico, and other North American Hispanic genealogy.

Wrapping Up

- Once you find your immigrant ancestor, you can use archives and ships' passenger lists to identify his or her home town.

- Many National Archives have Web pages describing research techniques for that country.

- At FamilySearch, you can download and print research guides for immigrant origins and for specific countries, as well as word lists of genealogical terms in non-English languages

- There are specific sites for genealogy of many nationalities.

Chapter 14

Ethnic Genealogy Resources

The International sources cited in Chapter 13 can also help you with ethnic research within the United States and Canada for well-documented ancestry such as Croatian or Chinese. For other groups, however, the search is a little more complex.

African American genealogy often presents special challenges. For example, when researching the genealogy of a former slave, it's necessary to know as much about the slave owner's family as you do about the slave. Wills, deeds, and tax rolls hold clues to ancestry, as do legal agreements to rent slaves. Tracking down all these items can be difficult. Native American genealogies are also difficult because in many cases, very little was written down in the eighteenth and nineteenth centuries. A genealogist must contact the tribe involved and look at many different kinds of records. Mixed ethnic heritages such as Melungeon are problematic to research because these mixed groups suffered from stigma for many years. If you are researching a Melungeon family line, the true genealogy may have been suppressed or even forgotten by your ancestors. These special cases have led to many online resources.

The sites mentioned in this chapter provide good information on how to begin to search for specific genealogy information, as well as history and culture of different groups. The challenges you will face can be discussed in the forums and mail lists; you will often find tips on which records to seek and how to get them. Don't forget, however, that new pages are being added to the Web all the time. Search for "genealogy" plus the name of whatever ethnic group you're seeking on your favorite search engine about once a month to see if new information has come online.

And stay on the mailing lists or newsgroups for the ethnic groups; when you hit a brick wall, perhaps someone on the list can help!

In 2001, the Statue of Liberty-Ellis Island Foundation published an online database of records from Ellis Island during the peak immigration years (1892-1924). This database of 22 million names—representing 60 percent of all United States immigration records—has opened the floodgates for a huge increase in the number of amateur genealogists. Jupiter Media Metrix listed the Ellis Island site in its latest "Top Newcomers" list. See Chapter 11 for an explanation of how to use this site.

African American

You will find many African American resources in the Caribbean sites listed below, and plenty of Caribbean information among the African American genealogy pages listed here.

AfriGeneas, (see Figure 14-1) at www.afrigeneas.com, is the best starting place for African American research. Transcribed records, discussion groups, monthly articles, and more will help you get started.

The Library of Michigan has a list of books to help with African American genealogy at www.libofmich.lib.mi.us/genealogy/ afroamer.html.

The Afro-American Historical and Genealogical Society (AAHGS) is a non-profit, membership organization committed to the preservation of the history, genealogy, and culture of those with African heritage.

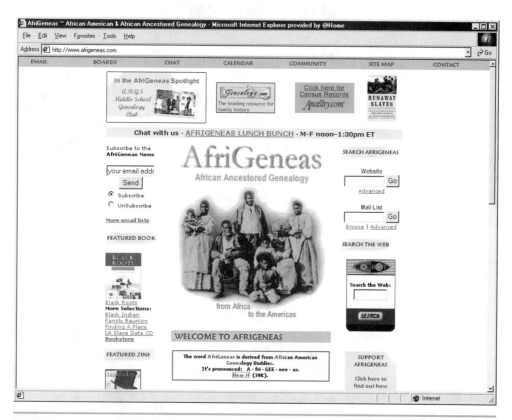

FIGURE 14-1. *AfriGeneas is the best starting place for African American genealogy.*

AAHGS stresses the importance of genealogy by encouraging active participation in recording research and documenting personal family histories. You'll find AAHGS at www.rootsweb.com/~mdaahgs/homepage.html.

The African-American Genealogy Ring is a cooperative of sites linking different resources. Start at www.afamgenealogy.ourfamily.com.

Christine's Genealogy Web site has links to articles, census transcriptions, fugitive slave information, and more at www.ccharity.com.

The Freedman's Bureau Online, www.freedmensbureau.com, allows you to search many records. The Freedman's Bureau supervised all relief and educational activities relating to refugees and freedmen, including issuing rations, clothing, and medicine. The Bureau also assumed custody of confiscated lands or property in the former Confederate States, border states, District of Columbia, and Indian Territory. The bureau records were created or maintained by bureau headquarters, the assistant commissioners, and the state superintendents of education. They included personnel records and a variety of standard reports concerning bureau programs and conditions in the states.

The Alabama African American Genealogy site is part of the AlaGenWeb. The opening page at www.rootsweb.com/~alaag has links to The Village (a listing of resources online), Alabama Slave Project, Alabama Black Indians, Alabama Civil War Colored Troops, Alabama African American Marriages, Slave Queries, and Slave Surnames.

The African-American Genealogical Society of Northern California is a local group, but its Web site with monthly articles, online genealogy charts, discussion groups, and more is worth a visit. Find it at www.aagsnc.org.

AAGENE-L is a moderated mailing list for African American genealogy and history researchers. Subscribe to the list by sending a message to aagene-l@upeople.com with SUBSCRIBE in the subject line.

Another significant genealogical resource is the Freedman's Bank CD. Released in February 2001 by the Church of Jesus Christ of Latter-day Saints, this database contains biographical information on the roughly 500,000 African Americans who deposited money into Freedman's Bank following the Civil War. It is estimated that 8 million to 10 million African Americans living today have ancestors whose records are contained in the Freedman's database. Available from the

FamilySearch site (see Chapter 10), the CD has records that cover from 1864 to 1871 and document the names and family relationships of those who used the bank.

The information contained in these records is rather fragmentary by normal genealogical standards, but they are some of the very few records that document these individuals and are a vital source of information for those with African American ancestry. There are approximately 480,000 names in the file, which have been entered in a pedigree-linked GEDCOM format. This means that they are indexed for searching; before this CD-ROM the records were available but unindexed, making them very hard to use. It took 11 years to complete the indexing and formatting for the CD-ROM.

The Freedman's Bank Records CD is available at cost for $6.50. It can be ordered over the Internet at www.familysearch.org or by calling Church distribution centers at 1-800-537-5971 and asking for item #50120.

Arab

Genealogy.com has a discussion group for United Arab Emirates genealogy at www.genforum.genealogy.com/uae.

A discussion of Arab names is at Arab Net's page, www.arab.net/arabnames/welcome.html.

Australian Aborigines

The Aboriginal Studies WWW Virtual Library Web site, www.ciolek.com/WWWVL-Aboriginal.html, has links to resources and articles. All links are inspected and evaluated before being added to this Virtual Library.

The National Library of Australia has a page on genealogy, www.nla.gov.au/oz/genelist.html, which includes links to many specific ethnic and family sites.

The Australian Institute of Aboriginal and Torres Strait Islander Studies has a page just for family historians at www.aiatsis.gov.au/lbry/fmly_hstry/fmly_hstry_hm.htm.

The Genealogy in Australia and New Zealand page has a link to the mail list for A/NZ genealogy at www.rootsweb.com/~billingh.

Caribbean

Caribbean Genealogy Resources, at www.candoo.com/genresources/ index.html, lists links to archives, museums, universities, and libraries with historical and genealogical information for countries in the Caribbean. Another page from this site is www.candoo.com/surnames/index.html, which is a list of Caribbean surnames. The text files list surnames, places, and dates, as well as e-mail contact information for researchers looking for them.

SearchBeat, an Internet catalog (see Chapter 5) has a collection of links for Caribbean genealogy that isn't as extensive, but includes some links that aren't in Candoo's, including some to Jewish Caribbean genealogy. Go to www.searchbeat.com and click on Regional | Caribbean | Society and Culture | Genealogy.

The AOL Hispanic Genealogy Special Interest Group has many Caribbean links. The main page is at users.aol.com/mrosado007/ index.htm.

RootsWeb, of course, has mail lists, WorldGenWeb pages, and transcribed records for most Caribbean countries. Go to www.rootsweb. com and search for the country of interest. Then go to www.rootsweb. com/~caribgw for the Carribbean GenWeb pages.

Creole/Cajun

The Acadians/Cajuns were the French settlers ejected from Nova Scotia by the British in the mid-eighteenth century. Some went to Quebec, and some to Louisiana.

The term "Creole" means different things in different places. In Latin America, it means of pure Spanish blood. In the Caribbean, it means a descendant of Europeans. In the Guineas, it means descended from slaves. In the southern United States, the term refers to landowners and slaveholders before the Civil War, aristocrats who took pride in gracious living and courtly manners, who were part of the overall French/Cajun culture of the Gulf Coast. For almost all Creole research, parish records are your best bet—those and mailing list discussions!

Acadian-Cajun Genealogy and History, at www.acadian-cajun.com/, publishes records, how-tos, history, mailing lists, maps, genealogies, and more.

The Encyclopedia of Cajun Culture, at www.cajunculture.com, will give you good background information.

Vive La Cajun, www.vivelacajun.com, has information on how to research Cajun genealogy.

The Cajun and Zydeco Radio Guide also has a list of family histories posted to the Web at www.cajunradio.org/genealogy.html.

The Canada GenWeb has a section on Acadian Genealogy in Canada at www.geocities.com/Heartland/Acres/2162.

The St. Augustine Historical Society (Louisiana) has some church records online at www.cp-tel.net/creole/creole_genealogy.htm.

The Louisiana Creole Heritage Center is located on the campus of Northwestern State University in Natchitoches, Louisiana, and on the Web at www.nsula.edu/creole/index.htm.

The Confederation of Associations of Families Acadian, www.cafa. org/index.html, is an organization to promote the culture and genealogy of Acadian Families in America.

From July 31 to August 15, 2004, Nova Scotia will host the 3rd World Acadian Congress; details are at acadien.com/2004. The Acadian Museum and Archives in Nova Scotia holds many genealogies. A listing of them, plus hours of operation and so on, can be found at www.ccfne.ns.ca/ ~museum/english/archives/genealogies/index.htm.

Search RootsWeb's list of mailing lists; there are several for Acadian/ Cajun research and data are in Louisiana and Canada. See the following pages: lists.rootsweb.com/index/usa/LA/misc.html, for Louisiana mail lists and www.rootsweb.com/~jfuller/gen_mail_country-can.html for Canadian mail lists.

Cuban

Even as you read this, University of Florida researchers are working to preserve and copy about 10 million records in the Cuban National Archives. These records cover Cuban life, business and shipping from 1578 to 1900, but they were sealed with the revolution of 1959. These records were collected by the Notaries of Cuba, and stored by the government.

Called *The Notary Protocols*, these records document births, deaths, property and slave ownership transactions—basically, data on everything and everybody who passed through Havana from Spain to America and back. Once they're made public, these records will enable slave descendants to trace their genealogy to the time their ancestors were first brought to the Americas.

This resource won't become available overnight, of course. The researchers still need to secure funding. Once they begin, the first stages of the project will take 12 to 18 months. Realistically, it will probably be 2003 or later before you can look at the indexes. The University of Florida will post a guide to the materials and you will then be able to obtain copies of individual documents on compact disc.

Doukhobors

The history of this small sect of Russian pacifist dissenters is outlined in "Who are the Doukhobors?" at www.kootenay.org/Doukhobor.html. Genealogy is covered at Doukhobors Saskatchewan Genealogy Roots at www.rootsweb.com/~cansk/Saskatchewan/ethnic/doukhobor-saskatchewan.html.

The RootsWeb message boards at Ancestry have several topics on this group.

Gypsy, Romani, Romany, and Travellers

A list of links on Gypsy lore, genealogy, and images is at sca.lib.liv.ac.uk/collections/gypsy/links.htm.

Romani culture and history are covered at Patrin, www.geocities.com/Paris/5121/patrin.htm. Type **genealogy** in the search box at the bottom of the page and several past articles will come up in the results (see Figure 14-2).

Hmong

The Hmong people came to the United States from Laos at the end of the Vietnam War. The Hmong Homepage, at www.hmongnet.org, has culture, news, events, and general information.

Jewish

The first site to visit for Jewish genealogy is JewishGen.org, www.jewishgen.org. Mail lists, transcribed records, GEDCOMs, and more are at the site. You can also find links to special interest groups, such as geographic emphasis or genetics. The next stop should be The Israel GenWeb Project Web site, which serves as a resource to those researching their family history in Israel at www.rootsweb.com/~isrwgw.

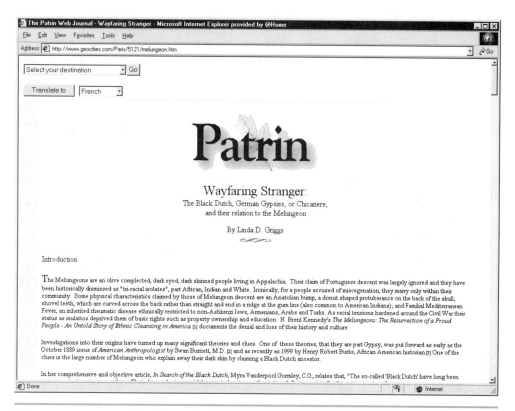

FIGURE 14-2. *"The Wayfaring Stranger" is just one article on Gypsy genealogy at Patrin.*

Sephardic Genealogy, www.orthohelp.com/geneal/sefardim.htm, has links to articles and historical documents, as does Sephardim.org at www.sephardim.org, which has an article on Jamaican-Jewish history.

Australian Jewish researchers should check out www.zeta.org.au/~feraltek/genealogy. Canadian Jewish genealogists should begin at The Jewish Genealogical Society of Montreal, www.gtrdata.com /jgs- montreal, with a history of the first Jewish settlers there.

Native American

A good site with how-to information for researching Native American genealogy is at hometown.aol.com/bbbenge/front.html.

Native American Heritage is an online book. To read it, you must submit your e-mail address and create a password, but access is free. Go to www. nativeamericanheritage.com and fill out the form. The book is also offered for sale as a video.

Aboriginal Connections is a site presenting categorized information to Canadian Aboriginal, Native American Indian, and International Indigenous sites on the Web. The genealogy page at www.aboriginalconnections. com/links/History_and_Culture/Genealogy lists links to eight genealogy pages and four language pages.

The African-Native American History & Genealogy Web page at www.african-nativeamerican.com is mostly concerned with the history of Oklahoma and surrounding areas.

Access Genealogy, www.accessgenealogy.com/native, Native American Genealogy page has transcribed records and a state-by-state list of online sites.

All Things Cherokee is a site about many aspects of Cherokee culture, genealogy included (see Figure 14-3). The genealogy page is at www.allthingscherokee.com/genealogy.html. The Potowami Tribe has a site at www.potawatomi.org, with a history of the tribe. The Cheyenne Genealogy site, www.mcn.net/ ~ hmscook/roots/cheyenne.html, has a database of some ancestors, a bibliography for further study, and other Montana links. Many other tribes also have sites. Simply use any search engine for the tribe name, plus the word "genealogy" and you'll likely get a hit.

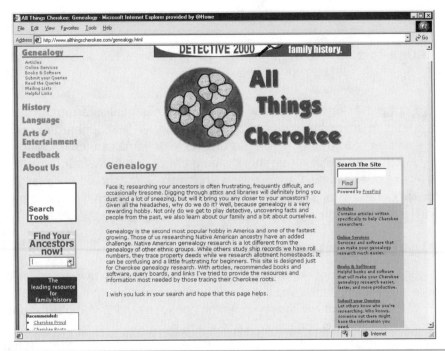

FIGURE 14-3.   *All Things Cherokee has a set of pages devoted to genealogy.*

Métis

Métis is a name for those of Native American heritage, but mixed tribes.

Gail Morin's Métis Families at www.televar.com/~gmorin is a place for sharing information on the history of the Métis people. This site contains census indexes, stories, family genealogies, marriage records, and sources for research. The region includes the Red River Settlement (Manitoba), Saskatchewan, Alberta, Quebec, Montana, and North Dakota.

The Métis of North America Genealogy, www.metis-woman.com/genealogy/index.htm, has a list of links to home pages, societies, organizations, and records.

Melungeon

The origins of the people and even the name are controversial, but the Appalachian ethnic group called Melungeon seems to be of European, African, Mediterranean, and Native American descent. They may have settled in the Appalachian wilderness as early as 1657, or possibly earlier. Melungeons are found in the Cumberland Plateau of Virginia, Kentucky, North Carolina, West Virginia, Tennessee, and, some argue, North Alabama. Recently, Melungeon genealogy has taken on new and exciting relevance with the publication of *The Melungeons: The Resurrection of a Proud People* by Dr. N. Brent Kennedy (Mercer University Press, 1997).

Melungeons and other Mestee Groups, www.geocities.com/mikenassau, by Mike Nassau, is an online book on the subject.

An informational page is "Avoiding Pitfalls in Melungeon Research," at www.public.usit.net/billiam/melungeon.html. This is the text of a talk presented by Pat Spurlock Elder at "Second Union, a Melungeon Gathering" held in Wise, Virginia, in July 1998.

The Melungeon Resource page includes an FAQ file at homepages.rootsweb.com/~mtnties/melungeon.html.

The Appalachian Mountain Families page includes information on Melungeons, members.nbci.com/Appalachian/.

Under One Sky, www.geocities.com/BourbonStreet/Square/5018/Page_1x.html, is a newsletter dedicated to research into the history, genealogy, and origins of the Melungeons and other mixed-ethnic people in Appalachia. Publication began in 1995 as The Southeastern Kentucky Melungeon Information Exchange.

Everton's site has an FAQ article on the "Black Dutch" at www. everton.com/FHN/weekly_index.php?show = yes&id = 566, who are often included in Melungeon genealogies.

Some rare diseases are characteristic of Melungeons. The Melungeon Health Education and Support Network at www.melungeonhealth.org describes some of them and has links to resources about them.

A Melungeon mailing list exists for people conducting Melungeon and/or Appalachian research including Native American, Portuguese, Turkish, Black Dutch, and other unverifiable mixed statements of ancestry or unexplained rumors, with ancestors in Tenessee, Kentucky, Virginia, North Carolina, South Carolina, Georgia, Alabama, West Virginia, and possibly other places. To subscribe, send an e-mail message to melungeon-l-request@rootsweb.com (mail mode) or melungeon-d-request@rootsweb.com (digest mode).

Wrapping Up

- Many ethnic groups have started mail lists, newsgroups, and history sites.

- Once a month, use your favorite search engine to find new sites.

- Stay on mailing lists to discuss your ethnic "brick walls" with others.

Chapter 15

The National Genealogical Society

The National Genealogical Society (NGS) is the granddaddy of genealogical societies in the United States. On its Web site, www.ngsgenealogy.org, you'll find announcements of NGS seminars, workshops, and programs, information on its home study course, youth resources, and other NGS activities. This is an excellent site for learning genealogy standards and methods.

NGS was organized in Washington, D.C., in 1903. The preliminary first meeting was held on 24 April and the formal organization effected 11 November. Now, the NGS has over 17,000 members: individuals, families, genealogical societies, family associations, libraries, and other related institutions.

National Genealogical Society

The NGS is one of the best umbrella organizations for family history. Its workshops, meetings, and publications are invaluable. You can see its home page in Figure 15-1.

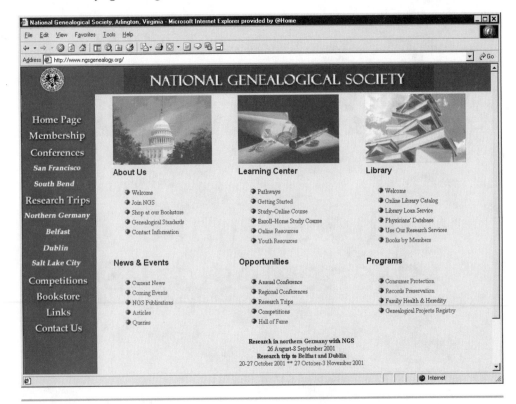

FIGURE 15-1.   *The NGS home page gives you links to many resources.*

On the home page, you'll find links to the newest and most relevant items on the site, including upcoming meetings, trips, courses, and competitions. And, on every page of the site, you'll find a navigation bar at the left, which leads to different sections, including the following:

About Us   These pages describe the missions and objectives of the society, how the organization is set up, and the many interesting committees of the NGS. *Pathways* presents an overview of the educational offerings from NGS. *Getting Started* is a set of pages about how to do genealogy. *Study Online Course* and *Enroll-Home Study Course* describe options for taking NGS classes on family history from home. American Genealogy costs about $300 for members and $375 for nonmembers. *Youth Resources* has information concerning genealogy and family history, suitable for children from ages 5 to 18. Among these are lesson plans, Web sites, books, and activities. Youth Resources also describes the rules for the Rubicam Youth Award for the best-prepared genealogy by a student in grades 8 through 12. The annual winner receives a $500 cash prize, a certificate, and a one-year NGS membership. An article about the winner and the winning presentation appears in the *NGS Newsmagazine.*

Library   The NGS has a circulating library available to members. Reference, records, and members' ancestral charts are among the holdings available online. Among the online services are the online card catalog (see Figure 15-2) and a form for loan request, a request form for research in the Physician Data Base, a listing of AMA records of American physicians who died after 1905 and before 1965, and a list of books by NGS members.

News and Events   This section includes news about the organization and its members, news from the world of genealogy, articles from recent genealogy conferences, and press releases from other organizations. Of special interest are the online articles on aspects of genealogy and the queries.

Opportunities   Here you find links to information on the annual conference, regional conferences, research trips, competitions, and the NGS Hall of Fame. The conferences are excellent. Any level of research from beginner to expert will be taught by experts from all over the world at NGS conferences. You can also find many supplies and genealogy-related items from vendors at the conferences.

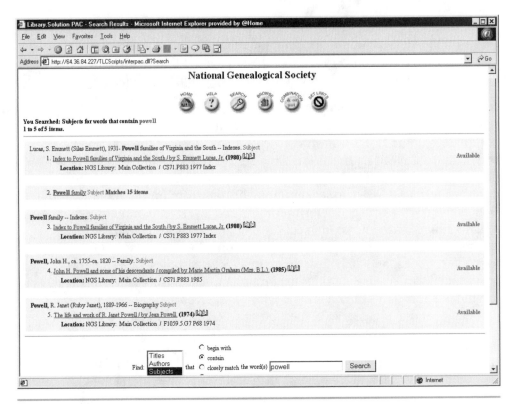

FIGURE 15-2. *You can search the NGS library card catalog online.*

Programs   Programs include the Consumer Protection Committee, which maintains a page on how to recognize a scam, such as those described in Chapter 2. Another page in this section describes the activities of the Records Preservation and Access Committee of NGS. The committee's task is to develop a consistent and logical long-term strategy to deal with the preservation of records and access issues at all levels, from local to national. Most of the effort currently expended on such issues is in reaction to specific threats to the access of records (people don't get as excited about preservation!). The strategy being developed is intended to get "out ahead of the curve," so potential problems can be identified and resolved before they become issues. Another committee under the Programs section is the NGS Family Health and Heredity Committee, whose mission is to advance and promote the value of researching and recording ancestral medical information in genealogy.

NGS Membership   Membership costs from $40 per year for an individual to $500 a year for a benefactor. The NGS Bookstore has books, forms, CD-ROMS, and more. Members, of course, get discounts.

As with any good Web site, the NGS has a Links page at ngsgenealogy. org/links.htm. Here you'll find leads to sites for general genealogy; libraries and archives online; societies and organizations; ethnic and immigration resources, records, and miscellaneous.

Contact Us   This page has street address, phone numbers, a map to the NGS headquarters, e-mail addresses, and the hours of the library.

Finally, the NGS has a set of guidelines for your genealogy. The standards are listed on the page www.ngsgenealogy.orgcomstandards.htm. You will also find the standards at the end of this book in Appendix A.

Wrapping Up

♦   The NGS is an umbrella institution for education and resources in genealogy.

♦   You can take online and at-home genealogy courses from NGS.

♦   National and regional meetings also offer genealogy courses.

Chapter 16

RootsWeb

Now would you like a place where you can search dozens of databases of genealogical material, hundreds of genealogical Web pages, and subscribe to thousands of mail lists? A place where you can publish your own page, upload your own data, and create your own mail list?

Welcome to "Online Genealogy Heaven," which is called RootsWeb, www.rootsweb.org. This began as a site for a group of people working at the research center RAND who dabbled in genealogy on the side. Once upon a time, they had a little mailing list, hosted by the University of Minnesota, and a little database on the RAND server. That was 11 years ago. Today, RootsWeb is the largest all-volunteer genealogy site on the Web.

Note

Both www.rootsweb.org and www.rootsweb.com work as URLs for this site.

The Merger

When the cost of storage and hosting this treasure trove became prohibitive, Ancestry.com and RootsWeb merged in June 2000. In other words, the largest commercial genealogy site and the largest volunteer site joined forces. (The use of RootsWeb remains free and contributions are completely voluntary.)

This means two things. First, people are no longer asked to contribute $25 a year to RootsWeb to help defray the costs the volunteers were incurring. And second, Ancestry.com now subsidizes the hardware and software to keep RootsWeb up and running.

In the months immediately following the merger, many were concerned that RootsWeb's privacy and fair use policies would change, but so far they haven't. To date, if you submit data to RootsWeb, it won't be slapped on to a CD-ROM and sold by Ancestry (of course, you still need to be sure that data on living people isn't included in your submissions because anyone can copy publicly posted data and slap it anywhere). For the user, little has really changed.

The mission of RootsWeb is summed up in the following statement, published on its home page.

Note

Sometimes you're on the "free" side of RootsWeb and sometimes you're on the "subscription" side (which is Ancestry.com). You must pay attention to the layout and typeface of the pages. Ancestry.com sites have lots of green on them, for example.

The RootsWeb project has two missions:

1. To make large volumes of data available to the online genealogical community at minimal cost.

2. To provide support services to online genealogical activities, such as USENET newsgroup moderation, mailing list maintenance, surname list generation, and so forth.

A quick guided tour of RootsWeb only scratches the surface of all the helpful and informative services available at this site. The following story gives you an idea of the unique possibilities RootsWeb offers.

RootsWeb Leads to a Reunion

About three years ago, I started searching for my Powell (on my father's side) ancestors, but about the only thing I knew how to do was search the surname and message boards.

One night, after having done nothing in about two months, I decided to get online and read the [RootsWeb] surname message boards. On a whim, I went into the Hubbard message boards (on my mother's side). The first message I read was about someone searching for descendants of my grandmother's parents.

When my grandmother was about three or four, her mother passed away and she went to live with an aunt and uncle. Eventually, my grandmother lost contact with her brothers. She did see her oldest brother once when she was about 15 but, after that, she never saw or heard from him again. That night, I found him, a person my grandmother had not seen in over 70 years.

We flew to Washington State and met all kinds of new cousins, aunts, and uncles. Over the next two years, my grandmother spoke with her brother many times. Unfortunately, he passed away last summer, but she did see him twice and was able to speak with him on numerous occasions.

We figured out that the message I responded to had been posted for about a minute before I discovered it. The surname message boards are a wonderful tool in searching for the ancestors and relatives you never knew you had, or those you had, but didn't know who they were.

—Jennifer Powell Lyons

What You'll Find at RootsWeb

RootsWeb has more genealogical information than you can shake a stick at. Some of this is secondary source information, such as what genealogies members have submitted. Some of this information is close to primary information, for example, transcripts of wills, deeds, census forms, and vital records, with citations of where exactly the original information can be found. Some of it is primary information, for example Ancestry's Census Images (covered in Chapter 17).

At the top of all the RootsWeb pages, you'll see a navigation bar of tabs: Home, Boards, Lists, Searches, Sites, Passwords, Contribute, and Help.

Home and Help are self-explanatory. The following explains Boards, Lists, Searches, and Sites. Passwords is a help page for retrieving lost passwords to mailing lists and Web sites. Contribute tells you how to upload your own family information to share on RootsWeb.

When you log on to RootsWeb, you'll find on the homepage a search template to input a surname, first name, or any keywords (see Figure 16-1). After you enter this information, click a button to search the databases and text files, the World Connect GEDCOMs, the RootsWeb Surname list, or the Social Security Death Index. If you choose a keyword, you can choose to search the major text files or the GenSeeker database of uploaded documents.

Finding information on RootsWeb can be that simple, but you can use many tools on the site to get more targeted results.

Getting Started   The home page of RootsWeb is an index to the site. Under Getting Started, you'll find links to informative files with information on how to use RootsWeb, how to do genealogy, how to subscribe to

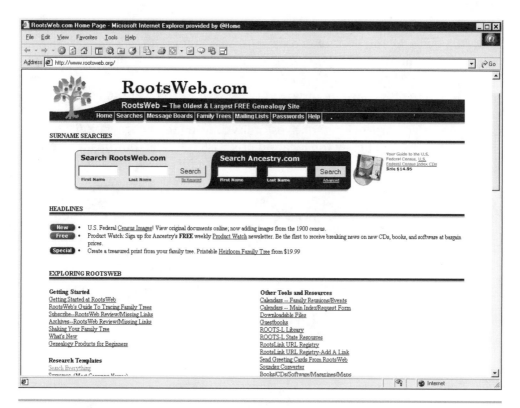

FIGURE 16-1. *Search for your surnames on RootsWeb on your first visit.*

the site's newsletters, the weekly column "Shaking Your Family Tree," What's New on the site, and a link to Ancestry's genealogy products for beginners.

Under *Research Templates* and *Search Engines and Databases,* you'll find links to several ways to search for genealogy. *Search Everything*, for example, leads to a page with links to several RootsWeb indexes: databases of vital records, GEDCOMS, and the RootsWeb Surname list. This resource is worth a careful look.

RSL The RootsWeb Surname List (RSL) is a registry of who is searching for whom, and in what times and places. The listings include contact information for each entry. If you find someone looking for the same name, in the same area, and in about the same time period, you might be able to help each other. That's the intent of the list. You don't have to pay to submit your own data or to search for data.

To search the list, you can use the form on the opening page or go to the page rsl.rootsweb.com/#search.

On the RSL page, you type in the surname you want to search for. You can narrow your search by inputing a location where you think the person you are looking for lives or lived, using the abbreviations you'll find at the link below the location box. Use the radio buttons to choose whether you want to search by surname (names spelled exactly as you've spelled them) or by soundex or metaphone (names that sound like the one you typed, but that are spelled differently). In future attempts, you can limit the search to new submissions within the last week, month, or two months. The list is updated once a month.

The Migration field shows you the path the family took. SC > GA, for example, shows migration from South Carolina to Georgia.

You can also send e-mail search commands to the RSL database: simply send a message with the surname you want to rsl-search@rootsweb.com. The results will be e-mailed back to you, just as they would be displayed on the Web page.

In the blink of an eye, you'll get a chart that shows the surname, date range, and locations that match, as well as a link to the person who submitted the data, showing how to contact him or her (see Figure 16-2). You can use the information to contact that person explaining what information you have on that surname and what you need.

Other Search Engines and Databases   RootsWeb has several other ways for you to search both the site and the Web at large. GenSeeker, for example, enables you to search the contents of all the registered WWW documents at RootsWeb, SearchThingy looks at all the databases and text files, MetaSearch looks for names across RootsWeb, and so on.

Other databases include the following:

♦ Social Security Death Index, which lists the deceased

♦ Surname Helper, which looks at the RootsWeb Message Boards and personal Web sites

♦ U.S. Town/County Database, which looks for locations

♦ The World Connect Project, which searches GEDCOMS of family trees submitted by RootsWeb members

- The USGenWeb Archives Search, which looks for pages posted across the United States in the GenWeb project

- WorldGenWeb, which searches for genealogy resources in nations outside the United States

The Surnames search index, United States Counties/States index, and the Countries index all search different subsets of the RootsWeb information. All of these are worth looking at.

World Connect Project   As explained in Chapter 8, the World Connect Project is one of several GEDCOM databases searchable through the Web. Searching it from the RootsWeb home page, you can only input first and last names. The results page will have another input form at the bottom, enabling you to fine-tune the search by adding places and dates.

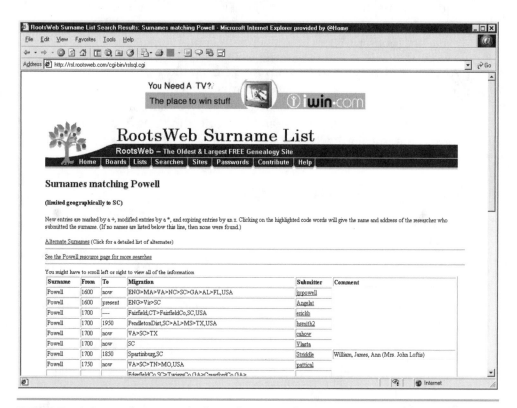

FIGURE 16-2.   *When I searched RSL for Powell in South Carolina, I got several hits.*

If you go to the World Connect page at worldconnect.rootsweb.com, you can find links to tips and hints for using World Connect. Remember, all the data here is uploaded by volunteers, so errors might exist!

Automated Surname Search   Clicking this button from the search form on the RootsWeb home page will search various text and database files on RootsWeb. You'll get a results page for hits within the Obit Times, World Connect, RSL, SSDI, and many other records on RootsWeb. Essentially, this is a metasearch on the RootsWeb site—a sort of RootsWeb's Greatest Hits!

SSDI   The Social Security Death Index searches the federal records of deaths. Anyone who died before Social Security began in the 1930s won't be in this database.

Searching from the RootsWeb home page, all you can input is the first and last name, but the results page will let you link to the Advanced Search page. Here you can narrow the search by location and date. This is an excellent tool for researching twentieth century ancestors.

Automated Keyword Search and GenSeeker   These two options from the RootsWeb search page are metasearch engines, which will look at text files and databases uploaded to RootsWeb such as obituaries, wills, deeds, and so on. Surname searches work using this, but so do searches for place names or keywords such as "census." Combine the two and you can get some good hits.

Other Search Engines

These searches can be helpful in your research, but they assume you're a rank beginner with no more than a name or a place to launch your inquiries. Perhaps you know for sure you're looking for a land record in Alabama or a cemetery in Iowa. RootsWeb has several searchable resources for items such as these. You'll find the search engines for the RSL and the other databases at searches.rootsweb.org (see Figure 16-3).

Message Boards and Mailing Lists

Among the best resources on RootsWeb are the mail lists and message boards, now hosted at Ancestry. A *message board* is a place where messages are read, sent, and answered on the Web, using a browser to read them. A *mail list* is where messages are e-mailed to and from

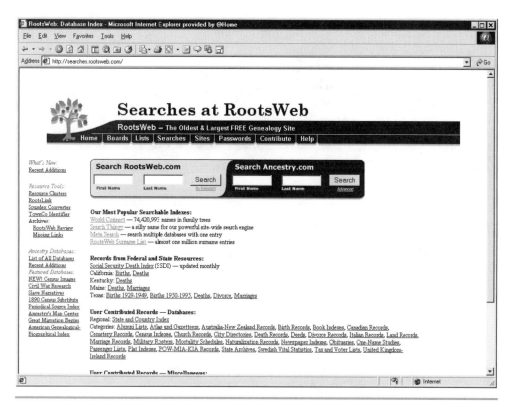

FIGURE 16-3. *From this page, you can reach dozens of specific searchable databases on RootsWeb.*

the members, whereas a mail client is used to read them. Both the message boards and the mail lists are archived and searchable. Figure 16-4 shows a typical message board on RootsWeb since the Ancestry merger.

Perhaps the easiest way to understand message boards is to visit their site at boards.ancestry.com/mbexec?htx = main&r = rw. Someday, you might want to administer a GenConnect board or even a suite of boards. If so, you'll find information on how to request a board(s) at resources.rootsweb.com/adopt.

The Mail Lists at lists.rootsweb.com cover many topics, such as the RootsWeb newsletters, described later in this chapter. Lists exist for specific surnames, every state in the United States, other countries—

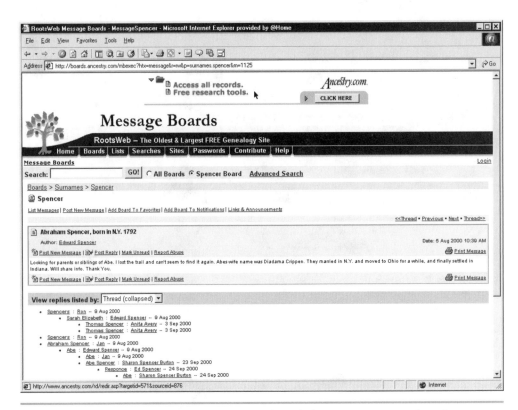

FIGURE 16-4. *You can search all message boards for a surname—such as Spencer— and find messages old and new.*

from Aruba to Zimbabwe—and lists for topics such as Adoption, Medical Genealogy, Prisons, and Heraldry. From the Mail Lists page, you can click a link to each one and you'll get instructions on how to use the list: subscribing, unsubscribing, sticking to the topic, and so on. The page for the Heraldry mail list on RootsWeb is shown in Figure 16-5.

Besides Roots-L, which is the grandparent of genealogy mailing lists on the Internet, RootsWeb hosts literally thousands of mailing lists. As mentioned in Chapter 7, you can find lists for surnames or family names, regions, or topics being researched. The index at www.rootsweb.org/ ~maillist has thousands of lists you can join, along with instructions explaining how to subscribe. It won't include all the mailing lists at RootsWeb, however, because it's a voluntary listing and not all list owners choose to be featured.

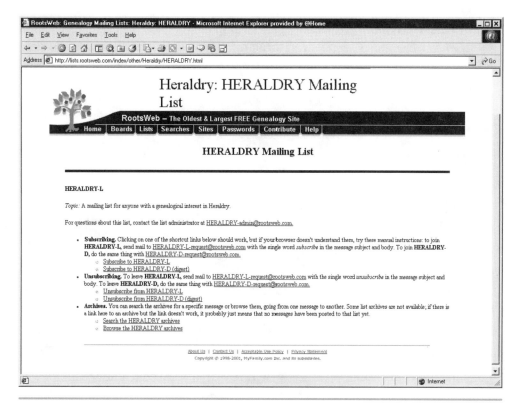

FIGURE 16-5. *Each mail list has a page describing its topic, use, and archives.*

A good rule of thumb: be choosy in joining lists! Take on only a few at a time. Read the lists for a while, sign off if they don't prove useful, and then try some others. Some lists are extremely active, sometimes, overwhelmingly so. One RootsWeb user who signed up for every possible mailing list for the United Kingdom had 9,000 e-mails in his inbox within 24 hours! Be careful what you wish for …

And remember, some lists are archived, so you needn't subscribe to see if that list is talking about subjects of interest to you. Just search the archive for your keywords and save the important messages.

You might even want to start a mailing list of your own someday, which contributors can do. You can learn more about what's required of a listowner by following the link titled Information for Listowners and Potential Listowners at the main page for Mailing Lists.

GenNewbie

GenNewbie started as an electronic mailing list for people who were new to computers and/or genealogy to ask questions, help others, and generally share information, research techniques, brick walls, and computer/genealogy woes. It began on October 31, 1996, as an offshoot of the renowned Roots-L. Since then, we've gained over 1,000 members, a unique community that supports the honest and open newbie questions in a flame-free, tolerant atmosphere concerning genealogy/computers.

GENMTD-L

Genealogical methods and resources are the topics for GENMTD-L. This isn't a queries list. Instead, it's a list about the nuts and bolts of genealogy research. You can participate through e-mail or through USENET news. The discussions are archived and intended to be searchable and retrievable, although they are—continually, we sometimes think—in a state of transition on exactly how to do this. More at a later time on this topic!

GENMTD-L is a moderated group intended for helpful discussions of the (noncomputing) research methods, resources, and problems genealogists have in common, regardless of the different families or different cultural groups they study. Those who develop specific questions or problems in their own research may solicit suggestions from the group on how to resolve a research problem. Those who discover useful research resources and strategies are encouraged to share their expertise.

Postings from both experienced and inexperienced participants are welcome. The philosophy of the list's moderators is to be light-handed and to offer extra help behind the scenes for new participants, who might be experiencing problems with e-mail addresses, Net customs, and so forth.

Newsletters

A newsletter, like a mailing list, comes straight to your e-mail inbox. Unlike the lists above, however, they are not for discussion; the communication is one-to-many. Like a print magazine, it will have news, notes, stories, and the occasional (text) advertisement. RootsWeb has several e-mail newsletters, all of which are worth reading. Here are some descriptions of them.

RootsWeb Review

RootsWeb is always growing and you can't depend on luck to find out about the latest and greatest sites! For help in this area, use the *RootsWeb Review,* a free weekly newsletter sent to contributors and users via e-mail. You'll find announcements of programs and services for RootsWeb users, new mailing lists, GenConnect boards, and Web sites, plus success stories from other cybergenealogists.

If you're interested in reading through previous issues, go to ftp://ftp. rootsweb.org/pub/review. You can subscribe by sending an e-mail to RootsWeb-Review-L-request@rootsweb.org with only the word "subscribe" in the subject line and message area.

Missing Links

Missing Links is a weekly compilation of articles about genealogical research methods and sources from all parts of the world. You'll also find delightful, amazing, and otherwise wonderful tales of genealogical research at *Successful Links*, as well as articles acknowledging the efforts of particularly helpful librarians, archivists, town or county clerks, and other unsung heroes, in an appreciative digest titled *Virtual Bouquets.* You can contribute your own stories by e-mailing your submissions as plain-text messages (not as attachments) to rwr-editors@rootsweb.com. To subscribe, send a message to rootsweb-review-subscribe@rootsweb.com.

Somebody's Links

Somebody's Links is a monthly collection of uncovered genealogical treasures, such as photographs, diaries, letters, and family Bibles. The contributors describe each item as accurately as possible, hoping someone out there is looking for it. Back issues of the newsletter are available as plain-text files at ftp://ftp.rootsweb.com/pub/somebody. Files are named according to the date of the issue (for example, 19991201.txt).

All back issues of *RootsWeb Review* and *Missing Links* are searchable at search-rwr.rootsweb.org.

Web Pages at RootsWeb

RootsWeb hosts thousands of genealogy Web sites. Some, like Cyndi's List at cyndislist.com or the USGenWeb Project's main site at www.usgenweb.com, you already read about in this book. RootsWeb also hosts the WorldGenWeb Project at www.worldgenweb.org and a majority of the country sites. Some examples follow:

Books We Own, at www.rootsweb.org/~bwo, is a list of resources owned/accessed by volunteers who are willing to look up genealogical information, and then e-mail or snail mail it to others who request it. This is a free service: volunteers might ask for reimbursement of copies and postage if information is provided via snail mail. The project began in 1996 as a way for members of the ROOTS-L mailing list to share their resources with one another. Today, over 1,500 volunteers exist. Resource owners are volunteers with a limited amount of time and resources to spend looking up information. Jenny Tenlen has served as the Webmaster of Books We Own since February 1997 and is the third Webmaster since this project began.

Cemetery Photos, at rootsweb.org/~cemphoto/Cemetery_Photos.html, is the same sort of idea, applied to cemeteries. Volunteers will go to a cemetery and take a picture of a tombstone for you if you know the exact names, dates, and locations for them to look for. Cemetery Photos is a project designed to help people obtain photos of headstones in areas they can't get to themselves. Over 3,500 volunteers cover 24 countries. Some ask to be reimbursed for the film and postage. You can volunteer to be part of this effort, too!

FreeBMD (England and Wales), at freebmd.rootsweb.com, stands for Free Births, Marriages, and Deaths. The *FreeBMD* Project's objective is to provide free Internet access to the Civil Registration index information for England and Wales. The Civil Registration system for recording births, marriages, and deaths in England and Wales has been in place since 1837. This is one of the most significant single resources for genealogical research back to Victorian times.

Immigrant Ships Transcribers Guild, at istg.rootsweb.com, is a group of volunteers dedicated to making the search for our ancestors' immigration easier. The aim is to make as many ship's passenger lists as possible available online. This group would also be happy to have your help!

Random Acts of Genealogical Kindness, at raogk.rootsweb.com, is a cooperative effort. Once a month, the volunteers of this movement agree either to videotape cemeteries or to visit county courthouses in the county (or an area of a country) they live in to transcribe records. The cost to you would be reimbursement of costs incurred in granting your request (video tape, copy fees, and so forth). This means if we can find one person living in each county of the United States, as well as folks from other countries, to volunteer once a month, our odds of obtaining what we need, anywhere we need to look, increase tremendously!

State Resource Pages, one of the main areas of RootsWeb, is at www.rootsweb.org/roots-l/usa.html. It offers a wealth of information to those researching in the United States. Just the upper portion of one page appears in Figure 16-6, listing articles on federal censuses, old ports, and all the counties in the Unites States. This is a great place to begin your search for records within a certain geographic area. Another to see is www.rootsweb.com/ ~ websites/uspages.html.

The HelpDesk

The HelpDesk maintains a page to help you find an FAQ file about RootsWeb and its services. If you have a question or problem, check

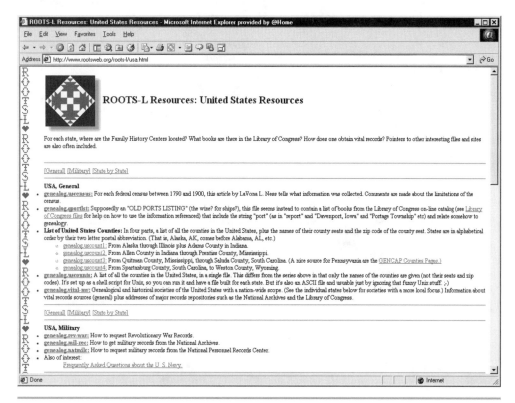

FIGURE 16-6. *The State Resources Pages help you zero in on a specific type of record in the United States.*

here first. If you can't find an answer here, you can follow the links from that site to the message board where you can post a question for the HelpDesk team to answer.

More and More

This quick tour is just enough to whet your appetite. Spend some time getting to know RootsWeb. Then get acquainted with Ancestry.com, the subject of Chapter 17.

Wrapping Up

- The RootsWeb site is a great place to begin your family history research.

- Message Boards are now hosted on Ancestry.com.

- RootsWeb mail lists cover a broad range of topics.

- Online files at RootsWeb have transcribed primary source records.

- Newsletters from RootsWeb help you stay on top of the latest in genealogy.

- Search engines on RootsWeb make using the site easier.

Chapter 17

The Ancestry.com Family of Sites

Ancestry.com, based in Salt Lake City, publishes books, magazines, and other genealogy materials. The online service, which is less than ten years old, has grown rapidly, and includes a research site, an interactive site, and a community site. All these sites are designed to help the amateur family historian in a variety of ways.

As mentioned in the previous chapter, Ancestry, a commercial venture, and RootsWeb, a volunteer cooperative, merged. The two sites are still different from each other, however, except in the area of the message boards. The files, chats, and other online functions are different among the Ancestry family of sites.

RootsWeb, covered in Chapter 16, still has free downloads of files and information. Ancestry's other sites—Ancestry.com, MyFamily.com, and FamilyHistory.com—have some free areas and some to which you must pay a yearly subscription to access.

Ancestry.com

Ancestry.com, the company's first Web site, is designed to help genealogists exchange information with other genealogists and to learn new techniques for family history. Features include the following:

- ◆ A large online genealogy library, searchable from the Web. The library includes such records as land, birth, marriage, death, census, and immigration records; the PERiodical Source Index (PERSI); Daughters of the American Revolution Lineage Books; the 1790 Census Collection; and the Early American Marriages Collection, to name just a few.

- ◆ Name databases, which are updated frequently, so future searches may turn up what today's search did not.

- ◆ Regular genealogy columns from George G. Morgan, Dick Eastman, Kip Sperry, Juliana Smith, Elizabeth Kelley Kerstens, and Drew Smith are available free of charge.

Several levels of membership are available to Ancestry.com: a "super subscription" with access to standard data and the U.S. Federal Census images for about $100 a year; access to standard data for $70 a year;

access to the U.S. Federal Census images for $70 a year; quarterly access to standard data or U.S. Federal Census images for $25 a quarter each; and a membership that's free of charge. Sometimes the company will run free access specials, especially around Christmas time, to encourage people to give subscriptions as gifts. Their free daily newsletter (you sign up by putting your e-mail in the box on the opening page of the site) has alerts on when the free offers begin and end.

Even if you don't sign up for a paid subscription, you can find loads of useful information in the free sections of Ancestry.com. Every business day, Ancestry.com adds a new database such as Andersonville Prisoners of War or New York City wills, and when a new database is added, it's free for a few days.

The most popular part of the site is its searchable database of the free Social Security Death Index. If you're looking for someone who died after the 1930s, this is a good place to start.

Another popular free area is the Ancestry.com World Tree database. Visitors to the site are welcome to submit what data they have for this database, the largest collection of its kind on the Internet. It's all-volunteer, and Ancestry.com has pledged to keep the searches free. Be aware, however, that Ancestry.com, as with most other sites that accept an individual's data, doesn't check the data submitted, so it all must be considered secondary material at best. Nevertheless, it can give you some good clues.

To use the Ancestry.com World Tree database, simply enter a name and the person's birth and death dates, if you have them. The matches in the databases are presented in a table, as shown in Figure 17-1.

You can click the links in the far right to view the person's pedigree, look at data for that individual, e-mail the submitter, or download the GEDCOM.

Other good links in the free area include the regular columnists (Dick Eastman, Dear MYRTLE, and others), genealogy lessons, phone and address searches, Juliana's Links, a searchable database of Web sites, and maps and gazetteers. In addition, it's always worth looking at the daily news page (www.ancestry.com/library/view/news/articles/d_p_1_archive.asp).

The site also features a chat area, bookstore, and sample articles from *Ancestry* magazine, the print version.

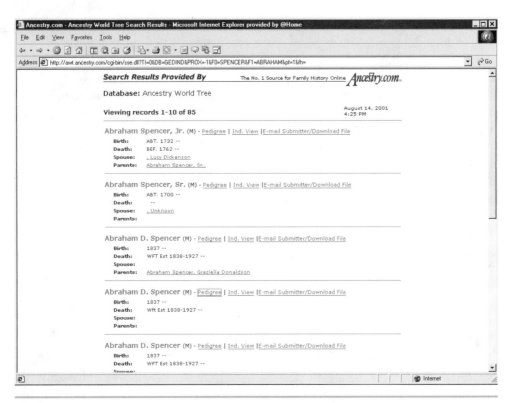

FIGURE 17-1. *In the Ancestry.com World Tree, you can find information from other genealogists. You can download the GEDCOM or contact the submitter.*

FamilyHistory.com

Message boards, uploaded GEDCOM databases for exchange, and Society Hall make up the genealogy community FamilyHistory.com. This part of the Ancestry.com empire is an online community, along the lines of RootsWeb or GenealogyForum.com. The main sections are World Tree and the Society Hall (see Figure 17-2). The mission of FamilyHistory.com is to give everyone interested in family history a community to swap information and improve their research by working together. The message boards have been moved to the

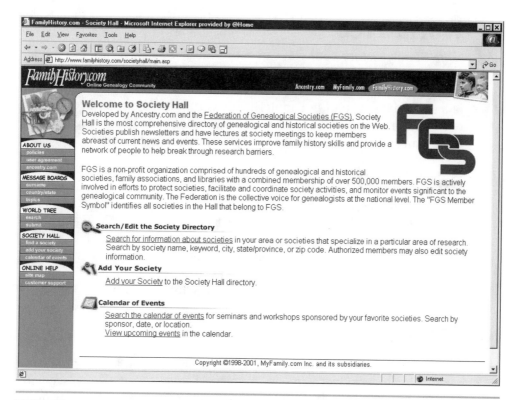

FIGURE 17-2. *FamilyHistory.com has a comprehensive directory of genealogy societies and associations.*

Ancestry.com site, as have the message boards of RootsWeb (see Chapter 16).

Message Boards

The message boards of FamilyHistory.com have been incorporated into the Ancestry.com system. The message boards are divided into three broad categories: surnames, geography, and research. You can search all the message boards with the form on the Message Boards page and use Soundex to get close matches (Spencer, Spenser, Spence, for example). You can also browse an alphabetical list of the board topics.

World Tree

From FamilyHistory.com you can get to the *Ancestry World Tree,* a free database of genealogies online. With the Ancestry World Tree, you can view pedigree charts, download files, and contact the original submitter of a set of data. As part of FamilyHistory.com, this data will never be sold or restricted in any way. You can also contribute your genealogy research to the Ancestry.com World Tree, so other researchers can contact you.

Society Hall

FamilyHistory.com also hosts the Federation of Genealogy Societies (FGS) Society Hall. This set of pages has listings of hundreds of genealogy societies and hosts many society Web sites. Use the Society Hall to find organizations in your area or to locate societies that focus on specific research. The Society Hall can help you learn about genealogy society events, publications, recent news, and other information.

MyFamily.com

The free MyFamily.com site is a portal. Portals are good places to start when you log on to the Internet. And, portals might be the last place you visit online before you log off because they offer so many features and activities—you might never need to surf anywhere else.

MyFamily.com's portal is a family history/community portal. The tools on the MyFamily.com site include a family calendar, family chat, family history features, message boards, a photo album, and more. Access to each family's site has both private password-only areas and public areas. You can use up to 5MB of free space per site you create. To use more space, you have to pay a yearly fee of $20 to $100, depending on the amount of space you need. The details are at www.myfamily.com/ isapi.dll?c = Site&htx = SiteUpgrade&siteid = BubD.

Still, 5MB of space is ample room to create a site for your family, with a short family tree. You can store photos, sounds, and video clips in your album, and you can upload games or shareable applications to the file cabinet.

Other features are on the MyFamily.com site (they have much less to do with genealogy), but for this book I will only cover those areas related to genealogy.

At the My Sites link (on the MyFamily.com home page), you can create a private message board, calendar, and file cabinets. You can also put together online scrapbooks of image, sound, and video files, upload your genealogy, and host private chats among members of your family you choose to invite. Once you create the site, your MyFamily home page looks like Figure 17-3.

Creating a site is just a matter of clicks. You define a name and login, and then draw up a list of relatives. You input their birthdays, anniversaries, and other important calendar dates, and then invite them to join you by creating a list of their e-mail addresses. Everyone on the list is e-mailed a specific logon name and password for that site (no one can access your site without them). You can also create an address book with phone numbers and so forth for you to access when you're online.

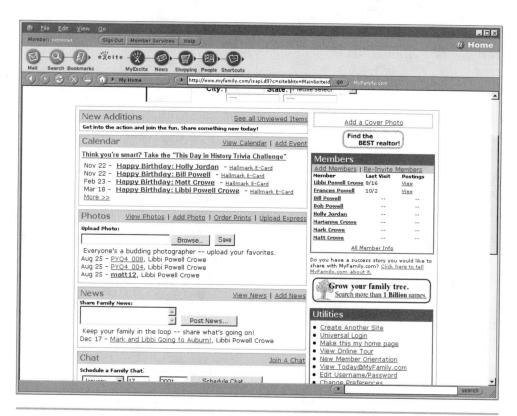

FIGURE 17-3. *When you create a site, you'll have your own My Sites page for adding messages, genealogy, and more.*

Family Tree

Now it's time to begin constructing your online family tree. To do this, use the Family Tree link in the navigation bar at the top of every page on your MyFamily site. You can create this by typing in entries online or by uploading a GEDCOM (by far the most recommended method!). I uploaded a GEDCOM, which looks like Figure 17-4.

By clicking the globe icon on the Family Tree creation page, you can make the GEDCOM available to Ancestry's World Family Tree or click it again to remove it. Updates are simple: you can do them offline, and then upload to overwrite the old tree, or click any individual's name in the display in Figure 17-4 and correct data on the fly. Those who have logon privileges to your site can download the data and submit trees of their own.

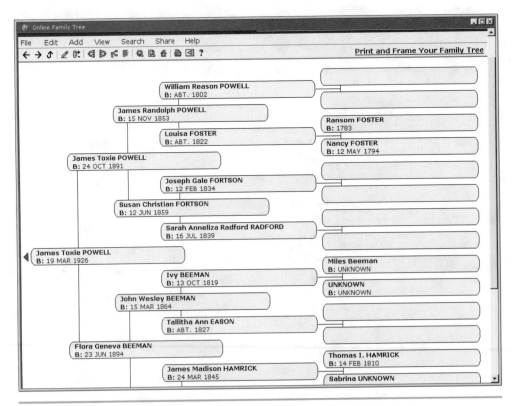

FIGURE 17-4. *The family tree on MyFamily.com can show descendant or ancestor views, as well as family groups.*

History

A nice feature is the "Our Family History" (listed as History on the navigation bar). Every family member you invited to participate can log on, click Add History, and contribute memories of events, stories, and experiences. By clicking List History, the members can view all the contributions. When reading one, they can "Reply" and add their perspectives, ask questions, and so on (see Figure 17-5).

Remember, all this information is available only to those people you invited to join your family site.

Chats

Whenever you like, all the members of your family site can sign on together for private, real-time chats. To do this, scroll down the first page of your site to the Chat listing, and pick a day and time. Everyone who

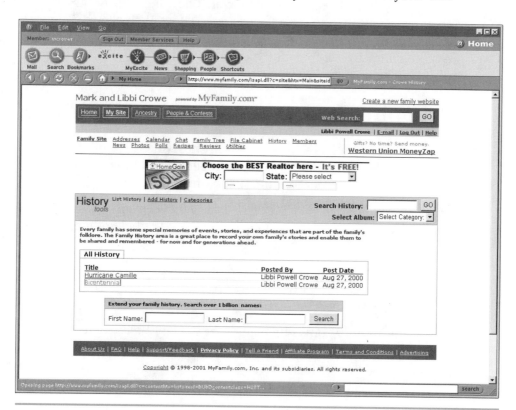

FIGURE 17-5.   *You can collect family history stories on your MyFamily site.*

is a member of your site will then be e-mailed regarding when to sign on. This is good for planning family reunions, interviewing relatives about family history, or swapping genealogical data.

Other Features

Other features include news (where you can post current family events); photo albums (where you can post pictures); a recipe swap area; a reviews area, where you can share opinions on current movies, music, and art; and utilities for maintaining the Web site you created. Furthermore, the site offers a gift center, channels on health and parenting, contests, and so on. All of these are fun, even if they aren't related to genealogy!

A Nice Collection of Sites

The Ancestry.com collection of sites, which now includes RootsWeb, is a great place to start your genealogical quest. RootsWeb allows you more creativity in your Web site design than MyFamily, but the MyFamily sites are more interactive. Either way, both sites can be useful in continuing and sharing your genealogy research.

Wrapping Up

- Ancestry.com has several different sites: Ancestry.com for research, FamilyHistory.com for societies and organizations, and MyFamily.com for interaction, though all three do at least a little bit of everything.

- Many Ancestry.com features are free, but the bulk of the data is only available to paying customers.

- MyFamily.com allows you to create a family site with genealogy data, messages boards, and so on. Recently, this portal started charging for members' sites over 5 megabytes.

- FamilyHistory.com is the site of the Society Hall, where you can find genealogy societies, associations, and clubs.

Chapter 18

Everton Publishers

One of the most venerable publishing companies in genealogy, Everton Publishers (www.everton.com) produces books, CD-ROMs, the print magazine *Everton's Genealogical Helper,* and an excellent Web site.

The Everton Web page offers several free features, although you do have to register your name, address, and e-mail address to access them. Figure 18-1 shows those features available to you in the Free Guest Area.

Databases

Like Ancestry, Everton accepts GEDCOM files from genealogists, but the database is available for free search use only on a limited basis. Submitting your own GEDCOM files gets you one month free searching on this database. For $50 a year (which includes a subscription to *Everton's Genealogical Helper*), you can have access to that database, as well as

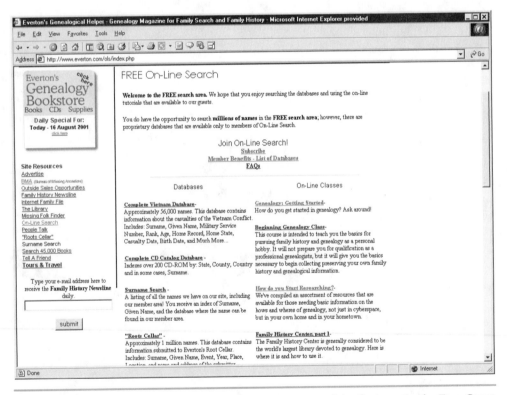

FIGURE 18-1. *Databases and online classes are some of the features in the Free Guest Area on Everton's Web site.*

many others. Everton also has a searchable database of the Social Security Death Index (SSDI), included in the free guest databases. Other guest privileges include a searchable catalog of genealogical CDs, a photo database, and a relationship chart. Some of the databases you can search in the free area include the following.

Vietnam Database

This database of 56,000 names has information regarding casualties of the Vietnam conflict. You can search this database by surname, given name, military service number, rank, age, home record, home state, casualty date, and birth date.

CD-ROM Catalog

If you're wondering whether to buy a CD-ROM from Everton's Web site, check out this index. You can search over 200 of them by state, county, country, and, in some cases, surname. If you get many hits on one CD-ROM, buying this might be worthwhile.

Surname Search

A listing of all the names Everton has on the site, including the paid member area. The results displayed are an index of surname, given name, and the database where the name can be found in the member area. If the hit is within a paid database, you'll be given a chance to subscribe.

Roots Cellar

One of the oldest and most popular features on the Everton site, this is a collaborative, volunteer collection of genealogical data. With about 1,000,000 names, this database contains information submitted by people who want to share information. You can search by surname and given name. Remember, as with many such sites, no one has checked the data for accuracy, but you can still benefit from this database by finding genealogists searching for the same lines and people you seek.

To submit to the Roots Cellar costs $5 for three entries (persons). To do so, click the link from the Roots Cellar search page and fill out the form.

Internet Family File

Like the Roots Cellar, this has genealogical data, but in GEDCOM form. You can add your own GEDCOM free. You can also search by surname and given name, and then receive information on how to download matching GEDCOMs. Remember, no one has validated the data you find here. You must contact the submitters to discover their sources.

You can submit your own GEDCOM by File Transfer Protocol (FTP) or by e-mail. Send the GEDCOM as an attachment to gedcom@everton.com or upload by FTP to ftp://www.everton.com.

Social Security Death Index (SSDI)

This is the same database offered by many other sites, searchable by surname, first name, Social Security number, and birth and death dates. You can have the output downloaded to your disk or displayed on the screen.

Family History Centers

This search page helps you find The Church of Jesus Christ of Latter-day Saints' Family History Center addresses and telephone numbers throughout the world.

The page contains a list of all the workshops sponsored by Everton Publishers, including location address, date, and time. Search it by state or by ZIP code.

AllCensus Images Search

A try-before-you-buy feature, this page lets you search census images from over 2,000 counties and, if you have hits on your search, purchase the CD-ROM. Included in the database are the United States Federal Census records from 1790 to 1920. Each CD has a different price, starting at $6.

Online Classes

Everton's online classes are a free collection of text files to help you get started in the world of genealogy, learn proper research techniques, and use various resources, such as the Family History Centers. Because a lot of material is here, you might want to download the files so you can read them later offline. The following are the classes listed.

Genealogy: Getting Started

This online course gives you a set of questions to start asking older members of your family: how to write down what you learned for later reference, how to organize your information, and an overview of the common forms used in genealogy.

Beginning Genealogy Class

This course teaches you the basics for pursuing family history and genealogy as a personal hobby. This class isn't aimed at certification as a professional genealogist but, instead, gives you the basics necessary to begin collecting and preserving your own family history and genealogical information.

How Do You Start Researching?

This course is an overview of resources available for basic information on the how's and where's of genealogy, not only in cyberspace, but also in your own home and in your hometown.

Family History Center, Parts 1-4

The Family History Center (FHC) is generally considered the world's largest library devoted to genealogy. This is a set of four lessons:

- What the FHC is

- How to use the Family History Library Catalog

- How to use the services in the Family History Library

- How to use the affiliated Family History Centers

African American Research

Census records have undergone a number of transformations in the United States. The depiction of blacks in United States censuses has undergone a similar transition, as shown in this series of three censuses from the Southeast. A sample lesson in this series is shown in Figure 18-2.

Vital Records in England and Wales

In England and Wales, vital records go back hundreds of years. Vital records information was compiled at the local level in several different registration and subregistration offices. Every three months, the local registrars were required to send copies of their records to the General Register Office, creating a central repository for all the vital records for the 40 counties in England and Wales. This set of lessons explains how to use them.

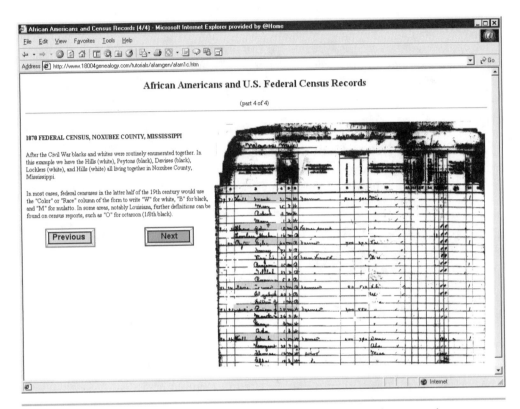

FIGURE 18-2. *The free lessons on African American research show sample census forms.*

How to Use Federal Mortality Schedules

From 1790 through 1840, federal censuses in the United States were largely numeric enumerations, confining themselves to listing only the names of household heads, rather than the name of every resident in the nation. In 1850 that changed, with a population census that attempted, for the first time, to record the name of every resident of the United States. That was the first year data was gathered on who died within the census year, before the census taker came around. This is an important adjunct to your census research.

The Hamburg Passenger Departure Lists

This set of informative files includes a historical background of the lists, the lists themselves, and an analysis of what was learned. It points out that the vast majority of emigrants passed through a relatively small number of major ports in Europe, and arrived in a similarly small number of ports in the United States.

United States-Canadian Border Crossing Records

To many people, the term *port* refers to seaports. But ports can be overland, too. Our ancestors immigrated to the United States using whatever entryway seemed best to them, whether by land or by sea. This set of pages explains how to track such migration.

Cemetery Records in Genealogical Research

Whether you view cemeteries as the natural backdrops for horror movies or as placid settings for honor and reflection, as a family historian you should also consider them as one of the finest storehouses of family information. This five-part series steps you through how to search cemeteries and record your findings. The page on photographing tombstones is shown in Figure 18-3.

Other Features

In addition to online lessons, Everton Web site includes other features useful to genealogists.

Family History Newsline

A newsletter delivered by e-mail, the *Family History Newsline* comes every weekday with tips and news from Frank Beacon. Subscribe to it on the page www.everton.com/FHN/mailinglist_manager.php. You can read back issues at www.everton.com/FHN/weekly_index.php.

RV-n-Genealogist

RV-n-Genealogist is a free site dedicated to genealogy and the RV lifestyle.

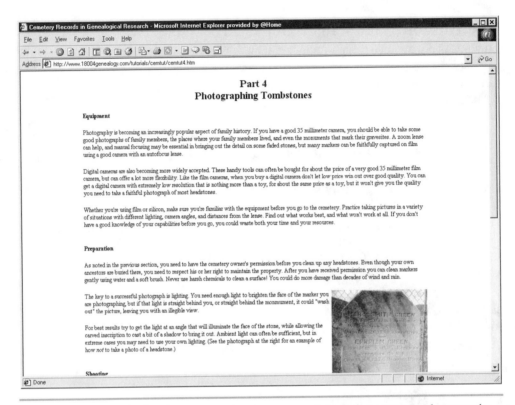

FIGURE 18-3. *The free lessons on cemetery research include a page on photography in cemeteries.*

Everton's Genealogical Helper (EGH)

For $24 a year, you can have access to a complete Web version of the print magazine, *Everton's Genealogical Helper,* and its article archive (more than 200 articles).

Genealogy Supply Store

The *Genealogy Supply Store* is a safe, secure place to find archival quality forms, binders, software, CD-ROM, books, magazines, gifts, and computers!

The Family Letter

A free service for members of On-Line Search, *The Family Letter* is secure because you must use a password and a user name. You can post letters and photos, keep current address lists, and/or post a family newsletter. This site can be used for organizations, family associations, and societies.

Subscribing

By subscribing to Everton's Web site, you gain access to more databases, magazine articles, and features.

Rates at press time:

- One-Week Subscription: U.S. $9.95

- One-Month Subscription: U.S. $15.00

- Six-Month Subscription: U.S. $29.50

- One-Year Subscription: U.S. $49.50

Wrapping Up

- The resources and how-to articles in Everton's Web site free area are excellent for the beginner and intermediate genealogist.

- The Genealogical Helper is one of the most respected journals in genealogy and worth subscribing to, with or without the online access.

- Other databases are available for subscription.

- Try the site at least once. You might find many treasures to take away with you.

Chapter 19

CompuServe's
Genealogy Forums

CompuServe is one of the oldest—and best—online services. For years, CompuServe was based on a text interface: you typed in a command, such as GO ROOTS, and a text menu would appear for looking at messages, files, and announcements in the genealogy forum. A graphics interface was introduced in the early '90s and has continued to evolve. After CompuServe was bought by America Online in 1998, the service's software got a major overhaul. CompuServe still uses GO words to navigate the system's features but, other than that, little remains of the CompuServe interface of 20 years ago.

The essence of CompuServe is still there, though. Despite sporting quite a few AOL-like features in the new interface, it's still the premier service for serious, mature users ("adult" in the good sense). CompuServe users tend to be those who work for a living and use CompuServe to do their work and their hobbies faster, better, and cheaper. CompuServe has little nonsense and lots of common sense.

Web Access

The genealogy forums on CompuServe are now available to nonsubscribers via the Web at www.rootsforum.com. All the CompuServe Genealogy Forums are now free and open to everyone. After more than 12 years within the closed systems of CompuServe, the files, messages, and chats of the Roots Forum are now available via the Web. You only need to have any one of the following:

- ◆ CompuServe Instant Messenger (CSIM)

- ◆ America Online Instant Messenger (AIM)

- ◆ Netscape Instant Messenger User ID

- ◆ An active CompuServe membership (simply enter your CompuServe User ID and password when prompted for a screen name)

- ◆ An active AOL membership (simply enter your AOL User ID and password when prompted for a screen name)

Note

On CompuServe, message boards, files, and chats on a topic grouped together are called a forum.

With any of these programs, you have a screen name to register with the forum. Then, you simply navigate to www.rootsforum.com and you can access all the forum's features.

This is the place to view the best genealogy message board, file upload/download areas, chat rooms, private clubs for specific family names and geographic interests, loads of how-to information for beginners, more than 2,000 genealogy book reviews, and more.

Note

You needn't have the Instant Messenger software installed and running. You only need to have a User ID and password with one of the previously shown versions of Instant Messenger. In fact, you needn't download or install any software; simply register the User ID and password.

Plenty to Offer

CompuServe's online genealogy resources have much to offer:

- ♦ Social Security Death Records online (link to Ancestry.com)

- ♦ Nearly 2,000 genealogy book reviews available online in the Roots Forum

- ♦ More than 8,000 genealogy-related files available online, including shareware and free genealogy programs for Windows, MS-DOS, Macintosh, Amiga, UNIX, and even older computers

- ♦ A genealogy page within the Research area with news, notes, and pointers, plus links to other genealogy sites, such as FamilySearch (see Chapter 10)

- ♦ Three main genealogy forums (Web and CompuServe access) and several other forums that occasionally touch on genealogy

Each forum on CompuServe has its own GO word. Each separate forum's messages and files can be searched for keywords. Each forum's chat schedule is different. You join a forum by clicking Join. You type in your forum name and your preferences for how the files and messages will display. On all the CompuServe genealogy forums, a *handle* (nickname) is strongly discouraged. You're urged to use your real first and last name for your forum name. The forum managers, who keep things running smoothly, are called *sysops,* which is short for system operators.

> **Note** ———————————————————————
>
> *To get a complete list of the GO words on CompuServe, go to GO SITEMAP.*

A Quick Overview

The CompuServe software is based on the Microsoft Internet Explorer (IE) browser. You can either have a local ISP account and use that TCP/IP connection to get to CompuServe or you can use the Dial-Up Network connection and surf from CompuServe. Microsoft IE is so well integrated into the software, you don't realize that's what you're using if you want to jump from the Genealogy Techniques Forum straight to the Library of Congress site. You can only tell the difference in one way: if you're still on the service, the page box in the top of the screen has a URL with CompuServe somewhere in the name.

> **Note** ———————————————————————
>
> *The CompuServe software will be familiar if you've ever used AOL. For example, there's a check mark to add a forum or other service to your list of favorites instead of a heart, but the process is the same. Click the check mark, choose from Add To Favorites, and either add to an instant message or add to an e-mail message (the latter two as links).*

As of press time, CompuServe software lacks the capability to download forum messages that interest you to read and answer offline. This has been available on CompuServe since the beginning of the service, right up to this 1999 version of the software and it's available with AOL's software. But the current CompuServe requires you to be online to read and answer messages. This is a grave error, in my estimation, and makes the software much less usable. For this reason, many people are choosing to stay with the CompuServe Classic software, which lets you download forum messages and file them in your filing cabinet.

Many useful features have been added in CompuServe 2000, however, such as the following:

♦   Instant Messaging, with buddy lists. This works only with other CompuServe members logged on at the same time you are. Instant Messaging is integrated into the Contact List, where you keep e-mail addresses of people you write to often. This also works with AIM (see Chapter 6).

♦   Spell Check, special fonts, pictures, and attachments in e-mail. In short, fully multimedia e-mail. CompuServe 2000 is also POP3-compliant, so you can use Eudora, Outlook, or any other POP3 e-mail reader.

♦   56K/V.90 access with many access points in the United States and around the world, which makes using CompuServe easy when you travel.

♦   The capability to have several member names under your main account.

♦   The capability to download Usenet and e-mail messages, and then upload them at specified times. Unfortunately, this doesn't include messages in forums at press time. For this, you have to stick with CompuServe Classic.

GO Genealogy

The GO word to get you started is GENEALOGY. Simply type **GENEALOGY** in the white box at the top of the CompuServe screen and click the green GO button. You'll get the screen in Figure 19-1. You can also access this page from the Web at www.compuserve.com/research/genealogy.asp.

Note

Capitalization doesn't matter with GO words. GENEALOGY will work as well as genealogy.

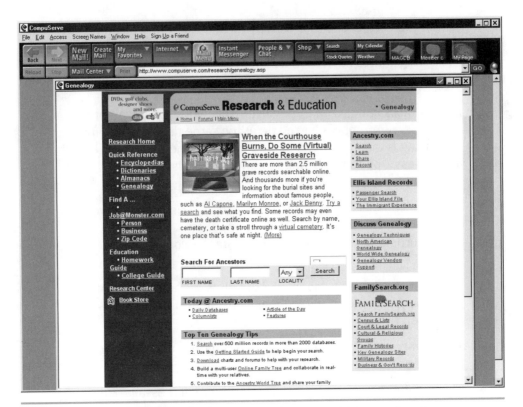

FIGURE 19-1.   *The keyword GENEALOGY takes you to the Research and
Learn Genealogy page.*

On this page, you have links to major genealogy sites, articles, and tips.
In the illustration, a recent article outlined searching cemeteries and had
links for several online cemetery search sites. You can also find links
to Ellis Island Records, Ancestry.com, and, of course, the CompuServe
genealogy forums.

Forums

CompuServe has four different genealogy forums, each useful for a
different type of genealogical research.

Genealogy Techniques Forum

The oldest genealogy forum on CompuServe is the *Genealogy Techniques Forum*. This is the place for beginners to share successes and to ask about how to get beyond a brick wall in their research. You can access it on CompuServe with the GO word ROOTS on the Web at www.rootsforum.com (see Figure 19-2 for the Web version).

You can also find links to all the messages files and chat rooms of the other genealogy forums here. Click Messages, Library Files, or Chat Rooms in the navigation bar to the left.

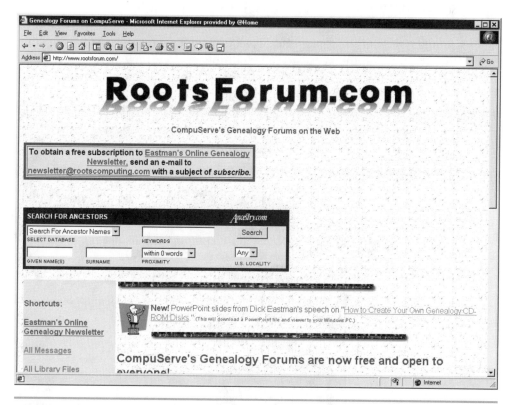

FIGURE 19-2.   *CompuServe's Genealogy Forum is available on the Web, as well as on the service itself.*

In the Genealogy Techniques Forum, you can learn how to use your computer for genealogy, how to use the Web, where to find professional genealogists, learn about coats of arms, learn how to conduct adoption searches, and more.

Eastman's Genealogy Newsletter (see Chapter 7), from Dick Eastman, is online here. You can subscribe, read the current issue, and search an archive of previous issues from this forum. Also, Dick Eastman has posted his PowerPoint presentation on how to create your own genealogy CD-ROMs and the reasons for doing so.

North American Genealogy Forum

The *North American Genealogy Forum* is for queries about ancestors in Canada, the United States, and Mexico. To get there, use the GO word NAROOTS or, on the Web, go to go.compuserve.com/NAGenealogy. As shown in Figure 19-3, this forum covers specific states and provinces in

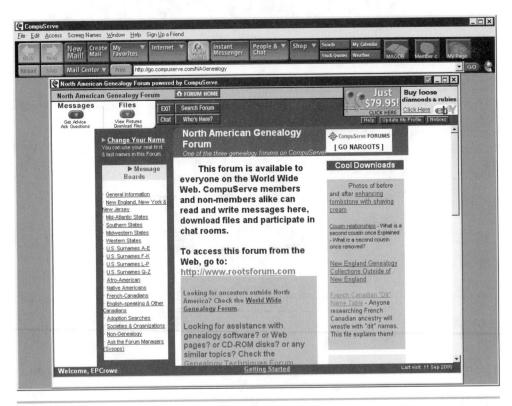

FIGURE 19-3. *The North American Genealogy Forum has more specific topics than the Genealogy Techniques Forum.*

Canada, Mexico, and the United States; societies and organizations (including their workshops, meetings, and seminars); and ethnic groups, such as Native Americans.

World Wide Genealogy Forum

For queries about ancestors anywhere but North America, check the *World Wide Genealogy Forum*. Use the GO word WWROOTS or the URL http://forumsb.compuserve.com/vlforums/default.asp?SRV = WWGenealogy.

Other Forums

You can also find genealogy discussed on other forums. For example, genealogy is often discussed in the Civil War and History Forums. The GO words are CIVILWAR and HISTORY.

Forum Decorum

Regardless of the version of CompuServe you use, with all the genealogy forums on CompuServe, you can exchange information with thousands of other members around the world, from experts and professionals to beginners. Everyone has something to contribute.

The goal of the forums is to create an atmosphere that encourages intelligent interaction and lively debate. The sysops are insistent on members using common sense and courtesy. If you have questions about how to proceed, you can contact the sysops by posting a message addressed To: SYSOP on the message board of any forum.

A forum is a place that values free expression; you'll often find lively discussions and spirited debates. The membership is international, from diverse ethnic backgrounds, and widely varied in education, something to remember when you're reading and answering messages. The give and take can get energetic!

Dick Eastman, the sysop of the genealogy forums, encourages people of all backgrounds to participate. Dick is especially eager for members of ethnic minorities to become active in genealogy to ensure preservation of both their heritage and the records of importance to their genealogy.

The Genealogy Forum has a few rules:

♦ Keep your language clean. No obscenities, slurs, or dirty jokes are allowed.

♦ No flames.

- ◆ Use smileys if your words could be taken the wrong way. Regardless, choose your words carefully.

- ◆ Use the spell checker. Also, avoid jargon, because the newbies also need to understand your messages.

- ◆ Forums have specific sections on different subjects. Post your information to the right one. If you simply place all your messages in the New to Genealogy... section, the people who can help you might miss them.

- ◆ Advertising is allowed under specific restrictions, as the following discusses.

Advertising on the Forums

Online advertising is a touchy subject. On the one hand, new products and services are a legitimate discussion topic among genealogists. On the other hand, some people feel they're already paying for CompuServe and to have to endure advertisements on top of that is insupportable.

In an attempt at compromise, the Genealogy Techniques Forum (GO ROOTS) has specific sections dedicated to announcements and discussions of commercial genealogy services and products. This way, if you want to see such information, you can find these messages and files quickly and easily. If you don't, just ignore those sections.

In the File Libraries, you can look at (and post to) products/services for advertising and announcements. The message board has two sections: Professional Genealogists, and Services and Products.

Professional Genealogists is also a place for professional genealogists to gather and ask questions or discuss the latest issues in their business, so this isn't strictly an advertising section. Still, you'll find a fair number of ads.

The catch to this permissible advertising is you're allowed to post only one message and only one text file per product. The file stays there until you ask a sysop to delete it. The message may scroll off as all messages eventually do. (You may answer any questions posted by others about your services or products at any time.) The text file should be in a press-release format, ending with the words "For further information, contact . . ." or something similar. You can encourage the reader to contact you online or by conventional means, as appropriate.

Don't post a message about goods or services that you produce or sell on any genealogy forum's message board without clearly stating your connection. Avoid jumping into threads to recommend products you create or sell. So-called *bombing runs* (posting many messages in different forum sections or by CompuServe Mail to promote your products or services) are rude, as is responding to forum messages by sending private e-mail advertisements.

In general, don't clutter the genealogy forums with nongenealogy, nonhistory, or nonadoption traffic without the express permission of the sysops. An exception is the sale of personal items, which is allowed but, even then, this should be genealogy related.

All this said, you're nevertheless encouraged to provide technical support of your customers on the Genealogy Techniques Forum. A major difference exists between providing support and the "advertising, soliciting, or promoting the purchase of goods or services."

If you see anyone breaking these general rules, you should contact the Genealogy Techniques Forum managers. Just post a message "To: SYSOP" on the forum and it will be read by the next manager who enters the forum.

Grand Tour

I'm going to take you on a tour of the North American Forum (GO NAROOTS). You'll find the Genealogy Techniques Forum (GO NAROOTS) and the World Wide Genealogy Forum (GO WWROOTS) work in much the same way. Sign on to CompuServe and use the Go word ROOTS. That is, type NAROOTS in the white box at the top of the screen and click GO or press ENTER. You can also get there on the Web by using http://go.compuserve.com/NAGenealogy. The screen, as you saw in Figure 19-3, has several components.

My user name is at the bottom, Welcome, EPCrowe/AL. The first time you sign on you're asked to choose a name to use in the forum. People often put the state they live in as part of their forum name. All genealogy forums ask that you use your real name, not a handle or your CompuServe sign-on ID. At the same time, I filled out profile to tell my interests to the other users of the forum. The tradition in the genealogy forums is to start with the surnames you're searching, perhaps with geographical locations, and other items of interest. You get to this screen by clicking

Update My Profile in the upper-right corner of the screen. You can search the forum's member database for surnames.

At the very top of the screen is the menu bar, where you find the usual commands; File, Edit, Window, and Help behave as you'd expect. Access enables you to change things like what number is dialed to log on, passwords, parental controls, and checking how long you've been on.

Under the menu bar is the CompuServe toolbar. You can customize it by choosing to have it large or compact, and you can drag the check mark of any window to create a toolbar button.

Under the CompuServe toolbar is the standard Microsoft IE toolbar: the round buttons are for forward and back, stop, reload, and home. The URL box is where you type in GO words or WWW URLs. Click the GO button to activate the GO word. Print and Search do what you'd expect.

Just below that you have a window within a window, the forum's opening page. The bar across the top has the name of the forum, the Forum Home button brings you back here from the other screens in the forum. This bar remains constant, no matter what you're doing in the forum.

The screen in Forum Home has links, news, and announcements pertinent to the specific forum.

The two buttons, Messages and Files, have similar functions. They will both change the window to show the sections of the forum and let you search or browse through them, as shown in Figure 19-4.

To access the files, which, in general, will have the same divisions of topics as the messages, click the Files button. As with the messages, you can search or browse through the files, as shown in Figure 19-5. You can display a description of the file and, if it's a text file, display it as well. Right-clicking the link to the file in the right-hand pane will bring up the download dialog box to save the file to your disk.

Browsing messages looks much the same as browsing files. Click the section, look at the topics, and then read specific items. You can also right-click and save messages to your file cabinet on disk, for later reference. This is a good idea as messages tend to scroll off, that is, the oldest get deleted to make room for the newest.

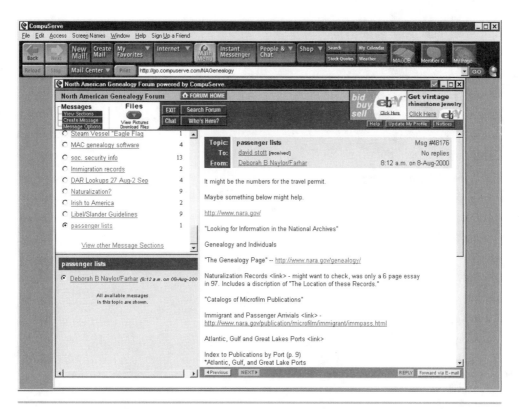

FIGURE 19-4. *Topics, authors, and messages are read in this window. The Files window layout is similar.*

To contribute a file, click the Contribute button. Choose the appropriate File Section, and then click the Contribute File button. Don't upload anything unless you have the rights (under copyright law, for example) to the files you contribute.

The first time you visit this page, CompuServe will attempt to download and install software (an ActiveX control) automatically on your computer. You might be asked for permission to download this control, depending on your security settings. Let the control be downloaded.

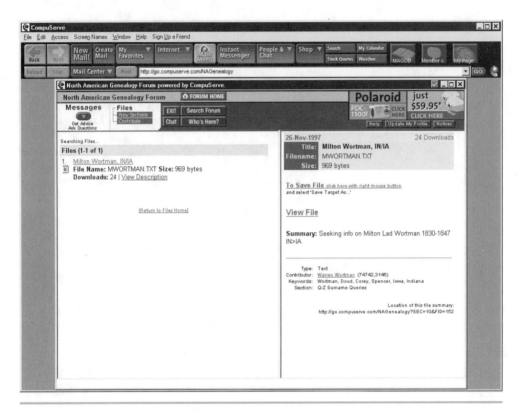

FIGURE 19-5. *To download a file on CompuServe, simply right-click the title and save it to your disk.*

As mentioned in Chapter 7, CompuServe has regularly scheduled chats on genealogy in all the forums. Anytime you're on, you can click the Chat button to see whether any chats are happening. Or, you can click the Who's Here? button and invite someone to an impromptu chat. Figure 19-6 shows you the windows that pop up when you click those buttons. These windows are separate from the main CompuServe window, so you can click the main window and send them to the back, or cascade or tile them all.

The hosted conferences (chats) on CompuServe are excellent. In one famous case, Forum Manager Dick Eastman saved the life of a member

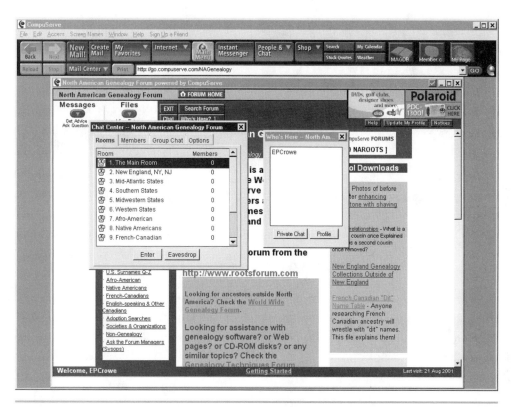

FIGURE 19-6.   *Click CHAT and choose a room for an impromptu chat.*

who was having a stroke during a live chat by noticing something was wrong and getting help to the member's home. Usually, however, chats are exciting only for the fun and interesting people who participate! You are free to host one whenever you like. Simply announce it in the messages.

The final button for you to notice is the Notices button (just beyond the Help button). Here is where you'll find text files with the latest information about the workings of the forum. News Flash, Messages, General, and so forth all have information the sysops want you to know.

Profile: Dick Eastman, Genealogy Forum Manager

"It's lots of fun, but no money," Dick Eastman says of being a forum manager. Along with several other Roots Forum members, Dick attends all GENTECH conferences to help promote the forum. That's just one of his many functions as forum manager. Dick also manages the files, checks for viruses, keeps the messages where they should be, and offers advice to new genealogists. And he recruits assistant sysops as well. Dick is the buffer between the technical people at CompuServe headquarters and the CIS user. His goal is to keep problems to a minimum, both in using the service and in doing genealogy.

"We're very much a referral service," Dick says. "Like a football coach, we won't play the game for you, but we'll help you learn the best game plans." Dick likes to do that on the forums but, amazing as it is to him, he says many people are too shy to post a public message. Instead, they send him private e-mail with their questions. Dick would prefer to answer questions where all can benefit from the answers, though.

"We're a social group," Dick says, "and we have a lot of fun. We get together at conferences like this [GENTECH] and meet face-to-face when we can. But I love the online environment. I'm a die-hard techie, and I think it's so much fun!"

Dick said that over and over, people have found relatives either on the Roots Forum or because of it. One of the most affecting, he says, was once when he was demonstrating Roots and the Phone*File system at a National Genealogical Society meeting. A woman found a name and number she thought might be her long-lost father, though she didn't dare hope. Still, she went to the pay phone, and sure enough, she was on the phone to him in minutes, arranging a reunion after 30 years. "She had tears running down her cheeks because she was flying to Philadelphia to see her father that next week. I could hardly talk the rest of the day, I was so choked up," Dick says.

Gaye Spencer, one of the forum managers, had a mysterious Amirilla Eastman in her lineage, whose parents she just couldn't place. That is, until one day a long message was posted on the Roots Forum about an Eastman family of the right period—along with all the siblings of that family—and there was Amirilla!

Dick Eastman himself found a relative he was able to help online. His French-Canadian Dubay line was hard to find, partly because of variant spellings. But Dick knew of a history professor by that name and, using Phone*File, Eastman discovered the fellow lived within 25 miles of where Eastman knew his ancestors to be from.

Calling the gentleman, he found out the professor had just self-published 1,200 copies of a genealogy of the family and was having trouble selling them. Eastman sent the professor gummed labels with every Dubay (and the variant spellings) he could find on Phone*File. The professor mailed each one a notice of the book and the result was a wonderful Dubay reunion, and a sold-out printing of the genealogy!

Dick Eastman is typical of the sort of person you'll find on CompuServe. The CompuServe Genealogy Forums were the first online genealogy resource I found, nearly 20 years ago. I still find them among the best of online resources.

Wrapping Up

♦ CompuServe's genealogy forums are full of useful information and helpful people.

♦ You can get to the forums using the GO word ROOTS on CompuServe, or over the Web using www.rootsforum.com.

♦ CompuServe offers three main genealogy forums: Techniques, North American, and World Wide.

♦ Other forums on CompuServe that might interest genealogists include the History and Civil War forums.

Chapter 20

America Online's Golden Gate Genealogy Forum

The history of America Online (AOL) is nothing short of amazing. Just ten years ago, AOL wanted to be as big as CompuServe and Prodigy. Now it's bigger than those two services combined. AOL owns CompuServe and Netscape, as well as other software companies, such as ICQ. If you live in North America, you probably got a free trial membership from AOL in the mail with your computer or with your modem.

The Genealogy Forum is one of the best offerings on all of AOL. You can get to parts of the Golden Gate Genealogy Forum on the Web without an AOL membership. Simply visit www.genealogyforum.com (see Figure 20-1.)

Like most commercial online services, AOL's proprietary content is available only through its proprietary front-end software. AOL's network has local access numbers throughout the world, but not necessarily in rural areas. The software package will find the phone number closest

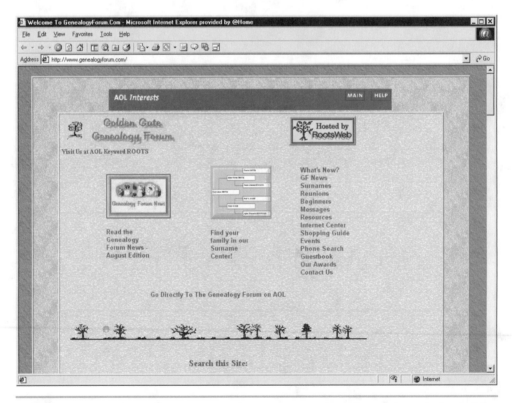

FIGURE 20-1. *The Golden Gate Genealogy Forum can be accessed through the Web.*

to you during the setup procedure but, every now and then, this list is expanded. It's a good idea to go to Keyword: ACCESS, to see whether you're using the best and closest connection.

Note

Keywords are quick ways to jump to different areas on AOL. Type CONTROL + K, *enter the keyword, and then click GO. Or, simply type a keyword into the URL box in the AOL toolbar. For genealogy, the keyword to remember is ROOTS.*

During the sign-up process, you choose a main screen name for your account. AOL added a new feature where you can take a current screen name from the list and start a new account with it, so you can start a new account by taking a name already in use from the current account. You can have up to seven screen names assigned to the main account, so each family member can have a mailbox, a set of favorites, and a place to file messages and downloads. To add and delete additional screen names, use the keyword NAMES.

Note

You can access AOL for a reduced monthly rate through another Internet provider. This is called "bring your own ISP." You pay the ISP's monthly rate, in addition to about $10 a month for AOL. This is handy if your town has an ISP but doesn't have a local AOL access number.

The Genealogy Forum (Keyword: ROOTS) is the center of genealogical activity on America Online. From the Beginners' Center to the Genealogy Chat rooms and the Resource Center, this forum is an incredibly rich resource. The Genealogy Forum's tens of thousands of members make it the largest genealogical society in the world, online or off. Figure 20-2 shows the Golden Gate Genealogy Forum main window in AOL 7.

Don't forget to add the Genealogy Forum to your list of Favorite Places. To do this, just click the heart on the top-right side of the forum main window. You can also add it to the toolbar of AOL 5.0 (or later versions). Just click-and-drag the heart up to the toolbar area. A window will pop up asking you to choose a picture and a name for the link. Make your choices and there you are.

> *Note*
>
> *In 1998, the AOL Genealogy Forum became the Golden Gate Genealogy Forum. The Golden Gate Genealogy Forum on America Online is a production of Golden Gate Services, Inc. of Franklin, Massachusetts, whose president, George Ferguson, has been the forum leader for years (screen name: GFL George). Much of the AOL content, although not all, is reflected at the Web site www.genealogyforum.com.*

Member Welcome Center

On your first visit to the Genealogy Forum, plan to spend some time in the Member Welcome Center (Figure 20-3). You get there by double-clicking the folder labeled Member Welcome Center in the Genealogy Forum Main Menu.

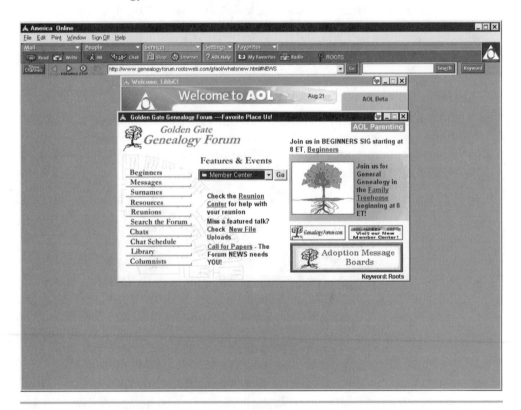

FIGURE 20-2.   *Details on the opening window will change occasionally, but the basic choices will remain the same.*

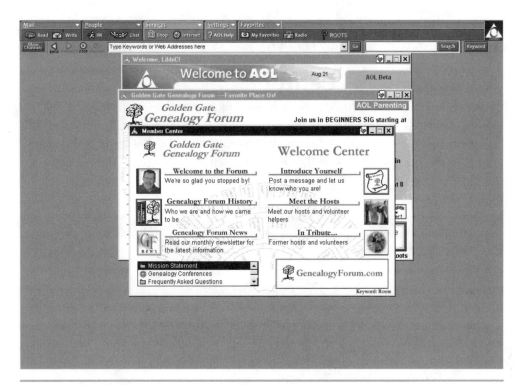

FIGURE 20-3.   *Visit the Member Welcome Center for background information on the Genealogy Forum and its staff.*

In the *Member Welcome Center* you can read about the people who keep the Genealogy Forum running, see how the forum is managed, and find out about upcoming genealogy conferences and events. Most importantly, you can read the Genealogy Forum Frequently Asked Question (FAQ) files.

As previously noted, FAQ files are indispensable reading, not only in forums (which are similar to real-world communities in that they have their own rules of behavior), but also in electronic mailing lists, newsgroups, and at Web sites. The FAQ files are collections of the most commonly asked questions pertaining to the forum, list, newsgroup, or site. Read these files before you start asking questions or posting messages to gain a basic understanding of the forum.

Once you finish with the Member Welcome Center, you have two paths you can follow: one is to head to the Beginners' Center, which is designed for people who are new to genealogy. Or, if you are already a genealogist, you can skip the Beginners' Center, and take the second path. Begin with the Quick Start Guide, which tells you how to start researching your roots with the Genealogy Forum.

Beginners' Center

To reach the *Beginners' Center,* you click the Beginners button on the Genealogy Forum main window. This takes you to the Beginners' Center on the www.genealogyforum.com Web site. Click this button and you'll see a window similar to the one in Figure 20-4. Some of the highlights of the Beginners' Center are described next.

FIGURE 20-4.   *The Beginners' Center gives you several links to how-to articles on genealogy.*

Beginner's Tool Kit

The *Beginner's Took Kit* is a collection of links to answer the most basic questions about genealogy. They include Information on Getting Started, Making Sense of It All, Obtaining Information, Organizational Ideas, Organizing Information, Other Genealogy Forum Centers, Other Related Forums, and DearMYRTLE. After you've paged through all these, especially DearMYRTLE's Beginners' Lessons, you'll be ready to begin your quest.

All sorts of gems are in the Beginner's Tool Kit. Do you want to learn about colonial diseases and cures? Or, what if you can't figure out a genealogical abbreviation? If so, this is the part of the Genealogy Forum for you. Here you'll find guides on getting started in genealogy, organizing your data as you get more experienced, tips on how to get information (who to write, how to ask), and links to related services on America Online.

FAQ/Ask the Staff

Click the *FAQ/Ask the Staff* link to see a list of FAQs. This list is identical to the one you'll find in the Member Welcome Center, except for the last item in the list: ASK THE STAFF. Click it and you'll get to send e-mail directly to one of the Genealogy Forum staff members.

The Five-Step Research Process

The *Five-step Research Process* is a systematic approach to doing any genealogical research. This is an excellent tutorial on how to get started in genealogy. According to the process outline, Family History Research is asking you the same questions, in order, and in cycles:

1. What do I already know?

2. What specific question needs to be answered?

3. What records might answer my question?

4. What do the records actually tell me?

5. What conclusions can I reach now?

Click the 5-Step Research Process link to open the window (Figure 20-5) and start applying the process to your research today.

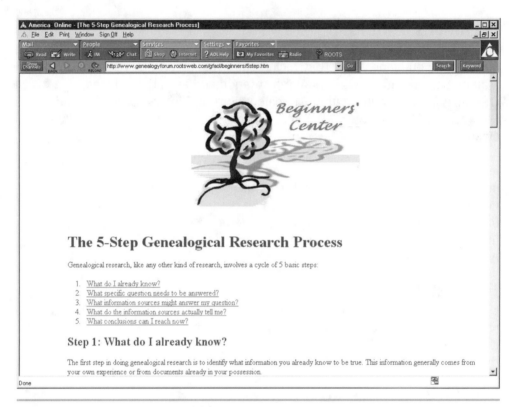

FIGURE 20-5. *The 5-Step Research Process is a system for making your genealogical research fast and efficient.*

DearMYRTLE's Beginner Lessons

Begun in January 1997, DearMYRTLE's Beginning Genealogy Lessons are weekly text files on aspects of genealogical research for the beginner. They are well-worth saving for future reference.

Internet Center

The *Internet Center* in the Genealogy Forum is where you'll find Web sites, FTP and gopher sites, newsgroups, and mailing lists that relate specifically to genealogy. This can save you a lot of time, as compared to searching randomly on the Internet for the same information. If you want to go farther afield, however, be sure to check out Net Help—the

Answer Man, where tips, tricks, and FAQs about the Internet in general, and AOL's connection in particular, are stored. You can subscribe to newsgroups here or at Keyword: USENET. Click Expert Add and type in the soc.genealogy newsgroups you want.

Note

See Chapter 8 for an in-depth discussion of Usenet.

Here's a newsgroup tip. You can use Automatic AOL to download Usenet messages that interest you. In Mail | Automatic AOL | Expert Setup, check the box Get Unread Postings, and put in Incoming Postings folder and the box Send postings from the Postings Waiting to Be Sent folder. Then, when online, go to Keyword: USENET. Click the Read Offline button. Your subscribed newsgroups will be listed on the left. Any newsgroups you add to the box on the right will be put in your filing cabinet during Automatic AOL. This will increase the time of your Automatic AOL with very busy newsgroups, but your online time will still be greatly reduced. You'll just have to remember to erase the old messages regularly to save disk space.

Note

This technique also works for the regular AOL message boards.

Quick Start

The guide tells you how to put the resources of the Genealogy Forum to work for you immediately. The Quick Start guide has four sections, each describing specific resources within the forum and telling you how to use them. The four sections are

- **Search by topic**   The fastest way to search in the Genealogy Forum. Most people begin by typing in a surname to see what pops up. You can also input a geographical term (Ohio, France) to see what files and articles are returned.

- **Surname message boards**   Use these to look up a surname directly.

- **Files library center**   Look in this area to see if other forum members have already uploaded useful material like GEDCOM files that are helpful to your research.

- **Special centers provide additional resources**   This is a quick introduction to some of the other useful resources in the Genealogy Forum, some of which are described next, such as the genealogy column DearMYRTLE.

Introduce Yourself Message Board

This is a link to the message board where the topic is member introductions: who you are, and where and what you're searching. Everyone who posts here will get personal e-mail with tips on how to use the forum.

Messages

The *message boards* in the Genealogy Forum are the place to post messages when you need information you can't find elsewhere in the forum. The boards operate on a volunteer basis. You're invited to post any questions you might have and encouraged to post a reply to anyone else's question if you have information. Also, don't forget to post the family names you're looking for in the message board under the Surname category.

To reach the message boards, click the large Messages button in the Genealogy Forum main window. Using the Message Board Center (Figure 20-6), you can post messages in any of six major subject areas. These are

- **Computer and General**   Post messages here about topics that don't fit into the other message board.

- **U.S.**   A place for messages about genealogy in the United States.

- **International**   Post messages in this area about research in countries other than the United States.

- **Surnames**   You can post messages here asking about specific family names you're researching.

- **Ethnic and Special Groups**   Post messages here about your research into ethnic or other special groups.

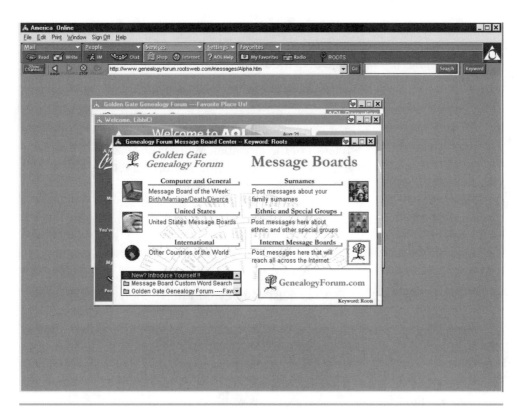

FIGURE 20-6. *The Message Board Center is the place to read and post messages about a wide range of genealogy topics.*

♦ **Internet Message Boards** These will be posted on the Genealogy Forum Web site and, therefore, reach people who are nonmembers of AOL.

Note

The first five subject areas will reach AOL members ONLY.

Before you start exploring the message boards, a good idea is to read the messages that appear in the menu on the lower-left side of the Message Board Center main window. These messages explain how the center and the message boards work. In particular, pay attention to the Set Personal Preferences First and How to Read & Compose Offline messages. They can make the Message Board Center much easier to use. Once you read these messages, you should set your preferences, and then start exploring the message boards.

Within each of these message board topic areas, you may find dozens of specific boards. For example, within Surnames are areas for surnames that begin with each letter of the alphabet. Within those areas are boards for surnames that begin with specific combinations of letters. These finally lead to the actual message boards themselves.

Each board also has a set of controls that make it easy to use and customize. Here's a rundown of the controls and what they do

- **Read Post**   Displays the contents of the message (or message thread) that's selected in the message list.

- **List Posts**   Displays a list of relevant information about the message (or message thread) selected in the message list.

- **More**   Click this to load more messages into the message list if you selected More in your preferences and if more messages are available than the message list holds.

- **Find Since**   Click this if you want to do a search of the message list.

- **Create Subject**   Click this to create a new subject in the message board.

- **Preferences**   Enables you to control how messages appear in the message list.

- **Mark Read**   Click this to mark the selected messages and threads in this list as read. The list will then treat them according to your preferences, as if you actually read them.

- **Mark All Read**   Click this to mark all the messages and threads in this list as read. The list will then treat them according to your preferences, as if you actually read all of them.

Offline Reading

Reading online isn't bad, but I find it much more efficient to read offline, using Automatic AOL and the File Cabinet's Search function. This can be a real time saver.

Here's how to go about it.

Let's say the topic of interest is messages about Powells. First, click Messages in the Roots Forum main window. A box of links is on the left, including Access all message topics here. Click that link, and you now have the window to search *all* of the AOL Genealogy Message Boards.

When the All Genealogy Forum Message Boards window appears (Tip: remember you can use that heart to put this window in your Favorites or on the toolbar!), click the Topic Genealogy Message Boards. For this example, you would click TOP SURNAMES IN THE U.S. When you open that window, keep clicking MORE until you get to the POWELL message board, highlight it, then click the Subscribe button. You'll get a message that the board has been added. To view your list, go to keyword My Boards. At the keyword My Boards (Tip: remember you can add Keyword My Boards to your shortcuts list!), you can click the button that says Read Offline.

Now, when you run an Automatic AOL session, the new messages are retrieved with your e-mail and placed in the Personal Filing Cabinet. Once a session is done, click My Files, and then Personal Filing Cabinet. Your message board will be a folder under Newsgroups. To read all the messages, just as you would e-mail or newsgroups, simply open the folder and click each message (even though you don't have to look at every one).

To save time, you can use the Find button in the Personal Filing Cabinet and look for messages that interest you. Say you want to learn about the name Powell in South Carolina. The Find button gives you the choice to search all folders or only open folders, and to search either full text or only the subject lines. To make the search faster, open the Powell Folder, closing all others, and choose Open Folders. Then, choose either Full Text or Titles Only (whichever you feel is most likely to get a hit). Next, enter the term **South Carolina** in the text box and click Find Next. If no messages match the search, you can delete all of that day's messages, compress the Filing Cabinet, and try another day.

Surnames

The *Surnames Center* (Figure 20-7) is another collection of message boards organized by surname. Here, however, individual surnames have their own boards, as opposed to the surname boards you can reach from the Quick Start Guide, which group surnames alphabetically.

The same rules and suggestions discussed earlier apply to these message boards. The only difference is that these message boards are each focused on a single surname, so you will likely find the messages more useful than on another board, even though fewer of them will exist.

Resources

Click the button marked *Resources* and you'll find The Resource Center chock full of information meant to save you lots of trial and error. Articles,

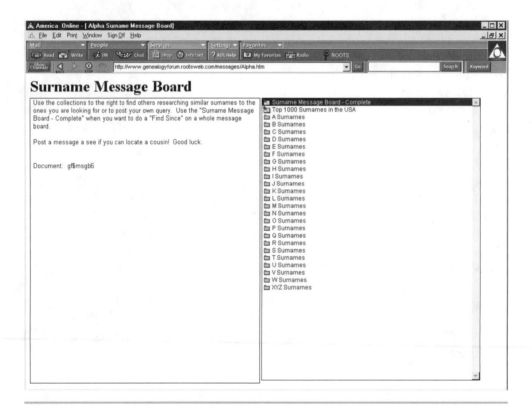

FIGURE 20-7. *The Surnames Center has hundreds of message boards, organized by surname.*

help texts, and tips under subject headings like Regions of the World, Ethnic Resources, and Vital all can make your research more productive.

Reunions

The *Reunions* button on the AOL Genealogy Forum main window will take you to www.genealogyforum.rootsweb.com/gfaol/reunion. Here you'll find archives of discussions, tips, and articles to help you plan and execute a successful family reunion, either online or in the real world.

Search the Forum

Clicking *Search the Forum* on the Genealogy Forum main window opens the Genealogy Search window. When you enter a search term in this window, the program will search the file libraries in the forum (the program doesn't search the messages). The result is a list of files that contain the search term.

Note

The AOL search will search more than library files. It also searches many of the resource center files, old issues of the newsletter, past DearMYRTLE files, and other information. This Search the Forum is for use in the AOL message boards (go to Keyword: ROOTS, Messages, and then look in the scroll box for the message board search option). The Search feature on the www.genealogyforum.com site will search uploaded GEDCOM files and the past message board postings (from the Web site only).

Chats

The *Chat Center* (Figure 20-8) is where you go to hold online, real-time conversations with other genealogists. To get to the Chat Center, click the Chats button on the forum's main window. Chat rooms exist for many different topics: Beginning Genealogy Chat, Southern Chat, and War Between the States Chat are three examples. Some chats are continuous and some are active at specific times. Schedules and lineups appear in the list on the left of the Chat Center main window.

As with the Message Board Center, the first order of business is to read the messages in the menu on the lower left of the Chat Center

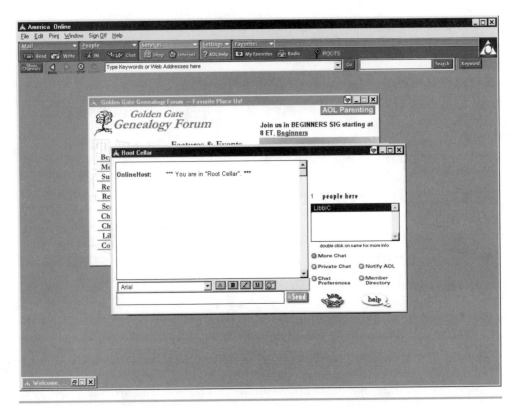

FIGURE 20-8. *Go to the Chat Center for real-time, live chat sessions with other genealogists from around the world.*

window. Pay particular attention to the Lineup lists. Because chat is a real-time activity, many sessions are scheduled in advance. If you just want to drop in, one of the five main chat rooms usually has someone in it.

The large window on the left is where the chat messages appear. As new ones arrive, the messages all shift up the screen, so the newest ones are at the bottom. Below the chat window is a box where you enter the text of your message. Click Send to transmit the message to the other participants in the chat. To the right of the chat window is a list of the people present in the chat room. Right now, I am the only one there, but the chat rooms can hold dozens of people. To find out more about someone in the chat room, double-click that person's screen name in this list.

Other controls in the chat window are

- **Private Chat**   This enables you to invite someone in the chat room to chat with you privately.

- **Chat Preferences**   Click this to set the five chat options available.

- **Notify AOL**   If someone is misbehaving in the chat, you can click this to report the infraction to AOL.

- **Member Directory**   This lets you request the profile of a person, whether that person is present in the chat or not.

Library

The *File Libraries Center* is a central location for all sorts of computer files of interest to genealogists. Divided into five sections, each containing multiple libraries, the center has thousands of files you can download.

You'll find files here ranging from trial versions of popular genealogy software to GEDCOMs and other genealogy information from members. You can use the new Library Sort feature to make finding specific files in the libraries easier. Or, you can click Search the Forum on the main Genealogy Forum window to use the Search Genealogy Forum feature.

Software Search

Start with AOL's Software Center (Keyword: FIND SOFTWARE). Here you have four choices: search for shareware (try-before-you-buy programs such as Brother's Keeper), search for commercial software (such as Family Tree Maker), check out the recommended Daily Download (usually a general purpose program), or visit the Computing Superstore.

To search for shareware, click the link. You'll get the Software Search window (Keyword: FILESEARCH). You can limit your search according to the time (All dates, Past month, Past week) the file was uploaded, and by categories: applications, operating system, and so on. Then type your keywords (genealogy programs, for example). In a few seconds, you have a list of matches. You can select one, read its description, and then decide whether to add it to your Download Manager (the list of files to be downloaded). When you have your list complete, you can choose Download Manager from the window that pops up when you choose Download Later and tell it to start.

Columnists

Links to several regular columns are posted to the AOL Genealogy Forum.

Note —————————————————————————

The quick way to get to these resources is Keyword: ROOTS, and then click the word Columnists.

The *Genealogy Forum News* is posted monthly on the Web and on AOL. It has a monthly theme, articles, and tips.

A daily column on genealogy topics, "DearMYRTLE Daily," is always helpful and informative. Use the keyword DearMYRTLE to come here directly. The "DearMYRTLE Daily" column area contains Myrtle's columns, as well as a message board, a collection of how-to guides, and much more. You can also access these by going to www.dearmyrtle.com from the Internet. "Bits of Blue and Gray," by Jayne McCormick, is a monthly column about the Civil War in the United States. "Pilgrims, Pioneers, and Aliens" is a monthly column about getting around "brick walls" in research. "Adventures in Genealogy" is published regularly on GenealogyToday.com and covers a broad range of topics.

Features and Events

The drop-down box in the Roots window on AOL has special features of the forum. This list changes occasionally because it's meant to be a list of shortcuts to highlights of the forum. The Member Center and GenealogyForum.com have already been discussed. Other links you might find here include the following:

Shopper's Guide   This page on the GenealogyForum.com Web site groups products by topic, such as genealogy software, ethnic genealogy, and miscellaneous supplies.

Genealogy in the News   This page list links to online news sources, such as CNN or U.S. News with recent stories on genealogy.

Genealogy Conferences   Genealogical organizations are invited to send announcements for inclusion in this Genealogical Events Listing. The listings are updated on a regular basis.

Genealogy Classes   This AOL-only area lists the online classes being offered in genealogy. The classes are usually held as chats on AOL (private chat rooms that you must have a password to log on to). An example class is Genealogy and Family History Centers, offered by Terry Ann Morgan. This course meets for four Mondays and costs $25.

Telephone Search Facilities   The Telephone Search Facilities window gives you access to nine Web sites you can use to track down the phone numbers and addresses of people (such as your long-lost cousin).

The best place to start your search is with AOL's own Switchboard (www.switchboard.com), which helps you find people, businesses, Web sites, and e-mail addresses.

The Staff of the Genealogy Forum

While the Genealogy Forum is full of interesting and useful treasures, by far the prize jewel of the forum is the people who staff it.

One of the forum staff, GFS Judy, said: "The Genealogy Forum provides a sense of family. Not only the 'real' relatives you are searching for, but the sense of family you get entering a chat room and being recognized; the information that total strangers go out of their way to type up and e-mail you, the forwarding of problems to others so that everyone can offer a suggestion or just encouragement to keep on going. I am constantly amazed that people who have spent 20 years of their lives, and countless dollars researching their family lines, will freely give out information just to help another researcher and perhaps get a tidbit in return. The materials people upload into the genealogy libraries save me hours of time traveling around the country, as does the Internet access. Computers truly make genealogy a realistic, global project that anyone can join in on regardless of age or income."

The Genealogy Forum is full of wonderful resources for the beginner, intermediate, and advanced genealogist. One of the best features is the excellent staff of experienced genealogists available to help you.

GFL George is the forum leader. Over 130 staff members are in the forum (anyone with HOST GFS at the beginning of their screen name is a Genealogy Forum staff member) and a list of them, with short bios, can be found in the Welcome Center folder named Volunteers. GFA Terry is one example. Director of a Mormon Family History Center (FHC), she's the Genealogy Forum expert on FHCs and the Family History Library in Salt Lake City.

"I have been working in the Genealogy Forum for years," GFA Terry says. "It started in about 1986 when I joined Q-Link (the first network from the owners of AOL—it was designed for Commodore computers). I worked in the genealogy area of Q-Link as a staff member. When AOL came about, and when my husband and I upgraded to an IBM, we joined this network. I was already a staff member on Q-Link (owned by the same company), so it was possible to become one here, too.

"My duties cover many things—I greet the new members, answer some of the questions on the message boards, do some librarian duties as I help make files go live, archive message boards, host meetings, and, well, there's a lot to do, but I enjoy it very much."

The network has helped her with her genealogy as well, and she says:

"I have made contact with several folks by posting the surnames I was looking for. I even found a distant cousin! This all works on a volunteer principal—folks helping other folks. One of them lived in Connecticut where I had ancestors and looked up some information for me. In turn, I looked up some information for her from Georgia. And the genealogy libraries have helpful text files, too."

Another person you should introduce yourself to is GFL George, the forum leader. A professional genealogist, George Ferguson has almost two decades of experience with online genealogy and is willing to share, help, and inform.

"The Genealogy Forum on AOL has been my love and my passion since its inception in 1988," George said. "With the help of many wonderful and dedicated volunteers, we have guided it to the place it is today. My Great Aunt Gertrude Durham started me on my genealogy work when I was a boy by presenting me with a ten-generation pedigree chart that was partially filled. I knew right then my life's work was to fill in the spaces." George started doing online genealogy research the day after he got his first modem.

George told me, "The best feature of the America Online Genealogy Forum would have to be the ability to get people from all over the country together in one online room to talk about genealogy. It's great because you don't have to leave the comfort of your own home, but you can get all kinds of questions answered. We also have an outstanding collection of downloadable files. We have programs and utilities for IBM-compatible systems, Macintosh systems, as well as Apple II systems. We have hundreds of lineage files, GEDCOM database files, genealogical records files, tiny tafel files, alphabetic surname files, as well as logs of past meetings. We have a surnames area where anyone can post a message about someone they are looking for. We also have message boards that are designed to exchange information about computer- and noncomputer genealogical subjects.

"We have started several special-interest groups (SIGs), which are becoming quite popular. On different nights, we have beginners' classes, an African American genealogy SIG, a Southern SIG, and a Scot-Irish SIG. In the near future, we hope to expand these offerings with expanded beginner services, a New England research SIG, and a reunion software users group."

George points out that the online real-time conversations are a valuable resource. There have been many meetings where somebody finds a cousin or a possible link. It is also an opportunity to chat with people who have similar interests to you. And you don't have to go out at night or drive into a big city to do it. Also, unlike the big genealogy groups that get together only once every month or so, AOL members can get out and talk almost any night of the week.

"We expect people to come and share the passion for genealogy," George said. "We expect nothing, but hope that everyone will share what they have with the rest of us and have fun doing it. What we find is that people freely give of themselves and that we can have a good time while learning different ways of investigating the past."

A former Forum host, GFH Ranch said, "Long before I assisted with a chat or had any formal involvement with AOL, I was a regular. For me, personally, the chats and message boards have been very instrumental in meeting cousins, which in turn leads to more sources, more information, and more options for research.

"I had used the genealogy newsgroups but prefer working with the breakdown of topics that AOL offers. Message boards are broken into portions of the alphabet and geographic locations, which dramatically reduces the amount you have to look through to find a possible connection," she added. "Chat sessions are narrowed to geographic areas (as well as general and beginner chats) and historical time periods."

Like many others on AOL, Ranch has had good luck finding real information there. "It is especially fun the first time you find a cousin. One time, I helped a lady find a missing link because I had an editor's note in a book. And another contact sent me an ancestor's photograph giving me a rare opportunity to share it with my family. I now have trouble remembering all the cousins I've met. Chats focus on families and heritage with a strong sense of 'helping our brother out.' We have folks in Tennessee offering to assist someone in Texas by calling the court house or photographing a tombstone."

Wrapping Up

♦ AOL's Genealogy Forum has a Web presence with message boards, a newsletter, and many other features at www.genealogyforum.com.

♦ The AOL-only portion includes online classes, files, and chats.

♦ You can use AOL's software to keep track of message boards, Usenet, and e-mail lists.

Chapter 21

Around the Web in 80 (or so) Sites

As you've no doubt noticed while reading this book, genealogy Web sites come in all categories. You will find portals that aim to be your Web home. You will find sites with scanned in primary records, transcribed records, and secondary sources, as well as sites with completed genealogies. As discussed in Chapter 1, you must remember to judge each source you find critically and carefully.

This list of Web sites reflects what I've found to be useful. Some of these sites will link you to sites I haven't found or that didn't exist at press time. Part of the fun is finding information you didn't know existed at all, much less on the Internet!

True Story: The Web Helps a Mobility-Challenged Genealogist

Being mobility challenged and on a very limited income, I have to depend mostly on the Internet at this time for my genealogy work, and I've had some success.

I had a query on an Irsch surname board for my great-grandfather and the fact he had married a Pitts in Noxubee, Mississippi in 1860. I just happened to decide to go to the Pitts surname board and posted the same query for a Lucretia Emmaline Pitts who had married a Frank Irsch.

I received a tentative confirmation from someone whose great-grandfather had a sister who had married an Irsch about that time. A few back-and-forths later we thought we might have a connection; I asked if she had ever heard the names Aunt Em and Uncle Henry Hill. I had heard my grandmother speak of them, but didn't know if they were blood relatives.

We both knew we had established the connection. "Aunt Em" was the sister of her great-great-great-grandfather, Lafayette Newton Pitts, and another sister, Lucretia, had married Frank Irsch. Their father's name was James W. Pitts and their mother's name was Mary. We still haven't discovered her maiden name.

She had a picture of some of the Irsch family that Lizzie Eaton/Bennett had identified for them as her brother and family and Grandma Pitts. She wasn't sure if the older woman was her Grandma Pitts, but didn't think so. Lizzie Eaton/Bennett was

MY grandmother, and if she identified the older woman as
Grandma Pitts, it would have been her grandmother, Mary ?-? Pitts. I
remember my mother telling me of Aunt Annie Irsch and Grandma
Pitts sending Christmas gifts when she was little.

Now we proudly know we have a picture of our shared great-
great-great-grandmother. We are working on other shared lines,
but I would call this a wonderful tale of success from the Internet!

—Louise McDonald

Four Score and Seven Sites to See

Since the first publication of this book, the number of genealogy-related
Web pages has gone from a handful to literally thousands. And, with
the rate at which things appear, disappear, and change location on
the Internet, you'll never be able to see them all. So, how do you find
genealogy sites that are worth seeing? The following is a list of some I
find useful.

The sites were included according to these factors:

♦ **Timeliness**   How often the site is updated and kept accurate

♦ **Usefulness**   How well the site matches the needs of genealogists

♦ **Uniqueness**   Information content (how rare the information is
and/or the unique manner in which it's presented)

♦ **Organization**   How easy the site is to find and how easy the
information is to retrieve

In the manner of Web sites everywhere, these sites will all lead you
to other sites, where (I hope) you'll find the information you need. Note,
this isn't even close to an exhaustive list. For that, see Cyndi's List and
Genealogy Resources on the Internet. In the list that follows, the sites
are cataloged alphabetically, not ranked.

Note

*All these links were active at press time but, considering how quickly
things change on the Web, it's likely some of the links listed will
already be gone.*

- **About.com Genealogy**
  (genealogy.about.com/hobbies/genealogy)   Has tips, discussion
  groups, and weekly articles on genealogy.

- **Adopting.org** (www.adopting.org/ar.html)   Has many adoption-
  related pages, including a birth-family search guide.

- **Adoptee/Birth Family Connections** (www.birthfamily.com)
  Has as its motto, "You existed before you were adopted." The
  site has articles on topics such as activism and reform of adoption
  laws, birth family registry, and warnings about scams.

- **Adoptee Search Resource** (www.theriver.com/Public/adoptee/)
  Is part of a portal called The River. This page has links to registries,
  vital records, and more resources for searching for birth parents.

- **Adoptees Internet Mailing List** (www.aiml.org/)   The list began
  in February 1996 to provide adoptees with a forum to discuss
  adoption search and reunion issues, as well as social, media,
  and legal issues related to adoption.

- **AfriGeneas Home Page** (www.afrigeneas.com)   The starting
  place for African American family history. Don't miss the in-depth
  profile of this site later in the chapter.

- **Alabama Department of Archives and History**
  (www.archives.state.al.us)   Has a specific genealogy page with
  links to what records are available. The site accepts credit cards
  for reference requests and is shown in Figure 21-1.

- **Allen County, Indiana Public Library Historical Genealogy
  Department** (www.acpl.lib.in.us/genealogy/genealogy.html)   Have
  over 220,000 printed volumes, 251,000 microfilms and microfiches,
  and 38,000 volumes of compiled genealogies in their collection.
  They also have census data going back to the 1700s, city directories,
  passenger lists, military records, Native American and African
  American records, and many other types. If you ever want to do
  a genealogy road trip, consider putting this library on your itinerary.

- **American Civil War Home Page** (sunsite.utk.edu/civil-war)   Has
  links to fantastic online documents from many sources, including
  those of two academics who've made the Civil War their career.

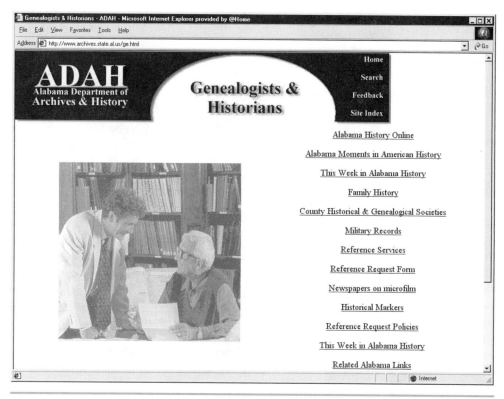

FIGURE 21-1. *The Alabama Archives has a page just for genealogists.*

♦ **Ancient Faces** (www.ancientfaces.com/cgi-bin/index.cfm)   Adds a personal touch to genealogy research by including photographs, documents, stories, recipes and more—all located under individual surnames.

♦ **Branching Out Online** (www.didian.com/branch)   One of many sites that uses "Branching Out" in its title, but this site is special. It's a tutorial on learning about online techniques and genealogy sites, and is great for beginners.

♦ **The British Heraldic Archive** (www.kwtelecom.com/heraldry) Dedicated to increasing interest in heraldry, genealogy, chivalry, and related topics. You can register to get an e-mail when the page is updated.

♦ **The Bureau of Land Management Land Patent Records**
(www.glorecords.blm.gov)   Is a searchable database. Invaluable,
especially for the western states when they were territories and
when local records were scarce. See Figure 21-2.

♦ **Byzantine.net** (www.byzantines.net/genealogy/INDEX.HTM)   Is
for persons of Ruthenian—Carpatho-Rusyn—ancestry and those
of the Byzantine Catholic/Orthodox faiths who came from the
former Austro-Hungarian Empire.

♦ **Calendars Through the Ages** (www.webexhibits.org/calendars)
Explores the fascinating history of how man has tried to organize
our lives in accordance with the sun and stars. See Figure 21-3.

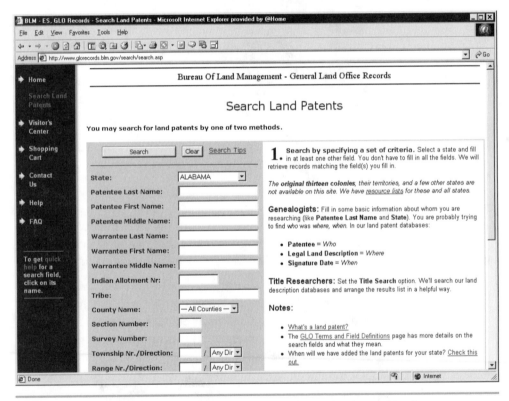

FIGURE 21-2.   *The Bureau of Land Management has a database of land patents you
can search from the Web.*

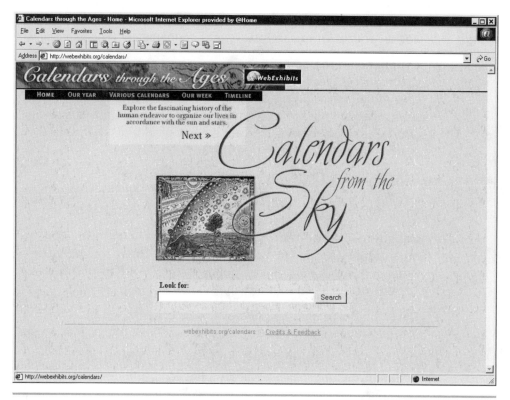

FIGURE 21-3.   *Learn the history of calendars at this site.*

♦   **Canadian Heritage Information Network** (www.chin.gc.ca)   A bilingual—French or English—guide to museums, galleries, and other heritage-oriented resources in Canada.

♦   **Cemetery Junction: The Cemetery Trail** (www.daddezio.com/cemetery/trail)   Has monthly articles on cemetery research and preservation.

♦   **Census Bureau Home Page** (www.census.gov)   Has a list of Frequently Occurring Names in the United States for 1990, Spanish surname list for 1990, age search service, and a Frequently Asked Questions (FAQ) file on genealogy.

- **Christine's Genealogy Web site** (ccharity.com) An excellent site about African American history and genealogy.

- **Cybertree Genealogy Database** (www.kuhnslagoon.net/cybertree/howto/index.html) Has a list of some words and phrases whose early meanings were different than today's. This site also contains obscure nicknames and abbreviations, as well as certain genealogical tools that might seem mysterious at first.

- **Cyndi's List of Genealogy Sites** on the Internet (www.cyndislist.com) The best-organized and annotated list of WWW genealogy sites on the Internet. A must see!

- **Daughters of the American Revolution** (www.dar.org) An organization for those who can prove an ancestor fought in the American Revolution. A free lookup in the DAR Patriot Index is just one of the site's many features.

- **David Eppstein's** home page (www.ics.uci.edu/~eppstein/gene) Has information on his shareware program Gene for the Macintosh.

- **Dan Mabry's Historical Text Archive** (http://historical textarchive.com) A compilation of articles and documents on various topics. Of special interest: the collections on African-American history and genealogy.

- **Directory of Royal Genealogical Data** (www.dcs.hull.ac.uk/public/genealogy/royal/catalog.html) A database containing the genealogy of the British Royal family and many other ruling families of the Western world—they all seem to be interrelated somehow. Contains over 18,000 names.

- **Distant Cousin** (distantcousin.com) Has several online databases, including marriages, military rosters, tombstone transcriptions, and ships passenger lists, which you can search free, as well as a large human-edited directory of genealogical Web sites, organized by surname, ethnicity, and geographical location.

- **Eastman's Online Genealogy Newsletter** (www.ancestry.com/home/eastarch.htm) A weekly all-text newsletter on genealogy topics. A typical issue will cover reviews of genealogy computer programs, news items of note to genealogists, a list of Web sites to visit, reviews of books, CD-ROMs, TV programs, and more.

◆ **Everton's Guide to Genealogy on the World Wide Web**
(www.everton.com)   Includes an online version of the venerable
Helper. This site has links to online resources and a tutorial for
genealogy beginners. Test drive their genealogical database
On-Line Search.

◆ **Family Chronicle** (www.familychronicle.com)   The Web site for
this magazine, which is dedicated to families researching their roots.
Check out their offerings and request a free sample of the magazine.

◆ **Family History, How Do I Begin** (www.familysearch.org) | Search |
Research Guidance | How Do I Begin?)   It's the Church of Jesus Christ
of Latter-day Saints' basic tutorial (see Figure 21-4).

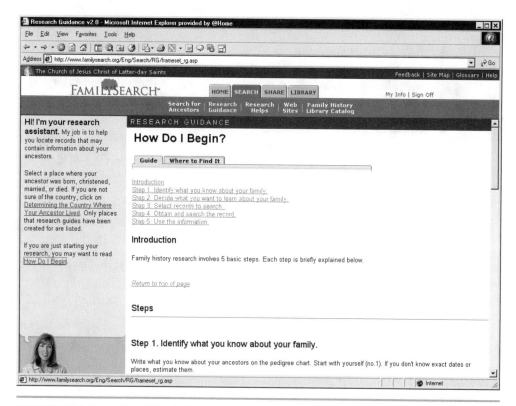

FIGURE 21-4.   *The LDS site has an excellent tutorial for the beginning genealogist.*

- **Family Tree Finders at SodaMail Archives** (www.sodamail.com/site/ftf.shtml)   A daily e-mail column on genealogy topics.

- **Family TreeMaker Online** (www.familytreemaker.com)   Boasts the FamilyFinder Index, which has genealogy data from users of their programs. Includes 153 million names you can search, the Internet FamilyFinder, and the Genealogy How-To—a 1,200 page guide to genealogy. This site is by Borderland Software, the publishers of Family Tree Maker.

- **FreeBMD** (FreeBMD.rootsweb.org)   FreeBMD stands for Free Births, Marriages, and Deaths. The FreeBMD Project is made up of volunteers transcribing the Civil Registration index information for England and Wales from the years 1837 to 1898 onto the Internet. Progress is sporadic; volunteer if you can.

- **Gathering of the Clans Home Page** (www.tartans.com)   Describes itself as a reference for people researching the Scottish clans. Includes information on 65 clans, as well as certain genealogical resources (specifically Scottish).

- **GENDEX** (www.gendex.com)   The home site of the GENDEX and GED 2HTML software. When you use GED2HTML to post your genealogy on the Web, you can register to be part of the worldwide GENDEX, a search engine for all such genealogy sites.

- **Gendoor** (www.gendoor.com)   A genealogy-only search page that finds sites related to genealogy, such as cemetery lists, family trees, and census data, which may not contain the word "genealogy."

- **Genealogy Dictionary** (home.att.net/~dottsr/diction.html)   For all those confusing terms such as "cordwainer" and "primogeniture."

- **Genealogy for Teachers** (earth.execpc.com/~dboals/geneo.html) Lists resources, organizations, guides, and tutorials. Aimed at educators, this site should help any beginner.

- **Genealogy Home Page** (www.genhomepage.com/)   A wide-ranging index of genealogy resources on the Internet. It includes links to maps, libraries, software, and societies. See Figure 21-5.

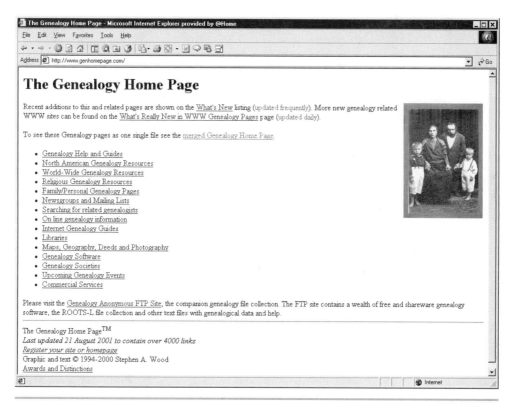

FIGURE 21-5.   *The Genealogy Home Page has links to many good sites.*

♦ **Genealogy Links.Net** (www.genealogylinks.net)   Includes over 9,000 links, most of them to online searchable databases, such as ships' passenger lists, church records, cemetery transcriptions, and censuses for England, Scotland, Wales, Ireland, Europe, USA, Canada, Australia, and New Zealand.

♦ **Genealogy of the Royal Family of the Netherlands** (www.xs4all.nl/ ~ kvenjb/gennl.htm)   A detailed genealogical history of the House of Orange-Nassau. Covers from Heinrich the rich of Nassau (born 1180) to Juliana Guillermo (born 1981).

♦ **Genealogy on the Web Ring** (www.geocities.com/Heartland/ Plains/5270/webring.html)   A group of genealogy Web pages and sites, all connected one to the other in a giant ring. From this page, you can explore the ring's sites in sequence or select random jumps to put some serendipity—wonderful surprises—into your research.

- **Genealogy Pages** (www.genealogypages.com)   A collection of links to free genealogical services, as well as to over 29,000 online resources.

- **Genealogy Resources on the Internet** (www.rootsweb.org/~jfuller/internet.html)   This site provides you with a quality-sorted list for finding the exact genealogical information you're looking for.

- **Genealogy Spot** (www.genealogyspot.com)   It's a free portal with links to online genealogy resources for beginners and experts alike. Sites featured on this site are hand-selected by their editorial team for quality, content, and utility.

- **Genealogy Today** (www.genealogytoday.com)   Announces and rates genealogy sites, has news updates, links to databases, lets readers vote for their favorite sites, and so forth.

- **GenServ** (www.genserv.com)   A GEDCOM exchange system you can search through e-mail or on the Web. This site is explored later in this chapter.

- **GENUKI** (www.genuki.org.uk)   This site is all about genealogy in the UK and Ireland.

- **GenWeb Database Index** (www.gentree.com)   Has links to all known genealogical databases searchable through the Web. This site now includes *GenDex,* an index of name databases with over two million entries.

- **Global: Everything for the Family Historian** (www.globalgenealogy.com)   The Global Genealogy Supply Web site. Shop online for genealogy supplies—maps, forms, software, and so forth—and subscribe to the "Global Gazette," a free e-mail newsletter covering Canadian genealogy and heritage.

- **Hauser-Hooser-Hoosier Theory: The Truth about Hoosier** (www.geocities.com/Heartland/Flats/7822)   Explains how genealogy solved the mystery of "What is a Hoosier?"

- **Headstone Hunter** (www.headstonehunter.com)   This site is all about cemetery research. People volunteer to find headstones for each other.

♦ **History Genealogy and Education** (www.ins.usdoj.gov/ graphics/aboutins/history/index.htm)   An informative page from the Immigration and Naturalization Service (INS). This site has information about the INS Historical Reference Library collection and services, documents concerning the history of the Service, as well as of immigration law, procedure, and immigration stations, plus instructions for historical and genealogical research using INS records.

♦ **Hungarian Genealogy** (www.rootsweb.com/ ~ wghungar)   A good place to start if your research leads you to Hungary.

♦ **HistorySeek! History Search Engine & Historical Information** (www.historyseek.com)   A directory search engine specifically made for historians, genealogists, scholars, and history enthusiasts. See Figure 21-6.

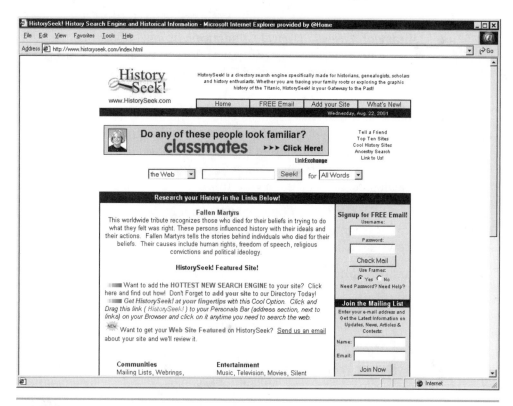

FIGURE 21-6.   *HistorySeek! is a targeted search engine.*

- **Immigration: The Living Mosaic of People, Culture & Hope** (http://library.thinkquest.org/20619)   A student project about immigration in the United States.

- **Internet Tourbus** (www.tourbus.com)   Patrick Douglas Crispen's e-mail course on how to use every part of the Internet. This site taught my mom everything she knows about the Net.

- **Janyce's Root Digging Dept**. (www.janyce.com/gene/rootdig.html) Yet another good place for beginners to start their online genealogical research.

- **JewishGen** (www.jewishgen.org/)   A comprehensive resource for researchers of Jewish genealogy worldwide. Among other things, it includes the JewishGen Family Finder, a database of towns and surnames being researched by Jewish genealogists worldwide, and it can be searched on the Web, or via e-mail (e-mail the server commands and results are e-mailed back to you).

- **Library of Virginia Digital Collections** (image.vtls.com)   A starting point where you can search Virginia colonial records, as well as Bible records, newspapers, court records, and state documents.

- **Lineages, Inc.** (www.lineages.com)   The Web site for a group of professional genealogical researchers who, for a fee, will help you find your roots. In addition, their site includes some free information, such as "First Steps for Beginners," a free genealogical queries page, and more.

- **Local Ireland: Genealogy** (www.local.ie/genealogy)   A portal with message boards, transcribed records, surname origins, and a newsletter.

- **Marston Manor** (www.geocities.com/Heartland/Plains/1638) This site offers numerous useful items for online genealogists, including a chart for calculating family relationships, and a detailed discussion of the terms proof and evidence as they relate to genealogy.

- **Mayflower Web Pages** (users.aol.com/calebj/mayflower.html) Contain the passenger lists of the Mayflower, the Fortune, and the Anne, plus many related documents.

♦ **Medal of Honor Citations** (www.army.mil/cmh-pg/moh1.htm)
Contains the names and text of the citations for the more than
3,400 people who've been awarded the Congressional Medal
of Honor since 1861.

♦ **Migrations** (www.migrations.org)   Has two separate parts. First
is a database of migration information submitted by volunteers
(secondary source information, of course!) searchable by name
and place. Second is a list of links to resources on migration.

♦ **New England Historic Genealogical Society** (www.nehgs.org)
Designed to be a center for family and local history research in
New England. The Society owns 200,000 genealogy books and
documents. If you're a New England genealogist, you should
check them out.

♦ **Online Genealogy Classes** (http://familytreemaker.
genealogy.com/university.html?Welcome = 998499542)
A short course for beginners.

♦ **Our Spanish Heritage: History and Genealogy of South Texas
and Northeast Mexico** (www.geocities.com/Heartland/Ranch/
5442/)   It's an interesting source if you're looking for relatives
from the South Texas/Northeast Mexico area. The database has
over 11,000 names, all interrelated as lineages.

♦ **Pitcairn Island Web Site** (www.lareau.org/genweb.html)   This
is the place to find information about the current inhabitants of
Pitcairn Island. But, more importantly for genealogists, this is the
place to go for information on over 7,500 descendants of the crew
of the H.M.S. Bounty, of *Mutiny on the Bounty* fame. See Figure 21-7.

♦ **Poland Worldgenweb** (www.rootsweb.org/~ polwgw/
polandgen.html)   Has maps and other information on Polish
provinces, as well as a surname search. You can also adopt
a province, becoming the provider of information about it.

♦ **Repositories of Primary Sources** (www.uidaho.edu/special-
collections/Other.Repositories.html)   A listing of over 2,500 Web sites
describing holdings of manuscripts, archives, rare books, historical
photographs, and other primary sources. This site is worth a look.

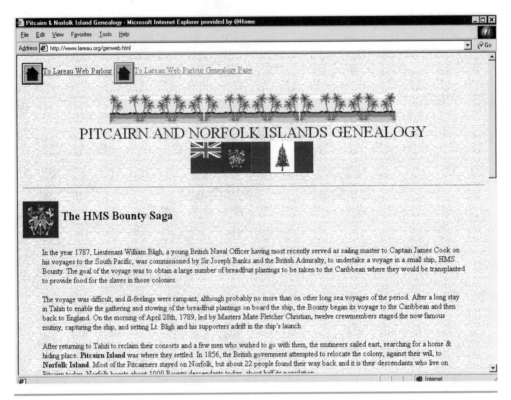

FIGURE 21-7. *Even if you aren't descended from the survivors of the Bounty, this site is fascinating.*

- **SBt Genealogy Resources** (www.cswnet.com/ ~ sbooks/genealogy) A collection of articles, links, and graphics for the genealogist. Especially interesting is the article, "Comparison of Four Search Engines for Online Genealogy Research."

- **Sons of the American Revolution** (www.sar.org) Has information on this organization's genealogical library, articles from its quarterly magazine, history of the American Revolution, and more. See Figure 21-8.

- **South Carolina Library** (www.sc.edu/library/socar/books.html) An online card catalog for the South Carolina Library, which houses an extensive collection of genealogy holdings.

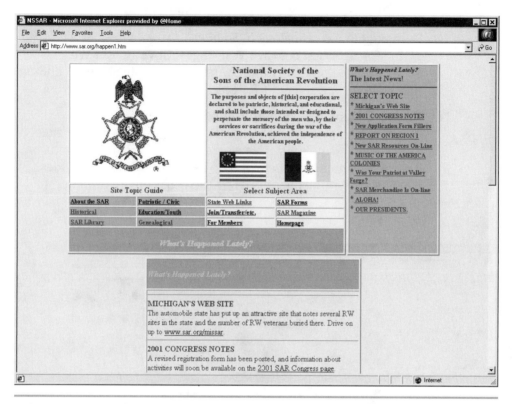

FIGURE 21-8.   *The SAR site has good background information.*

♦ **Spanish Heritage** home page (members.aol.com/shhar)   An AOL-based site, which is the home of the Society of Hispanic Historical and Ancestral Research.

♦ **StateGenSites** (www.stategensites.com)   Has monthly and weekly columnists on all aspects of genealogy. Uncle Hiram's weekly column is especially good!

♦ **Surnames.com** (www.surnames.com)   Discusses general genealogy, with some focus on the Arizona area. It includes a surname search and a map of genealogical organizations in the United States. The site also has a useful beginner's section.

♦ **SurnameWeb** (www.surnameweb.org)   Has free newsletters, Web sites, and secondary source materials.

♦ **Traveller Southern Families** (www.traveller.com/genealogy/)
Dedicated to the genealogy of Southern Families (see Figure 21-9),
with information about Civil War Pages, Government Web
Servers, Genealogy Software Companies, Family Societies and/or
Associations Pages, Books for Sale, and Genealogy Newsgroups.

♦ **Treasure Maps, the How-to Genealogy Site**
(www.amberskyline.com/treasuremaps)   One of the best sites
on the Web for novices. This site is aimed at providing hands-on,
how-to information to help you do research online. It includes
tutorials on writing queries, using the U.S. Census, and more.

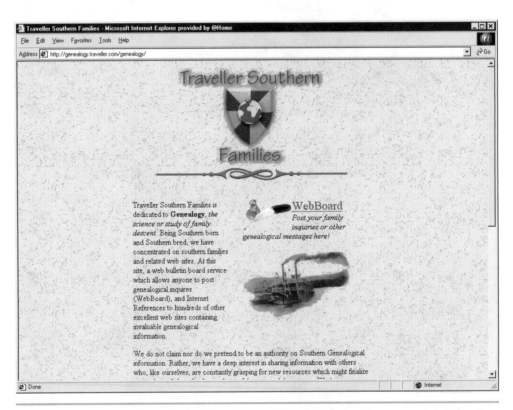

FIGURE 21-9.   *If you're researching the American South, you'll want to visit Traveller
Southern Families.*

To keep track of the latest news on Treasure Maps, you might want to subscribe to its monthly newsletter.

♦ **U.S. Gazetteer** (www.census.gov/cgi-bin/gazetteer) Just type in a city and/or state, and a map will appear showing the location. This service is run by the U.S. Census Bureau and uses information from the 1990 Census.

♦ **United States Civil War Center** (www.cwc.lsu.edu) Publishes book reviews, research tips, and articles about studying the War Between the States.

♦ **The USGenWeb Project** (www.usgenweb.com) A noncommercial project with the goal of providing Web sites for genealogical research in every county and every state of the United States. Much more information on this project appears later in this chapter.

♦ **Utah State Archives** (www.archives.state.ut.us) Here you can access the Research Center for the Archives' public services. This site includes research, places where questions can be answered, and where records can be ordered. Not everything here is free, but it's very convenient!

♦ **Xerox Map Server** (pubweb.parc.xerox.com/map) Offers interactive maps for finding any place in the world.

♦ **Yahoo! Genealogy Page** (www.yahoo.com/Arts/Humanities/ History/Genealogy/) A huge collection of links to guides, resources, and personal genealogies on Web sites. It also includes links to related resources.

A Closer Look

While one of the most exciting things about genealogy and Web browsing is the joy of discovery, some sites deserve a guided tour. These sites are particularly interesting or useful to online genealogists and each one has something special to offer. If you want to discover everything yourself, however, you have more than enough information to spend years researching online. Just skip past the rest of this section and be on your way.

AfriGeneas

AfriGeneas is a site for researching families of African ancestry (see Figure 21-10). The AfriGeneas Web site at www.afrigeneas.com is associated with a mailing list that gathers and presents information about families of African ancestry, as well as being a central point for genealogical resources around the world. Members of the mailing list are invited to contribute information and resources, sometimes going as far as taking responsibility for information for a certain area.

AfriGeneas provides leadership, promotion, and advocacy for genealogy resources devoted to researching African-related ancestry. It maintains a searchable database of surnames (in addition to slave data) from descendants of slaveholding families, as well as from other

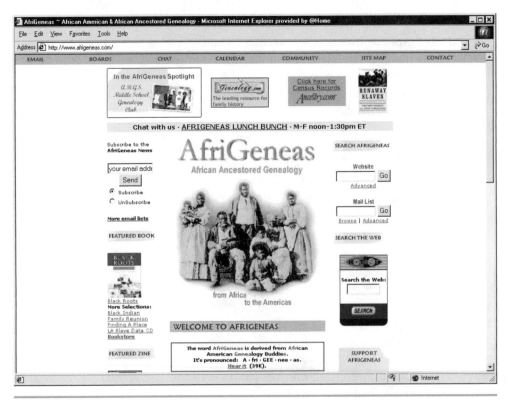

FIGURE 21-10. *The AfriGeneas Web site offers chat, message boards, and files.*

sources both public and private. Tips and topics to help people in their search for family history are distributed through mailing lists, chats, newsletters, and the Internet. Volunteers, who extract, compile, and publish all related public records with any genealogical value, do all of this. The site also maintains an impressive set of links to other Internet resources to help African Americans in their research.

◆ **Beginner's Guide**   This slide show-like presentation steps you through online genealogy. It's a no-nonsense approach, showing what can and can't be done online, and also includes some success stories.

◆ **Mailing List**   This is the discussion list. You'll find the rules and the archives, plus information about how to subscribe and unsubscribe to the mailing list.

◆ **State Resources**   With a clickable map, this page links to sites for each state in the United States with history, links to state resources, and queries.

◆ **World Resources**   This is along the same lines as State Resources, but only the United States and the Bahamas are up at press time. Volunteers are actively sought for other countries.

◆ **Surnames**   This is a set of queries with names, dates, and places of known ancestors. You can search the ones there, as well as post your own.

◆ **Slave Data**   This is designed to help you find a path to the last slaveholder or suspected last slaveholder. Records kept by the slave owner are frequently the only clue to African American ancestors, particularly during the period 1619–1869.

The site is also designed to assist descendants of slaveholders and other researchers, as well as share information they find containing any references to slaves, including wills, deeds, and other documents (see Figure 21-11). This site also houses a search engine and a form for submitting any data you might have.

To use the database, click the first letter of the surname you're interested in. This takes you to a list of text files with surnames beginning with that letter. Now, click a particular file name. The text file may be transcribed from a deed book, a will, or some other document. The name and e-mail address of the submitter will be included, so you can write to that person for more information, if necessary.

- **Census Records** These are transcribed census records. As a file is submitted, it's listed at the top of the What's New list on this page. Not all states have volunteers transcribing right now, so you can only click those states that show up as a live link.

- **Library** This contains guides, articles, chat transcripts, and images for you to look at online or download to your computer. Among the titles are "Researching in Southwest Louisiana" and "Cherokee Freedmen in Indian Territory."

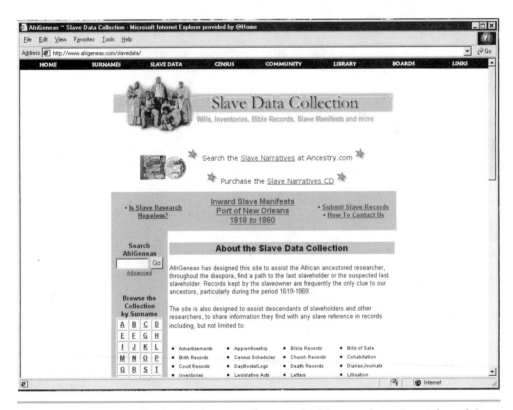

FIGURE 21-11. *Wills, deeds, slave manifests, and Bible records are just a few of the sources available at the Slave Database.*

◆ **Community**   This page shows how you can get involved, where and how to sign up as a volunteer, and testimonials about how much AfriGeneas has helped the people who use it.

◆ **Newsletter**   The monthly newsletter looks at genealogy news from the African American perspective.

◆ **Forum and Chat**   Chats on specific topics meet on a scheduled basis and open discussions are usually available 24 hours a day. The forum is a Web-based list of messages sorted by date, with the most recent at the top.

◆ **AfriGeneas Links**   Hundreds of fascinating links, sorted by topic, from good starting points like Christine's Genealogy Web site (see earlier listing) to WPA Slave Narratives to Canadian Black History.

◆ **Other sections**   The Storefront sells books and forms for genealogy. The About Us page gives a short history and a list of those who have helped develop AfriGeneas. The Feedback link launches your mail client, so you can tell the staff what you think.

AfriGeneas has come a long way from its beginnings as a mail list, and it keeps getting better and better.

DearMYRTLE

For the beginning-to-intermediate genealogist, there's no better spot than DearMYRTLE's Place at www.dearmyrtle.com. DearMYRTLE has helped hundreds of genealogists with her daily columns, weekly chats, newsletters, and online courses. Her site will help you learn and grow as a genealogist.

Note

AOL Members, keep in mind that DearMYRTLE has her own keyword: MYRTLE and her columns are archived on AOL back to 1995. The Web site includes columns beginning in 1999.

The first page of DearMYRTLE's site (see Figure 21-12) has announcements, links to features on the site, and often, a seasonal greeting.

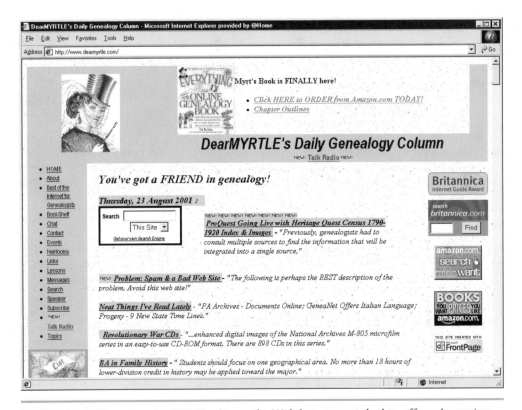

FIGURE 21-12. *DearMYRTLE's site on the Web has a great deal to offer a browsing genealogist.*

A quick look at parts of DearMYRTLE's site:

♦ **Chat**   This page leads you to Myrtle's scheduled chats, as described in Chapter 9. For the text chats, you need an IRC program such as mIRC or Microsoft Chat; for the Talk Radio Chats, you need Wonderhorse. Topics have included getting organized, using LDS resources, land records, and finding things on the Internet.

♦ **Links and Books**   Best on the Internet for Genealogists is DearMYRTLE's running series on the most useful sites she has found. Links is a page of pointers to other good sites. Books is the link to a page of book reviews by DearMYRTLE.

- **Subscribe**   This is the page that describes how you can get each DearMYRTLE daily column (in Digest form) via e-mail. Lessons include DearMYRTLE's free tutorials on genealogy research. If you subscribe to the List or Digest, you'll get the lessons by e-mail. You can read past lessons online and look at the topics coming up. The text of a new lesson is added each week.

- **Topics**   This is a collection of links to all her past columns, sorted by topic. Let the whole page load, and then use your browser's search or find function to look for your topic on the page—for example France or Internet Resources.

Bookmark DearMYRTLE's site. You'll be coming back often!

Genealogy Home Page

The *Genealogy Home Page* at genhomepage.com is a wide-ranging index of genealogy resources on the Internet. It includes links to maps, libraries, software, and societies. Right from the start, you can tell this site is more of a guide to genealogy resources available on the Web than a direct source of genealogical information. The home page (shown in Figure 21-13) starts off with two links to new, or newly discovered, genealogy sites. A URL Suggestion Form is at genhomepage.com/mail.html that enables you to submit a URL for inclusion on the Genealogy Home Page. If you decide to create your own genealogy Web site, this is one way to announce it to the world.

One of the most useful sections of the Genealogy Home Page is its collection of links under the heading Genealogy Help and Guides at www.genhomepage.com/help.html.

Another set of useful links from the Genealogy Home Page is on the Genealogy Societies page at www.genhomepage.com/societies.html. Here, you'll find direct links to more than 30 genealogical societies, divided into three categories:

- **Umbrella Organizations**   These are groups, such as the Federation of Genealogical Societies.

- **Geographic, National, Ethnic-based Societies**   Covers groups like the American-French Genealogical Society and The Computer Genealogy Society of San Diego.

♦ **Family-based Societies** These are organizations dedicated to research on specific surnames, like the Brown Family Genealogical Society or the Pelletier Family Association.

The Genealogy Home Page is the oldest effort at collecting worthwhile genealogy links together and it's still one of the most useful.

USGenWeb

The *USGenWeb Project* at www.usgenweb.org is a group of volunteers working to provide noncommercial genealogy Web sites in every county of every state in the United States. These sites are freely accessible to everyone—no memberships or fees are required. The online center of this effort is the USGenWeb Project Home Page at www.usgenweb.org (Figure 21-14).

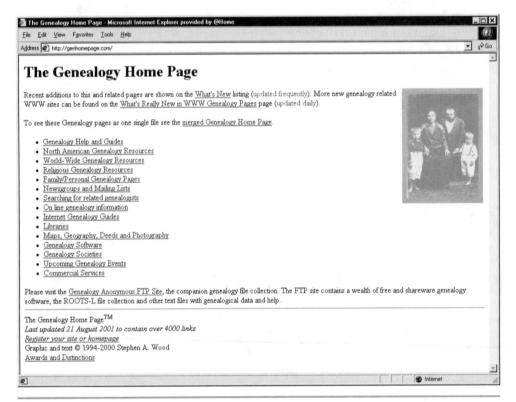

FIGURE 21-13. *The Genealogy Home Page is a guide to genealogy information on the Web.*

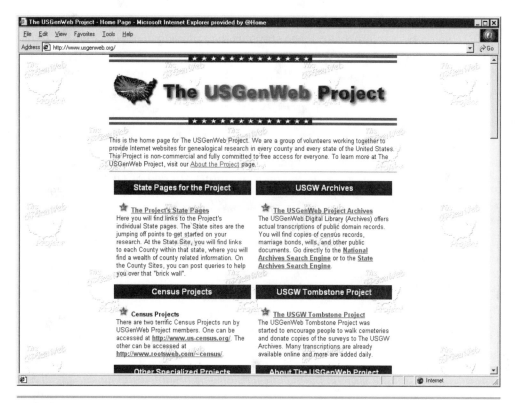

FIGURE 21-14.   *The USGenWeb Project Home Page is the place to start for county-by-county genealogical information.*

Originally, USGenWeb was envisioned as a single entry point for all counties in Kentucky, where collected databases could be stored. The databases would be indexed and cross-linked, so even if an individual were found in more than one county, he or she could be located. In the end, this initial concept snowballed far beyond its Kentucky home, growing so popular that today it contains links to every state in the union, including the District of Columbia. Each state site is unique, with its own look and feel, and serves as your gateway to the counties within the states. USGenWeb's state sites are also the best place for activities like unknown county queries, family reunion bulletins, state history research, and county maps. Some state sites are even working on special projects, such as transcribing Civil War troop records or reuniting families.

You'll see lots of variety at the county level. Every page or database is created by a volunteer and the resources they provide can be as individualistic as the people themselves. At a minimum, each county site provides links to post queries and access state archives. To put it simply, USGenWeb is an impressive accomplishment, and its volunteers deserve the thanks of every genealogist in the United States, both amateur and expert alike.

Note

If you have a lot of genealogical information about a particular county, check the listing on that county in the USGenWeb Project. Maybe you should join the volunteers who make this project possible. If you're interested, click the Information for Current and Prospective Volunteers link. This takes you to the Volunteers page at www. usgenweb.org/volunteers/volunteers.html where you can learn about being a volunteer.

While the main objective today for USGenWeb is to create county-by-county sites, they also have several special projects underway. You can find out about them on the USGenWeb Special Projects page at www. usgenweb.org/projects/projects.html. Some of the special projects underway at this writing are

- **Archives Project** USGenWeb was originally designed to provide information county by county. Unfortunately, some genealogical information can't be organized this way. Because of this, the *Archives Project* aims to put noncounty public domain information onto the Web. This project has several subprojects, including the Tombstone Project (www.rootsweb.org/ ~ cemetery). In the *Tombstone Project,* volunteers travel to cemeteries around the country where they transcribe tombstone inscriptions. These inscriptions are then made accessible through this Web page.

- **Lineage Project** For people who want to track down a particular ancestor, the *Lineage Project* provides a place to list information about the ancestor, with contact information—an e-mail address or Web page—for the researcher.

- **National and International Links Project** This is a collection of links from USGenWeb to sites of general genealogical interest around the world.

Returning to the USGenWeb home page, click the link to Information for Researchers at www.usgenweb.org/researchers/researcher.html. Here you'll find a page chock full of helpful research tips, plus an interesting section on preserving relics, such as old books, photos, and newspaper articles.

USGenWeb is one of the most important online genealogy sites, in my opinion. I hope you agree.

GENSERV

GenServ at www.genserv.com is a cooperative genealogy data exchange. You query the system through commands sent by e-mail, and you also receive the results by e-mail. Web-based queries are also supported, but I find e-mail easier to use. The opening page is shown in Figure 21-15.

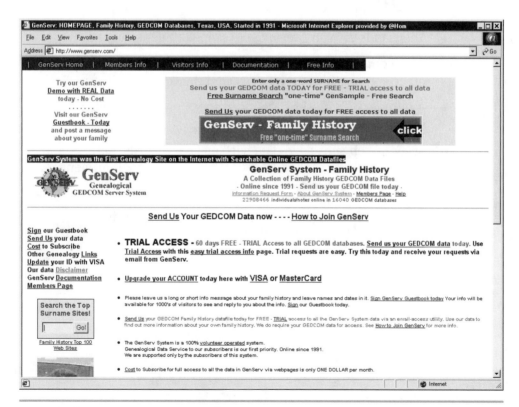

FIGURE 21-15.   *GenServ System was the first genealogy site on the Internet with searchable online GEDCOM data files.*

This ten-year-old project is a GEDCOM exchange and search site. People upload their GEDCOMs (which, of course, are secondary source information), and then members can search the different databases for matches on names, dates, and locations. The data in these databases is accessible through commands sent to the system via a regular e-mail message and also via WEB access. The system then formats the results and e-mails a report back to the user who sent the request. GenServ can generate several different kinds of reports from these e-mail requests.

Submitting your GEDCOM datafile is required for a 60-day free trial to this system and the system has data from over 50 countries. Membership costs from $12 to $35 a year. More money gets you more queries to the databases. The money goes toward disk drives and computers to run the system, and all the work is done by volunteers.

Wrapping Up

♦ Thousands of Web sites exist to help with genealogy.

♦ Some of the most useful Web sites are collections of links to other sites, such as Cyndi's List and the Genealogy Home Page.

♦ A number of Web sites are more specific with genealogies submitted from users such as GenServ.

♦ Several Web sites have data such as land records, family Bible entries, and transcribed Census data, for example, Afrigeneas, The Library of Virginia, and the Bureau of Land Management.

♦ Other pages have good information on how to proceed with your research, such as DearMYRTLE and the Adoptee Search Resource page.

Part 4

Appendices

Appendix A

Genealogical Standards from the National Genealogical Society

Often, a beginning genealogist's first problem is how to proceed. As with any endeavor, you can go about gathering your family history in good ways and in bad ways.

The National Genealogical Society (NGS) (covered in Chapter 15) has a committee on sound genealogical standards. The guidelines are intended to make the genealogist's task somewhat easier by giving a roadmap, so to speak, of how to navigate the collection, preserve, interpret, and share genealogical data. Study and follow these guidelines, and your quest for ancestry will be a rewarding one.

These standards are revisited at NGS meetings and may be updated in the future. Check the Web page at www.ngsgenealogy.org/comstandards.htm for updates.

Standards for Sound Genealogical Research

Recommended by the National Genealogical Society.

Remembering always that they are engaged in a quest for truth, family history researchers consistently—

- ◆ record the source for each item of information they collect.

- ◆ test every hypothesis or theory against credible evidence, and reject those that are not supported by the evidence.

- ◆ seek original records, or reproduced images of them when there is reasonable assurance they have not been altered, as the basis for their research conclusions.

- ◆ use compilations, communications and published works, whether paper or electronic, primarily for their value as guides to locating the original records.

- ◆ state something as a fact only when it is supported by convincing evidence, and identify the evidence when communicating the fact to others.

- ◆ limit with words like "probable" or "possible" any statement that is based on less than convincing evidence, and state the reasons for concluding that it is probable or possible.

- ◆ avoid misleading other researchers by either intentionally or carelessly distributing or publishing inaccurate information.

♦ state carefully and honestly the results of their own research, and acknowledge all use of other researchers' work.

♦ recognize the collegial nature of genealogical research by making their work available to others through publication, or by placing copies in appropriate libraries or repositories, and by welcoming critical comment.

♦ consider with open minds new evidence or the comments of others on their work and the conclusions they have reached.

Guidelines for Using Records, Repositories, and Libraries

Recommended by the National Genealogical Society.

Recognizing that how they use unique original records and fragile publications will affect other users, both current and future, family history researchers habitually—

♦ are courteous to research facility personnel and other researchers, and respect the staff's other daily tasks, not expecting the records custodian to listen to their family histories nor provide constant or immediate attention.

♦ dress appropriately, converse with others in a low voice, and supervise children appropriately.

♦ do their homework in advance, know what is available and what they need, and avoid ever asking for "everything" on their ancestors.

♦ use only designed work space areas and equipment, like readers and computers, intended for patron use, respect off-limits areas, and ask for assistance if needed.

♦ treat original records at all times with great respect and work with only a few records at a time, recognizing that they are irreplaceable and that each user must help preserve them for future use.

♦ treat books with care, never forcing their spines, and handle photographs properly, preferably wearing archival gloves.

- ◆ never mark, mutilate, rearrange, relocate, or remove from the repository any original, printed, microform, or electronic document or artifact.

- ◆ use only procedures prescribed by the repository for noting corrections to any errors or omissions found in published works, never marking the work itself.

- ◆ keep note-taking paper or other objects from covering records or books, and avoid placing any pressure upon them, particularly with a pencil or pen.

- ◆ use only the method specifically designated for identifying records for duplication, avoiding use of paper clips, adhesive notes, or other means not approved by the facility.

- ◆ return volumes and files only to locations designated for that purpose.

- ◆ before departure, thank the records custodians for their courtesy in making the materials available.

- ◆ follow the rules of the records repository without protest, even if they have changed since a previous visit or differ from those of another facility.

Standards for Use of Technology in Genealogical Research

Recommended by the National Genealogical Society.

Mindful that computers are tools, genealogists take full responsibility for their work and, therefore, they—

- ◆ learn the capabilities and limits of their equipment and software, and use them only when they are the most appropriate tools for a purpose.

- do not accept uncritically the ability of software to format, number, import, modify, check, chart or report their data, and therefore carefully evaluate any resulting product.

- treat compiled information from on-line sources or digital databases like that from other published sources, useful primarily as a guide to locating original records, but not as evidence for a conclusion or assertion.

- accept digital images or enhancements of an original record as a satisfactory substitute for the original only when there is reasonable assurance that the image accurately reproduces the unaltered original.

- cite sources for data obtained on-line or from digital media with the same care that is appropriate for sources on paper and other traditional media, and enter data into a digital database only when its source can remain associated with it.

- always cite the sources for information or data posted on-line or sent to others, naming the author of a digital file as its immediate source, while crediting original sources cited within the file.

- preserve the integrity of their own databases by evaluating the reliability of downloaded data before incorporating it into their own files.

- provide, whenever they alter data received in digital form, a description of the change that will accompany the altered data whenever it is shared with others.

- actively oppose the proliferation of error, rumor, and fraud by personally verifying or correcting information, or noting it as unverified, before passing it on to others.

- treat people on-line as courteously and civilly as they would treat them face-to-face, not separated by networks and anonymity.

- accept that technology has not changed the principles of genealogical research, only some of the procedures.

Standards for Sharing Information with Others

Recommended by the National Genealogical Society.

Conscious of the fact that sharing information or data with others, whether through speech, documents, or electronic media, is essential to family history research and that it needs continuing support and encouragement, responsible family historians consistently—

- respect the restrictions on sharing information that arise from the rights of another as an author, originator or compiler; as a living private person; or as a party to a mutual agreement.

- observe meticulously the legal rights of copyright owners, copying or distributing any part of their works only with their permission, or to the limited extent specifically allowed under the law's "fair use" exceptions.

- identify the sources for all ideas, information, and data from others, and the form in which they were received, recognizing that the unattributed use of another's intellectual work is plagiarism.

- respect the authorship rights of senders of letters, electronic mail, and data files, forwarding or disseminating them further only with the sender's permission.

- inform people who provide information about their families as to the ways it may be used, observing any conditions they impose and respecting any reservations they may express regarding the use of particular items.

- require some evidence of consent before assuming that living people are agreeable to further sharing of information about themselves.

- convey personal identifying information about living people— like age, home address, occupation, or activities—only in ways that those concerned have expressly agreed to.

- recognize that legal rights of privacy may limit the extent to which information from publicly available sources may be further used, disseminated, or published.

- communicate no information to others that is known to be false, or without making reasonable efforts to determine its truth, particularly information that may be derogatory.

- are sensitive to the hurt that revelations of criminal, immoral, bizarre, or irresponsible behavior may bring to family members.

Guidelines for Publishing Web Pages on the Internet

Recommended by the National Genealogical Society, May 2000.
Appreciating that publishing information through Internet Web sites and Web pages shares many similarities with print publishing, considerate family historians—

- apply a title identifying both the entire Web site and the particular group of related pages, similar to a book-and-chapter designation, placing it both at the top of each Web browser window using the < TITLE > HTML tag, and in the body of the document, on the opening home or title page and on any index pages.

- explain the purposes and objectives of their Web sites, placing the explanation near the top of the title page or including a link from that page to a special page about the reason for the site.

- display a footer at the bottom of each Web page which contains the Web site title, page title, author's name, author's contact information, date of last revision, and a copyright statement.

- provide complete contact information, including at a minimum a name and e-mail address, and preferably some means for long-term contact, like a postal address.

- assist visitors by providing on each page navigational links that lead visitors to other important pages on the Web site, or return them to the home page.

- adhere to the NGS "Standards for Sharing Information with Others" regarding copyright, attribution, privacy, and the sharing of sensitive information.

- include unambiguous source citations for the research data provided on the site, and if not complete descriptions, offering full citations upon request.

- label photographic and scanned images within the graphic itself, with fuller explanation if required in text adjacent to the graphic.

- identify transcribed, extracted, or abstracted data as such, and provide appropriate source citations.

- include identifying dates and locations when providing information about specific surnames or individuals.

- respect the rights of others who do not wish information about themselves to be published, referenced, or linked on a Web site.

- provide Web site access to all potential visitors by avoiding enhanced technical capabilities that may not be available to all users, remembering that not all computers are created equal.

- avoid using features that distract from the productive use of the Web site, like ones that reduce legibility, strain the eyes, dazzle the vision, or otherwise detract from the visitor's ability to easily read, study, comprehend, or print the online publication.

- maintain their online publications at frequent intervals, changing the content to keep the information current, the links valid, and the Web site in good working order.

- preserve and archive for future researchers their online publications and communications that have lasting value, using both electronic and paper duplication.

Appendix B

Forms of Genealogical Data

One of the reasons to get involved in the online genealogy world is to share the information you have—and to find information you don't have. To do this, standards have been set up for transmitting that information.

GEDCOMs, Ahnentafels, and Tiny Tafels

GEDCOMs, Ahnentafels, and tiny tafels are all designed to put information in a standard format. GEDCOMs and tiny tafels can be used by many different genealogical database programs and many utilities have been written to translate information from one to another.

GEDCOMs

In February 1987, The Church of Jesus Christ of Latter-day Saints (Mormon church) approved a standard way of setting data for transfer between various types of genealogy software, including its own Personal Ancestral File (PAF). The standard (a combination of tags for data and pointers to related data) has been adopted into most major genealogical database programs, including PAF MacGene, The Master Genealogist, Family Tree Maker, Family Ties, Brother's Keeper, Legacy, and so on.

If data from one database doesn't fit exactly into the new one even with GEDCOM's format, the program will often save the extraneous data to a special file. A good program can use this data to help you sort and search to determine whether it has what you're looking for. This is why so many people upload GEDCOMs to sites; perhaps someone somewhere can use the data. But because GEDCOMs tend to be large, many sites have a policy against uploading them. Instead, you upload a message that you're willing to exchange it for the price of the disk, or some other arrangement.

The current release of the GEDCOM standard is 5.5. At the page www.gendex.com/gedcom55/55gctoc.htm, you will find the standard spelled out in detail.

Ahnentafels

Ahnentafels aren't big tiny tafels. The word means *ancestor table* in German, and the format is more than a century old. An *ahnentafel* lists all known ancestors of an individual, and includes the full name of each, as well as dates and places of birth, marriage, and death. It organizes this information along a strict numbering scheme.

Once you get used to ahnentafels, reading them becomes easy, moving up and down from parent to child, and then back again. The numbering scheme is the key to it all. Consider this typical pedigree chart:

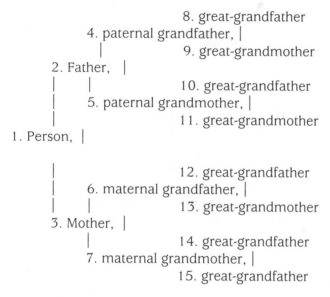

```
                        8. great-grandfather
        4. paternal grandfather, |
        |               9. great-grandmother
    2. Father,  |
    |   |               10. great-grandfather
    |   5. paternal grandmother, |
    |               11. great-grandmother
1. Person,  |

    |               12. great-grandfather
    |   6. maternal grandfather, |
    |   |               13. great-grandmother
    3. Mother,  |
        |               14. great-grandfather
        7. maternal grandmother, |
                        15. great-grandfather
```

Study the numbers in the previous chart. Every person listed has a number, with a mathematical relationship between parents and children. The number of a father is always double that of his child's. The number of the mother is always double that of her child's, plus one. The number of a child is always one-half that of its parent (ignoring any remainder).

In this example, the father of person #6 is #12, the mother of #6 is #13, and the child of #13 is #6. In ahnentafel format, the chart reads like this:

1. person

2. father

3. mother

4. paternal grandfather

5. paternal grandmother

6. maternal grandfather

7. maternal grandmother

8. great-grandfather

9. great-grandmother

10. great-grandfather

11. great-grandmother

12. great-grandfather

13. great-grandmother

14. great-grandfather

15. great-grandmother

Notice the numbers are exactly the same as in the pedigree chart. The rules of father = 2 × child#, mother = 2 × child# + 1, child = parent/2, ignore remainder, and so forth remain the same. This is an ahnentafel chart.

In practice, ahnentafels are rarely uploaded as text files, but it's one way to show what you do know about your tree quickly, and in few characters. Just clearly state that it's an ahnentafel. Some Web sites list genealogies as ahnentafels.

Tiny Tafels

Despite the similar name, a tiny tafel (TT) is a different animal. A *TT* provides a standard way of describing a family database, so the information can be scanned visually or by computer. It was described in an article entitled "Tiny-Tafel for Database Scope Indexing," by Paul Andereck in the April-May-June 1986 issue (vol. 5, number 4) of *Genealogical Computing*.

The concept of TTs was adopted by COMMSOFT first in its popular program, Roots-II, and later in Roots-III. TT has since been adapted by other genealogical programs, such as Brother's Keeper and GED2TT.

A TT makes no attempt to include the details contained in an ahnentafel. All data fields are of fixed length, with the obvious exceptions of the surnames and optional places. A TT lists only surnames of interest (with Soundex), plus the locations and dates of the beginning and end of that surname. TTs make no provision for first names, births, marriages, deaths, or multiple locations.

In the COMMSOFT TT, the name of the database, the version of the database, and any special switches used when the TT was generated are shown on the *Z* line. The definitions of the special switches are shown next.

- **D DATEFILLDISABLED**   When data for birth dates are missing (unknown), then the tiny tafel format can skip that field. When this switch is on, the TT generator has estimated missing dates. The TT program applies a 30-year per generation offset wherever it needs to reconstruct missing dates.

- **N NOGROUPING**   TT normally "groups" output lines that have a common ancestor into a single line containing the most recent birth date. Descendants marked with an interest level greater than zero, however, will have their own line of output. Or, when this switch is enabled, one line of output is created for every ultimate descendant (individual without children).

- **M MULTIPLENAMES**   Tiny Tafel normally lists a surname derived from the descendant end of each line. Specifying this option lists all unique spellings of each surname (up to five) separated by commas.

- **P PLACENAMES**   TT includes place names for family lines when this switch is enabled. Place names will be the most significant 14 to 16 characters of the birth field. When this option is enabled, the place of birth of the ultimate ancestor and the place of birth of the ultimate descendant of a line of output, respectively, are added to the end of the line.

- **S SINGLEITEMS**   TT normally suppresses lines of output that correspond to a single individual (that is, in which the ancestry and descendant dates are the same). This switch includes single-person items in the output.

- **#I INTERESTLEVEL**   TT normally includes all family lines meeting the previous conditions, no matter what its interest level. An interest level may be specified to limit the lines included to those having an interest level equal to or greater than the number specified. For example, with the interest level set to 1, all lines that have an ancestor or descendant interest level of 1 or higher will be listed.

Table B-1 shows the structure of a TT header. Table B-2 shows the types of headers in a TT. Table B-3 shows how TT data is arranged.

The Soundex code for any given line is obtained from the end of the line that has the highest interest level. But, if the interest level is

Column	Description
1	Header Type
2	Space delimited
3	*n* Text (n < 38)(n + 1)
	Carriage Return

Table B-1   *Header*

the same at each end, the name at the ancestor end will be used. If the application of these rules yield a surname that cannot be converted to Soundex, however, the program will attempt to obtain a Soundex code from the other end of the line.

Interest flag: The codes for interest level are
[space]   No interest (level 0)
. Low interest (level 1)
: Moderate interest (level 2)
* Highest interest (level 3)

Up to five surnames can be on one line where the surname has changed in that line. If more than five surnames are found in a line, only the latest five will be shown. The inclusion of additional surnames is enabled by the *M* switch.

Place names for the birth of the earliest ancestor and the latest descendant may be included by using the *P* switch. If a place name isn't provided for the individual whose birth year is shown, the field will be blank. The place for the ancestor is preceded by a backslash (\) and for the descendant by a slash (/).

Terminator:
W Date Tiny Tafel file was generated, DD MMM YYYY format.

That's how you build one manually. Most genealogical software packages now have a function to create and accept either a TT or a GEDCOM, or both, from your information in the database. Always be certain a downloaded GEDCOM or TT has verified information before you load it in to your database because taking it back out isn't fun.

The best way to use computers is to take some of the drudgery out of life. And, the best way to use TTs is to compare and contrast them with as many others as you can. Thus, the Tiny Tafel Matching System (TTMS) was born. This is a copyrighted software program from CommSoft, Inc.

Header Type	Description	Remarks
N	Name of person having custody of data	Mandatory first record
A	0 to 5 address lines, Address data	Optional
T	Telephone number including area code	Optional
S	Communication, Service/telephone number	0 to 5 service lines (MCI, ITT, ONT, RCA, ESL, CIS, SOU, etc., e.g., CIS/77123,512
B	Bulletin Board/ telephone number	Optional
C	Communications nnnn/X/P nnnn maximum baud rate X = O(riginate only), A(nswer only), B(oth) P = Protocol (Xmodem, Kermit, etc.)	Optional
D	Diskette format d/f/c d = diameter (3, 5, 8) f = format MS-DOS, Apple II, etc. c = capacity, KB	Optional
F	File format	Free-form, optional ROOTS II, ROOTS/M, PAF Version 1, etc.
R	Remark	Free-form, optional
Z	Number of data items with optional text	Required last item

Table B-2   *Defined Types*

and is on many bulletin board systems, which must be on The National Genealogy Conference (FidoNet) to carry the program. You have to be a qualified user of a site and submit your own TT file (which can have more than one tafel in it) to be allowed to use TTMS to the fullest.

Col	Description
1 through 4	Soundex Code (note 1)
5	Space delimiter
6 through 9	Earliest ancestor birth year
10	Interest flag, ancestor end of family line (note 2)

Table B-3   *Tiny Tafel Data*

To find a TTMS near you, call the CommSoft sites at 707-838-6373, register as a user, and look at the Files section under genealogy-related files. You can also get a description of the system there. Or, call Brian Mavrogeorge's board Roots(SF!) at 415-584-0697, which has an eight-page article about the system. Send Brian an e-mail message at brian.mavrogeorge@p0.f30.n125.z1.fidonet.org to ask for a copy.

The TTMS system has three main functions:

♦ Collecting and maintaining a local database of TTs

♦ Presenting "instant" matches on the local database

♦ Allowing "batch" searches of all other databases on the National Genealogical Society (NGS)

In this context, *instant* means while you sit waiting at your keyboard, hooked on to the BBS (which could take some time—with you and your line both tied up). For this reason, some BBSs will limit the time of day you can try this. A *batch* search means your query is sent out on the NGS and, in a few hours or days, you'll receive messages about other TTs that match yours. Then you can contact the persons who submitted the data.

Anyone who can sign on to a site can look for instant matches, but you have to submit a TT file of your own to do a batch search. The searches can be limited by dates, soundex, interest level, and so on to make the hits more meaningful.

Your TTs should be machine-generated (by Brother's Keeper, for example) to avoid formatting errors. Keep the TT as concise as possible and submit to only one board. For the batch system to be most efficient, redundancies must be minimal. And be sure to experiment with the date overlap features to keep the reports short. As you find new information, you can replace your old TT file with new information. This is especially important if your address changes.

Appendix C

Internet
Error Messages

The Information Superhighway is full of potholes, dead ends, and wrong turns. You know you've hit one when a message pops up saying "404 not found" or "Failed DSN lookup." Scratching your head, you wonder, "40what? Failed who? What do these cryptic messages mean anyway?"

These messages mean the Internet is trying to tell you something. Here's a short guide to some of the most common messages, their probable causes, and what you can do about them.

Browser Error Messages

403 forbidden   The Web site you're trying to access requires special permission—a password at the least. No password? You'll probably have to give up or find out how to register for the site.

404 not found   Your browser found the host computer, but not the specific Web page or document you requested. Check your typing, make sure you have the address (URL) right, and then try again. If this doesn't work, shorten the address, erasing from the right to the first slash you encounter. For example, if www.benchley.com/pub/dottie isn't working, try www.benchley.com/pub/. If that doesn't work, keep erasing the address back to the first single slash.

Bad file request   The problem: you're trying to fill out an onscreen form and you get this message. The cause: either your browser doesn't support forms or the function isn't turned on. Another possibility: the form you filled out or the HTML coding at that Web site has an error in it. If you're sure your browser isn't the problem, send e-mail to the site administrator and surf on.

Cannot add form submission result to bookmark list   A script— say, from a WebCrawler search—returns variables, such as the results from a query. You can't save the results as a bookmark because this isn't a permanent file on the Internet. It's just a temporary display on your computer at this moment. You can save only the address of a page or document stored on some computer on the Internet. You can, however, save the result of a search to your own hard disk and create a bookmark that points to it.

Connection refused by host   See 403 forbidden.

Failed DNS lookup The Web site's address couldn't be translated into a valid IP address (the site's officially assigned number). Either that, or the domain name server (DNS) was too busy to handle your request. What does this all mean? Well, the www.google.com site has the DNS address 216.239.33.100. The computer that translates the site's name into that number is a domain name server. If you see this message, the DNS couldn't take the word-based URL and translate it into an IP address (numbers). First, check your spelling and punctuation. If you still get the message, try to ping the site. Or, assume the DNS was busy and try again later.

File contains no data The browser found the site, but discovered nothing in the specific file. If you typed in a URL and got this message, check your spelling and punctuation. If you got this message after using an interactive page, perhaps you didn't finish the form or the script on the page is faulty. Try again, at least once.

Helper application not found Your browser downloaded a file that needs a viewer (like a video clip), but can't find the program to display it. Go to your browser's Option menu (or similar menu) and make sure you've properly specified the necessary helper program, its correct directory, and executable filename. Then try again. Note: You can usually ignore this error and download the file to view it later.

NNTP server error You tried to connect to your Internet service provider's (ISPs) newsgroup server—the computer that handles messages going to and from all newsgroups supported by your ISP. The problem: Your browser couldn't find it. This could be because the server is down or because you typed in the wrong server. Be sure you entered the news server correctly in the Preferences or Options dialog box. Try again.

Another cause could be you tried to access one ISP's news server from your account on another ISP. You can't use CompuServe's network to read Usenet off Prodigy Internet and vice versa.

Not found The link to a page or document or some other site no longer exists. Shorten the URL back to the first single slash and try again. If you still can't find the site, access a Web-search program like WebCrawler or Lycos and see if you can find the site's new address.

TCP error encountered while sending request to server Some kind of erroneous data got in the pipes and is confusing the easily confused Internet. This could be because of a faulty phone jack, line noise, sunspots, or gremlins. Try again later and if the problem persists, report it to your system administrator.

Too many users   Many servers, especially File Transfer Protocol (FTP) servers, have a limit on the number of users who can connect at one time. Wait for the traffic to die down and try again.

Unable to locate host   Your browser couldn't find anything at the URL you specified. The address could have a typo, the site may be unavailable (perhaps temporarily), or you didn't notice your connection to the ISP has ended.

FTP Error Messages

Hundreds of FTP programs probably exist for the PC and Mac, and the error messages will vary. Nevertheless, here are some errors, their causes, and resolutions.

Invalid host or Unable to resolve host   This is FTP's equivalent to "404 not found." It doesn't mean the site isn't there, it just means your FTP program couldn't find it. First, check your syntax and try again. If you still hit a brick wall, run a PING program and see what's going on. Most ISPs have a PING program on their server; in fact, Windows 9x and later versions come with one. Just type **PING < <sitename> >** in the DOS command window. If the site exists, PING will tell you how long it took a signal to travel there and back. If PING couldn't get through, then assume the site is down, at least temporarily. Try another day.

Another way to find out if a site exists is to run *nslookup,* a program available from many ISPs. nslookup looks up a server's IP address in a master Internet directory. When you're logged onto your ISP, type **nslookup < <hostname> >**.

Your FTP program connects and then suddenly freezes   If this happens shortly after you log in, try using a dash (-) as the first character of your password. This will turn off the site's informational messages, which may be confusing your FTP program.

Too many consecutive transmit errors   This means line noise has confused your FTP program and it can't continue.

The problem could be your modem. If you got a bargain 28.8 Kbps modem, it's possible that modem has less configurable options and cheaper interface circuits between the modem's real guts, the chipset, and the phone line. Modem connections above 9,600bps require real care in these circuits and cheaper modems cut corners. Call your manufacturer to see if they have some workarounds.

Another possibility is you're choking Windows, the communication program, or the modem by setting the COM port's speed to higher than

38.4 Kbps or 57.6 Kbps. Even though most 28.8 Kbps modems claim to handle communications at speeds up to 115 Kbps, something in the link may be unable to do so. Reset the COM port speed and try again.

This could also be a problem with the command string sent to your modem before dialing. Check with your vendor and be prepared to supply the model number, the current initialization string sent to the modem, and settings for hardware flow control, error correction, and so on.

Usenet Error Messages

Reading and participating in newsgroups is one of the Internet's oldest and most enjoyable pastimes. But, to avoid glitches and online faux pas, read some FAQ files first. You can find a good set at www.faqs.org/faqs/top.html.

Usenet error messages are usually specific to your news reader, but some common traps exist.

Invalid newsgroup This jarring note can appear for various reasons. You might have spelled the newsgroup name wrong. It's easy to put periods in the wrong place. Or, maybe the newsgroup no longer exists. This is common with the alt.* groups. Search your provider's list of newsgroups. You can also find a list of active newsgroups at www.faqs.org/faqs/active-newsgroups. If you try to "add" a Newsgroup to your subscription list, but you get the address wrong, you'll get this message. Finally, your news server might not carry this group. Talk to the sysop about adding it, or find the archived messages of the group. If all else fails, search for the newsgroup (or its archives) with Google (www.google.com).

No such message Sometimes, especially if you're using a browser, you'll get a list of messages that's out of date. The message you wanted to read is still listed in the index, but it has "scrolled off" the server. This means the message has been erased to make room for newer messages. Go to Google or one of the archive sites to search for the message you want.

Could not connect to server Either the news server is busy (you can try again later), it's down (you should notify your ISP), or you aren't allowed access to the news server. Another possible cause is you've set up your browser or newsreader client incorrectly. Check your typing in your configuration screen.

A Usenet message looks like gibberish This isn't really an error. It's a binary file—such as a picture, sound, movie, or program—that has been uuencoded into ASCII characters. You can copy the message to a file and use a decoding program to restore it. The newest and best newsreaders come with automatic decoding, however. Read the instructions for getting coded messages for your newsreader.

E-Mail Error Messages

E-mail is what the Internet was originally designed for and it's extremely dependable. Most mail errors are user syntax errors. When addressing a message, you must get the syntax exactly right. Commas and spaces are never allowed in e-mail addresses. The first thing to do when an e-mail you've sent is "bounced" back is to check your typing.

Unknown user   Usually you have typed the name wrong. Sometimes you have the wrong address. Call the person and ask for the correct e-mail address.

Mail from a mail list stops coming   If delivery from one of your favorite mail lists suddenly stops, it could be caused by a temporary glitch in that site or the Internet. If you aren't getting mail from anywhere else, the latter is probably the case. If you are, you might have been involuntarily "unsubscribed" by the mail list program at the site. (The usual reason is because the mail it sent you was bounced back with an error.) The solution is to resubscribe.

Another possibility is the list might have been discontinued and you weren't reading the messages closely. If you suspect this, send an e-mail to the site with only this in the body of the message: `review listname`, with listname being the name of the list. You should get back the list's current status, including the address of the owner, whom you might want to query.

Message undeliverable Mailer Daemon   You've just met the mail program that parses all messages. If something is wrong, the header will try to tell you what it is. Read the whole header and you'll probably find the problem. Usually, it's the spelling.

WARNING: Message still undelivered after xx hours   Sometimes, the Internet is kind enough to warn your when you mail isn't getting through. This message is typically followed by one saying the mailer will keep trying for so many hours or days to deliver the message. You needn't do anything about this message, but you might want to call the recipient and tell her the e-mail you sent will be delayed.

Glossary

ahnentafel   The word means "ancestor table" in German and the format is more than a century old. The ahnentafel lists all known ancestors of an individual and includes the full name of each ancestor, as well as dates and places of birth, marriage, and death. It organizes this information along a strict numbering scheme.

anonymous FTP (File Transfer Protocol)   The procedure of connecting to a remote computer, as an anonymous or guest user, to transfer public files back to your local computer. (See also: *FTP* and *protocol.*) Anonymous FTP is usually read-only access; you often cannot contribute files by anonymous FTP.

Archie   An Internet program for finding files available by anonymous FTP to the general public.

backbone   A set of connections that make up the main channels of communication across a network.

baud   A measure of speed for data transmission across a wire. A baud isn't equivalent to bits per second, but to changes of state per second. Several bits may go across the wire with each change of state, so bits per second can be higher than the baud rate.

BITNET   Originally, a cooperative computer network interconnecting over 2,300 academic and research institutions in 32 countries. Originally based on IBM's RSCS networking protocol, BITNET supports mail, mailing lists, and file transfer. It eventually became part of the Internet, but some colleges restrict access to the original BITNET collection of a computer.

browser   An Internet client for viewing the World Wide Web.

bulletin board system (BBS)   A set of hardware and software you can use to enter information for other users to read or download. In this book, a BBS is usually a stand-alone system you dial up with the phone, but many are now reachable by telnet. Most bulletin boards are set up according to general topics and are accessible throughout a network.

catalog   A search page for the Web where only an edited list is covered, not the whole Internet.

chat   When people type messages to each other across a host or network, live and in real time. On some commercial online services, this is called a conference.

client   A program that provides an interface to remote Internet services, such as mail, Usenet, telnet, and so on. In general, the clients act on behalf of a human end-user (perhaps indirectly).

compression   A method of making a file, whether text or code, smaller by various methods. This is so the file will take up less disk space and/or less time to transmit. Sometimes the compression is completed by the modem. Sometimes the file is stored that way. The various methods to do this go by names (followed by the system that used it) such as PKZIP (DOS), ARC (DOS), tar (UNIX), STUFFIT (Macintosh), and so forth.

conference   A live, online chat, or a forum (see definition below) or echo (see definition below) of e-mail messages.

CREN (Computer Research and Education Network)   The new name for the merged computer networks, BITNET and Computer Science Network (CSNET). CREN supports electronic mail and file transfer.

data base   A set of information organized for computer storage, search, retrieval, and insertion.

default   In computer terms, not a failure to meet an obligation but, instead, the "normal" or "basic" settings of a program.

directory   **1.** A level in a hierarchical filing system. Other directories branch down from the root directory. **2.** A type of search site where editors choose the Web sites and services in the catalog, instead of a robot collecting them indiscriminately.

domain name   The Internet naming scheme. A machine on the Internet is identified by a series of words from more specific to more general (left to right), separated by dots: microsoft.com is an example (See also: *IP address*.)

domain name server (DNS)   A machine with software to translate a domain name into the corresponding numbers of the IP address. "No DNS entry" from your browser means a name such as first.last.org wasn't in the domain name server's list of valid IP addresses.

door   A program on a BBS, which enables you to perform specific functions, for example, download mail, play a game, scan the files, and so forth. The BBS software shuts down while you are in a door and the door's commands are in effect.

downloading   To get information from another computer to yours.

echo   A set of messages on a specific subject sent to specific BBSs, which have requested those messages.

e-mail   An electronic message, text, or data sent from one machine or person to another machine or person.

firewall   Electronic protection against hackers and other unauthorized access to your files while you're connected to a network or the Internet.

flame   A message or series of messages containing an argument or insults. Not allowed on most systems. If you receive a flame, ignore that message and all other messages from that person in the future.

Flash ROM   A chip in a modem that can be used to upgrade the unit if new technology comes along after you bought it. The upgrade comes in the form of a program, which, when run, rewrites the read-only memory in the modem with the new standard, protocol, or whatever else has been improved.

forum   A set of messages on a subject, usually with a corresponding set of files. Can be on an open network, such as ILINK, or restricted to a commercial system, such as CompuServe.

FTP (File Transfer Protocol)   Enables an Internet user to transfer files electronically from remote computers back to the user's computer.

gateway   Used in different senses (for example, Mail Gateway, IP Gateway) but, most generally, a computer that forwards and routes data between two or more networks of any size or origin. A gateway is never, however, as straightforward as going through a gate. It's more like a labyrinth to get the proper addresses in the proper sequence.

GEDCOM   The standard for computerized genealogical information, which is a combination of tags for data and pointers to related data.

Gopher   An Internet program to search for resources, present them to you in a menu, and perform whatever Internet program (telnet, ftp, and so forth) is necessary to get the resource. (See also: *Veronica* and *Jughead*.) All three are read-only access.

hacker   Originally, someone who messed about with computer systems to see how much could be accomplished. Most recently, a computer vandal.

host computer   In the context of networks, a computer that directly provides service to a user. In contrast to a network server, which provides services to a user through an intermediary host computer.

hot key   When a BBS systems responds to one-keystroke commands, without an <ENTER> or <RETURN> key, that option is called hot key. Some BBS software enables it with no option to turn it off; others let you set your user configuration to choose this or not. To make a command take effect without a hot key, you must press an <ENTER> or <RETURN>. Also, without a hot key, some systems let you string together several commands on one line.

HTML (Hypertext Markup Language)   A coding system to format and link documents on the World Wide Web and intranets.

hub   A computer that collects e-mail regionally and distributes it up the next level. Collects the e-mail from that level to distribute it back down the chain.

Internet   The backbone of a series of interconnected networks that includes local area, regional, and national backbone networks. Networks in the Internet use the same telecommunications protocol (TCP/IP) and provide electronic mail, remote login, and file transfer services.

Internet Relay Chat (IRC)   Real-time messages typed over an open, public server.

Internet presence   A type of chat program that requires users to register with a server. Users build "buddy lists" of others using the same program, and are notified when people on their buddy list are available for chat and messages. Also called "instant message."

Internet service provider (ISP)   A company that has a continuous, fast, and reliable connection to the Internet and sells subscriptions to the public to use that connection. The connections may use TCP/IP, shell accounts, or other methods.

INTERNIC   The company that has contracted to administer certain functions of the Internet, such as maintaining domain names and assigning IP addresses. Its home page is at http://rs1.internic.net.

intranet   A local network set up to look like the World Wide Web, with clients such as browsers, but self-contained and not necessarily connected to the Internet.

IP (Internet protocol)   The Internet standard protocol that provides a common layer over dissimilar networks, used to move packets among host computers and through gateways, if necessary.

IP address   The alpha or numeric address of a computer connected to the Internet. Also called "Internet address." Usually the format is user@someplace.domain, but it can also be seen as ###.##.##.##.

Jughead   An Internet program that helps Gopher (see definition) build menus of resources, by limiting the search to one computer and a text string.

list (Internet)   Also called "mail list." Listserv lists (or listservers) are electronically transmitted discussions of technical and nontechnical issues. They come to you by electronic mail over the Internet using LISTSERV commands. Participants subscribe via a central service and lists often have a moderator who supervises the information flow and content.

lurk To read a list or echo without posting messages yourself. It's sort of like sitting in the corner at a party without introducing yourself, except it's not considered rude online. In fact, in some places, you're expected to lurk until you get the feel of the place.

mail list Same as *list*.

MNP (Microcom Networking Protocol) Data compression standard for modems.

modem A device to modulate computer data into sound signals and to demodulate those signals to computer data.

moderator The person who takes care of an echo, list, or forum. This person takes out messages that are off-topic, chastises flamers, maintains a database of old messages, and handles the mechanics of distributing the messages.

Mozilla A nickname for Netscape Navigator. In the early days, Netscape's mascot was a little dragon-like creature called Mozilla.

navigation bar A set of words and/or images that appears on every page of a Web site, with links to other sections or pages of the same Web site.

NIC (Network Information Center) A NIC provides administrative support, user support, and information services for a network.

NREN (The National Research and Education Network) A proposed national computer network to be built on the foundation of the NSF backbone network, NSFnet. NREN would provide high-speed interconnection between other national and regional networks.

offline The state of not being connected to a remote host.

online To be connected to a remote host.

OPAC (Online Public Access Catalog) A term used to describe any type of computerized library catalog.

OSI (Open Systems Interconnection) This is the evolving international standard under development at ISO (International Standards Organization) for the interconnection of cooperative computer systems. An open system is one that conforms to OSI standards in its communications with other systems. As more and more genealogical data becomes available online, this standard will become increasingly important.

PDF (Portable Document Format) An Adobe copyrighted format that allows a document to be saved to look a certain way, no matter what machine is used to display it. The machine, however, must use Adobe's Acrobat reader (a free program) to display the file.

PPP (Point-to-Point Protocol)   A type of Internet connection. An improvement on SLIP (see the definition below), it allows any computer to use the Internet protocols and become a full-fledged member of the Internet, with a high-speed modem. The advantage to SLIP and PPP accounts is you can usually achieve faster connections than with a shell account.

protocol   A mutually determined set of formats and procedures governing the exchange of information between systems.

remote access   The capability to access a computer from outside another location. Remote access requires communications hardware, software, and actual physical links, although this can be as simple as common carrier (telephone) lines or as complex as Telnet login to another computer across the Internet.

RAM (random access memory)   The working memory of a computer. RAM is the memory used for storing data temporarily while working on it, running application programs, and so forth. "Random access" means any area of RAM can be accessed directly and immediately, in contrast to other media, such as a magnetic tape, where data is accessed sequentially. RAM is called volatile memory; information in RAM will disappear if the power is switched off before it's saved to disk.

ROM (read-only memory)   A chip in a computer or a peripheral that contains some programs to run the unit. The memory can be read, but not changed under normal circumstances. Unlike RAM, it retains its information even when the unit is turned off.

search engine   A program on the World Wide Web that searches parts of the Internet for text strings. A search engine might search for programs, for Web pages, or for other items. Many claim to cover "the whole Internet" but that's a physical impossibility. Getting more than 50 percent of the Internet is a good lick.

server   A computer that allows other computers to log on and use its resources. A client (see the definition above) program is often used for this.

shareware   The try-before-you-buy concept in microcomputer software, where the program is distributed through public domain channels and the author expects to receive compensation after a trial period. Brother's Keeper, for example, is shareware.

shell account   A method of connecting to the Internet. You dial an Internet service provider with regular modem software and connect to a computer that's connected to the Internet. Using a text interface, usually with a menu, you use the Internet with this shell, using commands such as telnet. In this system, the Internet clients don't reside on your computer, but on that of the ISP.

signature   A stored text file with your name and some information, such as names you're searching or your mailing address, to be appended to the end of your messages. Your signature should contain only ASCII characters, no graphics.

SLIP (Serial Line Internet Protocol)   A system allowing a computer to use the Internet protocols with a standard telephone line and a high-speed modem. Most ISPs now offer PPP or SLIP accounts for a monthly or a yearly fee.

Social Security Death Index (SSDI)   A searchable database of records of deaths of Americans with Social Security numbers, if that death was reported to the Social Security Administration. It runs from the 1960s to the present, although a few deaths prior to the 1960s are in it. The records give full name, place and date of death, where the card was issued, and birth date. Many Web sites have online searches of the SSDI, some with SOUNDEX (see definition below).

SOUNDEX   An indexing system based on sound, rather than the spelling of a surname.

spider   A program that gathers information on Web pages for a database, usually for a search engine.

sysop   The SYStem OPerator of a BBS, forum, or echo. The sysop sets the rules, maintains the peace and operability of the system, and sometimes moderates the messages.

tagline   A short, pity statement tagged on to the end of a BBS e-mail message. Example: "It's only a hobby, only a hobby, only a. . . . " Taglines are rarely seen on commercial networks, such as AOL, MSN, and CompuServe.

TCP/IP (Transmission Control Protocol/Internet Protocol) A combined set of protocols that performs the transfer of data between two computers. TCP monitors and ensures correct transfer of data. IP receives the data from TCP, breaks it up into packets, and ships it off to a network within the Internet. TCP/IP is also used as a name for a protocol suite that incorporates these functions and others.

telnet   An Internet client that connects to other computers, making yours a virtual terminal of the remote computer. Among other functions, it enables a user to log in to a remote computer from the user's local computer. On many commercial systems, you use it as a command, for example, telnet ftp.cac.psu.edu. Once there, you are using programs and, therefore, commands from that remote computer.

terminal emulation   Most communications software packages will permit your personal computer or workstation to communicate with another computer or network as if it were a specific type of terminal directly connected to that computer or network. For example, your terminal emulation should be set to VT100 for most online card catalog programs.

terminal server   A machine that connects terminals to a network by providing host TELNET service.

thread (message thread)   A discussion made up of a set of messages in answer to a certain message and to each other. Sometimes worthwhile threads are saved into a text file, as on CompuServe's Roots Forum. Some mail readers will sort by thread, that is, according to subject line.

tiny tafel (TT)   A TT provides a standard way of describing a family database so the information can be scanned visually or by computer. All data fields are of fixed length, with the obvious exceptions of the surnames and optional places. Many TTs are extracted from GEDCOMs.

TN3270   A version of telnet providing IBM full-screen support, as opposed to VT100, or some other emulation.

Trojan horse   A type of malicious code. This is usually a program that seems to be useful and harmless. In the background, however, it might be destroying data or breaking security on your system. It differs from a virus in that it propagates itself as a virus does.

upload   To send a file or message from one computer to another. (See also: *download*.)

USB (universal serial bus)   A connection to a computer. Unlike a parallel port (where your printer probably plugs in) or a serial port (where your modem probably plugs in), a USB port enables you to "daisy chain" peripherals. If you have a USB printer, modem, and CD-ROM drive, you could plug only one into the USB port and the rest connect by USB cables in a chain (in theory, say, computer to modem to printer to CD-ROM). In practice, sometimes it's a little tricky to get them in an order that makes all the peripherals happy.

USENET   A set of messages, and the software for sending and receiving them on the Internet. The difference between USENET and a mail list lies in the software and the way you connect to them.

V.32   A data compression standard for modems.

Veronica   A search program for gopher.

virus   A program that installs itself secretly on a computer by attaching itself to another program or e-mail, and then duplicates itself when that program is executed or e-mail is opened. Some viruses are harmless, but most of them intend to do damage, such as erasing important files on your system.

World Wide Web (WWW or **the Web)**   A system to pull various Internet services together into one interface called a browser. Most sites on the Web are written as pages in HTML.

worm   A computer program that makes copies of itself and spreads through connected systems, using up resources in affected computers or causing other damage.

Z39.50 Protocol   A protocol used often by online library card catalogs. This is a way one computer can query another computer and transfer result records. This protocol provides the framework for OPAC (See also: *OPAC*). users to search remote catalogs on the Internet using the commands of their own local systems.

Smiley (Emoticon) Glossary

Because we can't hear voice inflection over e-mail, a code for imparting emotion sprung up. These punctuation marks used to take the place of facial expressions are called Smileys or emoticons. Different systems have variations of these symbols. Two versions of this "Unofficial Smiley Dictionary" were sent to me by Cliff Manis (Internet: cmanis@csf.com), and I've edited and combined them. Several versions are floating around, but I think this one sums up the symbols you're most likely to see.

:-)   Your basic Smiley. This Smiley is used to show pleasure, or a sarcastic or joking statement.

;-)   Winky Smiley. User just made a flirtatious and/or sarcastic remark. Somewhat of a "don't hit me for what I just said" Smiley.

:-(Frowning Smiley. User didn't like that last statement, or is upset or depressed about something.

:-I   Indifferent Smiley. Better than a Frowning Smiley, but not quite as good as a happy Smiley.

:->   User just made a biting sarcastic remark. Worse than a :-).

>:->   User just made a devilish remark.

>;->   Winky and devil combined.

Those are the basic symbols. Here are some less common ones.

Note: A lot of these can be typed without noses to make midget smilies.

- -:-)	Smiley is a punk rocker
- -:-(	Real punk rockers don't smile
;-)	Wink
,-}	Wry and winking

:,(	Crying
:-:	Mutant Smiley
.-)	Smiley only has one eye
,-)	Ditto, but he's winking
:-?	Smiley smoking a pipe
:-/	Skepticism, consternation, or puzzlement
:-\	Ditto
:-'	Smiley spitting out its chewing tobacco
:-~)	Smiley has a cold
:-)~	Smiley drools
:-[	Un-Smiley blockhead
:-[	Smiley is a Vampire
:-]	Smiley blockhead
:-{	Mustache
:-}	Wry smile or beard
:-@	Smiley face screaming
:-$	Smiley face with its mouth wired shut
:-*	Smiley after eating something bitter or sour
:-&	Smiley is tongue-tied
:-#	Braces
:-#|	Smiley face with bushy mustache
:-%	Smiley banker
:-<	Mad or real sad Smiley
:-=)	Older Smiley with mustache
:->	Hey hey
:-|	"Have an ordinary day" Smiley
:-0	Smiley orator
:-0	No Yelling! (Quiet Lab)
:-1	Smiley bland face
:-6	Smiley after eating something sour
:-7	Smiley after a wry statement
:-8(	Condescending stare
:-9	Smiley is licking his/her lips
:-a	Lefty smiley touching tongue to nose
:-b	Left-pointing tongue Smiley
:-c	Bummed-out Smiley
:-C	Smiley is really bummed
:-d	Lefty Smiley razzing you
:-D	Smiley is laughing
:-e	Disappointed Smiley
:-E	Bucktoothed vampire
:-F	Bucktoothed vampire with one tooth missing
:-I	Hmm
:-i	Semi-Smiley
:-j	Left-smiling Smiley

:-o	Smiley singing National Anthem
:-O	Uh oh
:-o	Uh oh!
:-P	Disgusted or nyah nyah
:-p	Smiley sticking its tongue out (at you!)
:-q	Smiley trying to touch its tongue to its nose
:-Q	Smoker
:-s	Smiley after a BIZARRE comment
:-S	Smiley just made an incoherent statement
:-t	Cross Smiley
:-v	Talking head Smiley
:-x	"My lips are sealed" Smiley
:-X	Bow tie
:-X	Smiley's lips are sealed
::-)	Smiley wears normal glasses
:'-(	Smiley is crying
:'-)	Smiley is so happy, s/he is crying
:^)	Smiley with pointy nose (righty). Sometimes used to denote a lie, a myth, or a misconception.
:^)	Smiley has a broken nose
:(	Sad Midget Smiley
:)	Midget Smiley
:[	Real downer
:]	Midget smiley
:*	Kisses
:*)	Smiley is drunk
:<	Midget unSmiley
:<)	Smiley is from an Ivy League school
:=)	Smiley has two noses
:>	Midget Smiley
:D	Laughter
:I	Hmmm
:n)	Smiley with funny-looking right nose
:O	Yelling
:u)	Smiley with funny-looking left nose
:v)	Left-pointing nose Smiley
:v)	Smiley has a broken nose
':-)	Smiley shaved one of his eyebrows off this morning
,:-)	Same thing, other side
~ ~ :-(	net.flame
(-:	Smiley is left-handed
(:-(	UnSmiley frowning
(:-)	Smiley big-face
(:I	Egghead
(8-o	It's Mr. Bill!
):-(	UnSmiley big-face

)8-)	Scuba Smiley big-face
[:-)	Smiley is wearing a walkman
[:]	Smiley is a robot
[]	Hugs
{:-)	Smiley with its hair parted in the middle
{:-)	Smiley wears a toupee
}:-(	Toupee in an updraft
@:-)	Smiley is wearing a turban
@:I	Turban variation
@ =	Smiley is pr-nuclear war
*:o)	Bozo the Clown!
%-)	Smiley has been staring at a green screen for 15 hours straight
%-6	Smiley is braindead
+-:-)	Smiley is the Pope or holds some other religious office
+:-)	Smiley priest
<:-I	Smiley is a dunce
<:I	Midget dunce
<|-(	Smiley is Chinese and doesn't like these kind of jokes
<|-)	Smiley is Chinese
=)	Variation on a theme
>:-I	net.startrek
|-)	Hee hee
|-D	Ho ho
|-I	Smiley is asleep
|-O	Smiley is yawning/snoring
|-P	Yuk
|^o	Snoring
|I	Asleep
0-)	Smiley cyclops (scuba diver?)
3:[	Mean pet Smiley
3:]	Pet Smiley
3:o[	Net.pets
8:-)	Smiley is a wizard
8:-I	Net.unix-wizards
8-)	Glasses
8-)	Smiley swimmer
8-)	Smiley is wearing sunglasses
8:-)	Glasses on forehead
8:-)	Smiley is a little girl
B-)	Horn-rims
B:-)	Sunglasses on head
C=:-)	Smiley is a chef
C=}>;*))	Mega-Smiley. A drunk, devilish chef with a toupee in an updraft, a mustache, and a double chin
E-:-)	Smiley is a Ham radio operator
E-:-I	Net.ham-radio

g-)	Smiley with ponce-nez glasses
K:P	Smiley is a little kid with a propeller beanie
O :-)	Smiley is an angel (at heart, at least)
O |-)	Net.religion
O-)	Megaton Man On Patrol! (or else, user is a scuba diver)
X-(	Smiley just died

If you see	The chatter means...
Afk	Away from keyboard
Y	why
U	you
C	see
BRB	Be right back
<g>	grin
<bg>	big grin
<vbg>	very big grin
BTW	by the way
CWYL	chat with you later
FWIW	for what it's worth
GIWIST	Gee, I wish I'd said that!
HHOK	Ha, ha! Only kidding!
HTH	Hope this helps
HTHBE	Hope this has been enlightening
IMHO	In my humble opinion
IMNSHO	In my not so humble opinion
IOW	In other words...
IRL	In real life
ITRW	In the real world
JK	Just kidding
LOL	Laughing out loud
OTP	On the phone
OTF	On the floor
OIC	Oh! I see!
OTOH	On the other hand
POV	Point of view
RL	Real Life
ROTFL	Rolling on the floor laughing
RTFM	Read the fine manual [or help file]
TTFN	Ta ta for now
TTYL	Talk to you later
WRT	With regard to

Index

A

AAGENE-L mailing list, 212
AAHGS (Afro-American Historical and
    Genealogical Society) Web site, 211-212
Aboriginal Connections Web site, 217
Aboriginal Studies WWW Virtual Library
    Web site, 213
aborigines
        resources for Australian, 213
        resources for Native American, 217
About.com, 110, 306
Acadian-Cajun Genealogy and History
    Web site, 214
Access Genealogy Web site, 85, 217
acronyms, online chats, 62
adapters, ISDN lines, 26-27
address book, AIM, 101-102
addresses, mailing list, 114. *See
    also* ROOTS-L
Adoptee/Birth Family Connection
    Web site, 306
Adoptee Search Resource Web site, 306
Adoptees Internet Mailing List, 306
Adopting.org Web site, 306
Advanced Search page, NARA, 152
advertisements
        forums and, 272

Usenet and, 130
AF (Ancestral File)
        FamilySearch Internet using, 160
        searching surnames with, 10
Africa, South African online resource
    (white), 206
African-American Genealogical Society of
    Northern California Web site, 212
African-American Genealogy Ring
    Web site, 212
African Americans. *See also* AfriGeneas
    Web site
        African American Odyssey page, 147
        African-Native American History &
            Genealogy Web page, 217
        Christine's Genealogy Web site, 310
        genealogy Web sites, 211-212
        online classes, 257-258
African genealogy newsgroups, 138
African-Native American History &
    Genealogy Web page, 217
AfriGeneas Web site
        African American genealogy
            and, 211
        Home page, 306
        overview of, 322-325

Afro-American Historical and Genealogical Society (AAHGS) Web site, 211-212

AFs (Ancestral Files)
overview of, 168-169
using information from LDS, 167

Ahnentafels, 344-346

AIM (America Online Instant Messenger)
blocking feature, 107
chats, 101-102
instant messaging, 99
overview of, 103-104
spam protection, 100

Alabama African American Genealogy Web site, 212

Alabama Department of Archives and History Web site, 306-307

All Things Cherokee Web site, 217

AllCensus Images search, Everton Publishers, 256

Allen County, Indiana Public Library Historical Genealogy Department Web site, 306

Alta Vista, search site, 92

alt.adoption newsgroup, 137

alt.culture.cajun newsgroup, 137

alt.genealogy newsgroup, 137

America Online (AOL). *See* AOL (America Online)

America Online Instant Messenger (AIM). *See* AIM (America Online Instant Messenger)

American Civil War Home Page, 306

American Family Immigration History Center, 174-175

American Memory, LOC research online, 146-149
African American Odyssey page, 147
Collection Finder, 147-148
Maps section, 148-149

Ancestor Detective Watchdog Web site, genealogy scams, 19

AncestorSuperSearch Web site, 205

Ancestral File (AF)
FamilySearch Internet, 160
searching surnames, 10

Ancestry Daily News, read-only mailing list, 124

Ancestry-GenPage Finder search site, 85-86

Ancestry World Tree database, FamilyHistory.com, 248

Ancestry.com Web site, 243-252
FamilyHistory.com, 246-248
MyFamily.com, 248-252
overview of, 244-246
RootsWeb merger with, 228
World Tree database, 245-246

Ancient Faces Web site, 307

AND operators, using, 83-84

Annotations, Ellis Island Records Online Community Archives, 176-177

AOL (America Online). *See also* Golden Gate Genealogy Forum
accessing, 283
binary files on Usenet, 139-140
blocking spam, 37-39
etiquette, 62
Genealogy Forum, 284
Hispanic Genealogy Special Interests Group, 213
Instant Messenger, 103-104
NetFind, 92
reading Usenet, 134-136
spam protection, 36-37, 100-101

Appalachia, research online, 219

Arab Net's Web site, 213

Arabs, online resources, 213

Archives Project, USGenWeb site, 330

Archivo Historico del Agua Web site, Mexico, 208

ASCII mode, using FTP, 78

Asia, online resources, 203

AskJeeves, search site, 92

AT&T Web site, White Page directories, 94

attachments, e-mail, 41-43

audio files, Family History Scrapbooks, 180-182

Australia
aboriginal online resources, 213
Jewish genealogy in, 217
online resources, 206

Australian Institute of Aboriginal and Torres Strait Islander Studies Web site, 213

avatar chats, 105

B

backups, virus protection, 45
Bad file request, browser error
    message, 352
Bailey, Duane A., 8
Bailey, Mary (Hagstrom), 8
bandwidth, avatar chats, 105
batch searches, TTMS, 350
Beginner's Center, AOL Golden Gate
    Genealogy Forum, 286-290
        Beginner's Tool Kit, 287
        DearMYRTLE's beginner lessons, 288
        FAQ/ Ask the Staff, 287
        Five-Step Research Process, 287-288
        Internet Center, 288-289
        Introduce Yourself message
            board, 290
        Quick Start, 289-290
Beginner's Guide, AfriGeneas Web site, 323
Beginner's Tool Kit, AOL Golden Gate
    Genealogy Forum, 287
Beginning Genealogy, online class, 257
Belgium, online resources, 203-204
Benelux, online resources, 203-204
BigFoot Web site, White Page
    directories, 94-95
binary files
        FTP, 78
        Usenet, 139-140
BINHEX files, 42
Biography Guide search site, members
    of Congress, 86
Black Sheep Web site, genealogy scams, 19
bookmarks
        creating desktop shortcut to, 72-73
        error message, 352
        saving Favorite sites with, 71
books
        Books We Own, RootsWeb, 118, 240
        DearMYRTLE Web site, 326
        Everton's Genealogy Supply
            Store, 260
        Genealogy Mall Web site, 8
        recommended reference, 18-19
boolean terms, 83-85
Branching Out Online Web site, 307
Britain. *See* England
The British Heraldic Archive, 307
browsers, 67-78

connecting to card catalogs, 184-188
defined, 68
error messages, 352-354
obtaining, 68
reading newsgroups, 134
terminology, 68-69
tips and tricks, 74-78
touring, 70-74
buddy lists
        AIM and, 101-102, 104
        ICQ and, 104-105
Bureau of Land Management Land Patent
    Records Web site, 308
Byzantine.net, 308

C

cable modems, 25
Cajun
        Cajun and Zydeco Radio Guide
            Web site, 214
        history newsgroups, 137
        online resources, 214-215
Calendars Through the Ages Web site,
    308-309
call-waiting service, connecting to ISPs, 25
Canada
        Aboriginal Connections
            Web site, 217
        Canada GenWeb site, 214
        Canadian Heritage Information
            Network Web site, 309
        Global Gazette email newsletter, 314
        Jewish researchers in, 217
        North American Genealogy Forum,
            270-271
        online resources for, 207
        United States-Canadian Border
            Crossing Records, 259
Caribbean
        African American resources, 211
        genealogy newsgroups, 139
        online resources, 213-214
Caribbean Genealogy Resources
    Web site, 213
Carpatho-Rusyn
        Byzantine.net, 308
        online genealogy resources for, 204
catalogs, defined, 80

CD-ROM catalog, Everton Publishers, 255
cell phones, connecting to Internet, 29-30
cemetery research
    Cemetery Junction, The Cemetery
        Trail Web site, 309
    Cemetery Photos on RootsWeb
        site, 240
    Cemetery Records in Genealogical
        Research online class, 259
    Headstone Hunter Web site, 314
census records
    AfriGeneas Web site, 324
    AllCensus Images Search, 256
    Census Bureau Home Page, 309
    Census Web site, 14
    Federal Mortality Schedules, 258
    USGenWeb Digital Census
        Project, 14
characters, limiting in chat programs, 63
Chat Center, Genealogy Forum, 295-297
chats, 97-112
    AfriGeneas Web site, 325
    AOL Chat Center, 295-297
    AOL Instant Messenger, 103-104
    avatar chat, 105
    chat channels, 98
    CompuServe, 276-277
    conducting, 106-108
    DearMYRTLE, 326
    e-mail vs., 100
    etiquette for, 56-63
    how they work, 101-102
    ICQ, 104
    mIRC, 105-106
    MyFamily.com, 251-252
    overview of, 98-99
    security risks in IRC, 102-103
    spam protection, 36-37
    voice, 103, 106
    warnings about, 100-101
    where to find, 109-110
Cherokee Web site, 217
Cheyenne Genealogy Web site, 218
China, online resources, 203
Christine's Genealogy Web site, 212, 310
The Church of Jesus Christ of Latter-day
    Saints. *See* LDS (The Church of Jesus
    Christ of Latter-day Saints)
church records, researching, 6

*Cite Your Sources: A Manual for
    Documenting Family Histories and
    Genealogical Records* (Lackey), 19
civil discourse, 54-61
    flames, 54-55
    getting along, 56-61
    rules of, 55-56
Civil War Forum, CompuServe, 271
clans, 4
classes, genealogy. *See* online classes
clients, defined, 33
C|Net Search, search site, 92
Collection Finder, American Memory,
    147-148
columnists, AOL Golden Gate Genealogy
    Forum, 298
CommSoft, Inc., tiny tafels, 346-350
community archives
    AfriGeneas Web site, 325
    Ellis Island Records Online, 176-177
Compose Mail icon, 115
compression, FTP, 78
CompuServe, 263-280
    2000 version, 266-267
    advertising on forums, 272-273
    blocking spam, 39
    forums, decorum of, 271-273
    forums, overview of, 268-271
    forums, success of, 278-279
    GO genealogy, 267-268
    offerings of, 265-266
    overview of, 266-267
    reading Usenet, 135-136
    rules, 55-56
    spam protection on, 36-37, 100
    touring North American forum,
        273-277
    Web access, 264-265
Confederation of Associations of Families
    Acadian Web site, 214
Congress
    searching ancestors of, 86-87
    spam protection and, 37
connections. *See* Internet connections
Consumer Protection Committee, NGS
    Web site, 224
Convicts to Australia Web site, 206
Coolist Web site, 122
court records, researching, 6

crackers, defined, 45
Creole, online resources, 214-215
Cuba, online resources, 215
Cybertree Genealogy Database
    Web Site, 310
Cyndi's List Web site
    chat etiquette, 63
    French genealogy, 204
    genealogy scams, 19
    list of FHCs, 170
    list of Palm programs, 29
    read-only mailing list, 125
    searching via, 86-87
    usefulness of, 310
Czechoslovakia, online resources, 204

D

D DATEFILLDISABLED, TT, 347
Daily Indexes, listing ROOTS-L in
    HTML, 120-121
data transmission standards, 343-350
    Ahnentafels, 344-346
    GEDCOMs, 344
    tiny tafels, 346-350
databases
    Everton Publishers, 254-256
    GenWeb Database Index
        Web site, 314
    NARA research online, 152-156
    ROOTS-L, 118-119
Daughters of the American Revolution
    Web site, 310
David Eppstein's Home Page, 310
Dead Person's Society Web site, 206
DearMYRTLE
    Beginning Genealogy Lessons, 288
    international resource, 199
    overview of, 325-327
    read-only mailing list, 124
    voice chats, 107-108
decompression, FTP, 78
demodulation, defined, 23
Denmark, online resources, 205
Deutsche Bahn, online resources, 204
dial-up connection settings
    choosing ISP, 31
    CompuServe software, 266
    disabling call-waiting, 25
    modems, 23-25

digest mode, ROOTS-L, 119
Digital Resources Netherlands and
    Belgium Web site, 203-204
Digital Subscriber Line (DSL)
    overview of, 27-28
    virus protection using firewalls, 45
directories, defined, 80
Directory of Royal Genealogical Data Web
    site, 310
Distant Cousin Web site, 310
documentation
    judging validity of, 15-19
    keeping track of information, 6-9
    resources for online, 12-15
Doukhobors, online resources, 215
drop-ins, chat room, 99
DSL (Digital Subscriber Line)
    overview of, 27-28
    virus protection using firewalls, 45

E

e-mail, 35-43
    choosing ISPs, 31
    CompuServe 2000, 267
    error messages, 356
    etiquette, 53
    file attachments and formats, 41-43
    filters, 35-36
    mailing lists, 114, 121-122
    private accounts, 37
    spam protection, 36-41
    using chat vs., 100
Eastman, Dick, 271, 278-279
Eastmans' Genealogy Newsletter
    overview of, 270, 310
    read-only mailing list, 124
Edit menu options, 71
EGH (Everton's Genealogical Helper), Web
    version, 260
Ellis Island Family History Day, 174-175
Ellis Island Immigration Museum
    overview of, 174-175
    visiting in person, 182
Ellis Island Library, 180-181
Ellis Island Records Online, 173-182
    amateur genealogy and, 210
    community archives, 176-177
    Family History Scrapbooks,
        177-182

free services, 176
grand opening, 174-175
registering and joining, 175
searches, 176
visiting museum in person, 182
Emazing's Genealogy Tip of the Day,
mailing list, 125
encoding, defined, 41-42
Encyclopedia of Cajun Culture
Web site, 214
England
The British Heraldic Archive
Web site, 307
Directory of Royal Genealogical
Data Web site, 310
genealogy newsgroups, 139
online classes for vital records, 257
online resources for, 205-206
error messages, Internet, 351-356
browsers, 352-354
e-mail, 356
FTP, 354-355
Usenet, 355-356
Escribe Web site, 122
ethnic genealogy, 209-220. *See also*
international genealogy
African American, 210-212
AOL message boards, 290
Arab, 213
Australian aborigines, 213
Caribbean, 213-214
Creole/Cajun, 214-215
Cuban, 215
Doukhobors, 215
Genealogy Home Page, 327
Gypsy, Romani, Romany and
Travellers, 216
Hmong, 216
Jewish, 217
Melungeon, 219-220
Métis, 218
Native American, 210, 217-218
overview of, 210
etiquette, net. *See* online society
Eudora mail
blocking spam, 37
overview of, 43
Europe
genealogy newsgroups, 137

Northern Europe genealogy
newsgroup, 139
online genealogy resources for,
203-206
Everton Publishers, 253-262
databases, 254-256
Family History Newsline
newsletter, 124, 259
The Family Letter, 261
Genealogical Helper, 260
Genealogy Supply Store, 260
Guide to Genealogy on the World
Wide Web, 311
online classes, 256-259
RV-n-Genealogist Web site, 259
subscribing to, 261
World Resources, 199
Everton's Genealogical Helper (EGH),
Web version, 260
*Evidence! Citation & Analysis for the
Family Historian* (Mills), 19
Excite, search site, 92
Exhibitions link, Library of Congress,
150-151

F

Failed DNS lookup, browser error
message, 353
Family Chronicle Web site, 311
Family History Centers. *See* FHCs (Family
History Centers)
Family History, How Do I Begin?, LDS
tutorial, 311
Family History Library Catalogs, 160-161
Family History Newsline, Everton, 259
Family Letter, Everton, 261
Family Tree Finders at SodaMail Archives
Web site, 312
Family Tree Maker (FTM), 47
Family Tree, MyFamily.com, 250
Family TreeMaker Online Web site, 312
family trees, online availability of, 14-15
FamilyHistory.com, 246-248
FamilySearch Internet, 159-172
interactivity, 165-166
international resources, 200
LDS and, 10, 168-170
Library tab, 167

opening page, 161-162
ordering products, 167
other resources, 167
overview of, 160-161
palmtop computers and, 28
recording research, 7
Research Guidance, 163
Research Helps, 164
Search for Ancestors tab, 161
using, 161-163
visiting FHCs, 170-171
FAQs (Frequently Asked Questions)
AOL, 285
chat programs, 56-57
etiquette, 53
Genealogy Forum, 287
online rules of, 55
Usenet, 140-141
FastSearch, search site, 92
faxes, choosing modem, 24
Featured Attractions, Library of
Congress, 150-151
Federal Mortality Schedules,
online class, 258
Federal Register Publications, 155
Fetch, FTP program, 77
FGS (Federation of Genealogy Societies)
Society Hall, FamilyHistory.com, 248
FHCs (Family History Centers)
background of, 168-169
Everton Web site, 256
online classes, 257
recording research, 10
using LDS information, 167
visiting, 170-171
fido.eur.genealogy newsgroup, 137
File Libraries Center, Genealogy Forum,
297-298
File menu options, 71
File Transfer Protocol. *See* FTP
(File Transfer Protocol)
files
adding to Family History
Scrapbooks, 180-181
browser error message, 353
e-mail attachments, 41-43
ROOTS-L, 118-119
Files button, CompuServe, 274

filters, e-mail
blocking spam, 37-39
overview of, 35-36
reading Usenet with Outlook
Express, 134
firewalls, 45
First Families of Australia 2001
Web site, 206
Five-Step Research Process, Genealogy
Forum, 287-288
flames
chat programs and, 57
conversation rules and, 55-56
cyberspace manners and, 53
overview of, 54-55
Usenet and, 128, 141
Flash Upgrade Modem technology, 24
FOOTER.HTM, 48
formats, e-mail, 41-43
forms, research, 7-8
forums, AfriGeneas Web site, 325
forums, CompuServe
advertising on, 272-273
decorum, 271-273
defined, 264
overview of, 268-271
promoting, 278-279
taking tour of, 273-277
what is offered, 265-266
France. *See* French
FrancoGene Web site, 204
fraternal organizations, researching, 6
FreeBMD (Free Births, Marriages, and
Deaths), RootsWeb, 205, 240, 312
Freedman's Bureau Online Web site, 212
French
FrancoGene Web site, 204
genealogy newsgroups, 137-138
online resources, 204
Frequently Asked Questions. *See* FAQs
(Frequently Asked Questions)
FTM (Family Tree Maker), 47
FTP (File Transfer Protocol)
browsers and, 76-77
conventions, 78
error messages, 354-355
software, 35
Fuller, John, 125

G

Gail Morin's Métis Families Web site, 218
Gathering of the Clans Home page
    Web site, 312
Gaunt, Christine, 125
GEDCOMs
    Everton Web site and, 254-256
    family trees and, 250
    GEDStar palmtops and, 28
    GenServ Web site and, 332
    overview of, 344
    publishing on Internet and, 46-47
    turning into HTML, 48
    uploading for FamilySearch
        Internet, 165-166
GedPage, 48-49
GENDEX Web site, 312
Gendoor Web site, 312
Genealogical Research in Latin America
    Web site, 206
Genealogical Society of Washtenaw
    County Web site, 8
Genealogy classes, AOL, 299
Genealogy conferences, AOL, 299
Genealogy Dictionary Web site, 312
Genealogy for Teachers Web site, 312
Genealogy: Getting Started, online
    class, 256
Genealogy Home Page Web site, 312-313,
    327-328
Genealogy in the News, AOL, 298
Genealogy Links.Net, 313
Genealogy Mall Web site, 8
Genealogy of Mexico Web site, 208
Genealogy of the Royal Family of the
    Netherlands Web site, 313
Genealogy on the Web Ring, Web site,
    313-314
Genealogy page, NARA research online,
    151-152
Genealogy Pages Web site, 87, 314
genealogy project, beginning, 4-20
    helpful sources, 6
    overview of, 5-6
    queries, 10-12
    review, 20
    scams, 19
    surnames, 9-10
    tracking information, 6-9
    verifying sources, 12-19

Genealogy Resources on the Internet
    Web site, 314
Genealogy Spot Web site, 314
Genealogy Supply Store, Everton, 260
Genealogy Techniques Forum,
    CompuServe, 269-270, 272-273
Genealogy Today Web site, 314
Genealogy.com
    overview of, 206
    United Arab Emirates, 213
Genealogy.net, 204
GenealogyPortal.com, 87-88
GenealogySearch.com, 90
GeneaSearch.com, 87-88
GenGateway search site, 88
GENMTD-L mailing list, 238
GenNewbie mailing list, 238
GenSeeker, RootsWeb site, 232, 234
GenServ search site, 89-90, 314, 331-332
GenSource search site, 90
GENUKI Web site, 314
GenWeb Database Index Web site, 314
GENWEB site, 8
geography
    Genealogy Home Page and, 327
    Maps section, LOC research
        online, 148-149
Germany
    genealogy newsgroups, 137-138
    GermanRoots Web site, 204
    online resources, 204
Global: Everything for the Family
    Historian Web site, 314
Global Gazette newsletter, 314
Go option, browser menu bar, 71
GO words, CompuServe
    forums and, 268-271
    genealogy, 267-268
    overview of, 265-266
    typing in URL box, 274
Go.com, search site, 92
Go.com Translator, 199
Golden Gate Genealogy Forum, AOL,
    281-302
    Beginner's Center, 286-290
    Chat Center, 295-297
    columnists, 298
    features and events, 298-299
    File Libraries Center, 297-298
    history of, 282
    Members Welcome Center,
        284-286

message boards, 290-293
overview of, 282-284
Resources button, 294-295
Reunions button, 295
Search the Forum, 295
staff of, 299-302
Surnames Center, 294
Golden Gate Services, Inc., 284
Google, search site, 92, 131-132
Government Land Office Land Patents
Web site, 14
Gypsies, online resources, 216

H

hackers, defined, 45
Haller, Judith, 8
Hamburg Passenger Departure Lists,
online class, 259
handles
avoiding in CompuServe, 266
login ID nicknames, 102
online chat etiquette, 63-64
The Handybook for Genealogists:
United States of America, 9th Edition
(Everton), 18
hardware, 22-33
cell phone, 29-30
choosing ISPs, 30-33
high-speed connections, 25-28
modems, 23-25
palm-top computers, 28-29
Hauser-Hooser-Hoosier Theory: The Truth
About Hoosier Web site, 314
HEADER.HTM, 48
Headstone Hunter Web site, 314
Help files
browser error message, 353
chat programs, 102, 106
FamilySearch Internet, 164
Library of Congress, 157
NARA, 157
RootsWeb, 241-242
HelpDesk, RootsWeb, 241-242
high-speed connections
overview of, 25-28
voice chats, 108
Hispanic genealogy
Hispanic Genealogical Society of
New York Web site, 208

Hispanic Genealogy Special
Interests Group Web site, 213
newsgroups, 138
Our Spanish Heritage: History and
Genealogy of South Texas and
Northeast Mexico Web site, 319
Spanish Heritage Web site, 319
History folders, browsers, 75-76
History Forum, CompuServe, 271
History Genealogy and Education
Web site, 315
History, MyFamily.com, 251
HistorySeek! History Search Engine
& Historical Information, search
engine, 315
Hmong, online resources, 216
hosts
browser error message, 354
FTP error message, 354
Hot Bot, search site, 92
How Do You Start Researching?, online
class, 257
HTML (Hypertext Markup Language)
editors, built-in FTP engines and, 77
editors, Internet publishing and, 48
listing ROOTS-L in Daily Indexes,
120-121
publishing on Internet, 46-48
turning GEDCOM into, 48
HTTP (Hypertext Transfer Protocol), 68-69
Hungarian Genealogy Web site, 315

I

ICQ
overview of, 104-105
spam protection and, 100
IFHAA (Internet Family History
Association of Australia) Web site, 199
IGI (International Genealogical Index)
overview of, 168-169
searching surnames, 10
using FamilySearch Internet, 160
using information from LDS, 167
IIGS (International Internet Genealogical
Society), 202-207
Africa, 207
Asia, 203
Australia, 206
Canada, 207

chats using, 109
Europe, 203-206, 203-206
Mexico, 207
overview of, 199, 202-203
South America, 206
image files, Family History Scrapbooks,
    180-181
Immigrant Ships Transcribers Guild,
    RootsWeb, 240
Immigration: The Living Mosaic of People,
    Culture & Hope Web site, 316
index cards, 6-7
index mode, ROOTS-L, 119-120
inoculations, 44-45
instant matches, TTMS, 350
instant message programs
    chats, 99
    CompuServe 2000, 265, 267
    etiquette for, 61-63
Integrated Services Digital Network
    (ISDN), 26
internal modems, defined, 24
International Genealogical Index. *See* IGI
    (International Genealogical Index)
international genealogy, 193-208
    Africa, 207
    AOL message boards, 290
    Australia, 206
    Canada and Mexico, 207
    Ellis Island Records Online, 174
    FamilySearch Internet, 161, 164
    International Internet Genealogical
        Society, 202-206
    LDS research guides, 199-200
    South America, 206
    success story, 194-199
    useful sources, 194
    World Wide Genealogy Forum, 271
    WorldGenWeb, 201-202
International Internet Genealogical
    Society. *See* IIGS (International
    Internet Genealogical Society)
Internet
    evaluating information on, 12-15
    genealogy and, 5
    mail clients, 43-44
    message boards, 291
    publishing on, 46-49, 341-342
    Usenet vs., 130
Internet Center, AOL Genealogy Forum,
    288-289

Internet connections
    browser error message, 352
    card catalogs, 184-188
    cell phones, 29-30
    CompuServe, 264-265
    dial-up modem, 25
    high-speed, 25-28
    palm-top computers, 28-29
    Usenet error message, 355
Internet, error messages, 351-356
    browsers, 352-354
    e-mail, 356
    FTP, 354-355
    Usenet, 355-356
Internet Explorer. *See* Microsoft IE
    (Internet Explorer)
Internet Family History Association of
    Australia (IFHAA) Web site, 199
Internet Relay Chat. *See* IRC (Internet
    Relay Chat)
Internet Service Providers. *See* ISPs
    (Internet Service Providers)
Internet Tourbus Web site, 316
intranet, defined, 99
Introduce Yourself message board, AOL
    Genealogy Forum, 290
Invalid host, FTP error message, 354
Invalid newsgroup, Usenet error
    message, 355
IRC (Internet Relay Chat)
    commands for, 106
    etiquette, 61-63
    how chats work, 101, 106-107
    overview of, 98
    security risks, 102-103
Ireland
    genealogy newsgroups, 139
    Local Ireland: Genealogy
        Web site, 316
    online resources, 205
The Irish-Canadian List files, ROOTS-L, 118
ISDN (Integrated Services Digital
    Network), 26
ISPs (Internet Service Providers)
    accessing AOL, 283
    blocking spam, 39-41
    choosing, 30-33
    CompuServe software, 266
    DSL lines, 28
    losing contact with mailing list,
        121-122

reading Usenet with, 134
software and, 34-35
Israel GenWeb Project Web site, 217
Italy, online resources, 204

J

Janyce's Root Digging Dept. Web site, 316
Java, chats
spamming, 101
using Quick Buddy, 103
JFK Assassination Records Collection, 155
Judaism
genealogy newsgroup, 138
JewishGen Web site, 122, 316
JewishGen.org, 217
online resources, 217

K

keywords
searching CompuServe's forums, 265-266
searching with RootsWeb, 234
using in AOL, 283
KiwiGen Web Ring site, 206
Klippel, Denzil J., 194-199

L

Latter-day Saints. *See* LDS (The Church of Jesus Christ of Latter-day Saints)
laws, genealogy and, 4
LDS (The Church of Jesus Christ of Latter-day Saints). *See also* Ellis Island Records Online, FamilySearch Internet
guides for international genealogy, 194
religion and genealogy, 168-170
searching surnames, 10
using information from, 167-168
Legacy.com, obituary search site, 90
lessons, genealogy. *See* online classes
Libdex Web site, online card catalogs, 191
libraries
AfriGeneas Web site, 324
AOL File Libraries Center, 297
NGS Web site, 223-224, 337-338
library card catalogs, 183-192
connecting by telnet, 188-190

connecting by Web browser, 184-188
finding, 190-191
Library Catalog, NARA, 155-156
Library of Congress. *See* LOC (Library of Congress)
Library of Michigan, 211
Library of Virginia
Digital Collections, 316
Internet documentation, 14
Web-based card catalog, 187-188
Library tab, FamilySearch Internet, 167
Library Today link, Library of Congress, 150
Lineage Project, USGenWeb site, 330
Lineages, Inc. Web site, 316
Lineup lists, AOL Chat Center, 296
links, defined, 69
list servers, defined, 118
list servers, ROOTS-L, 119-121
LOC (Library of Congress), 145-151
American Memory link, 146-149
Exhibitions link, 150-151
help when using, 157
The Library Today link, 150
online card catalogs, 191
overview of, 146-147
Research Tools page, 150
Using the Library of Congress link, 150
Local Catholic Church History and Ancestors Web site, 208
Local Ireland: Genealogy, 316
Location box, browser, 73
Louisiana Creole Heritage Center, 214
LusaWeb site, online resource, 205
Lycos Radio, voice chats, 107-108

M

M MULTIPLENAMES, TT, 347
mail mode, ROOTS-L, 119-120
mailing lists, 113-126
African American, 212, 323
Caribbean, 214
defined, 232-233
error messages, 356
Melungeon, 219-220
moderated vs. automated, 114
other sites for, 122-123
overview of, 114
proper addressing, 114

read-only lists, 124-126
RootsWeb, 234-238
subscribing to, 115
mailing lists, ROOTS-L, 115-122
communications, 117-118
files and databases, 118-119
losing contact, 121-122
rules for, 117
subscribing to, 116
using, 119-121
maintenance, virus checks, 45
manners, cyberspace. *See* online society
Manners, Miss, 52-54
Maps section, Library of Congress, 148-149
Marston Manner, 316
Martin, Judith, 52-54
Mayflower Web Pages site, 316
McAfee AntiVirus protection, 44-45
Medal of Honor Citations Web site, 317
medieval genealogy newsgroup, 138
Melungeon Health Education and Support Network Web site, 219
Melungeon, online resources, 219-220
Melungeons and other Mestee Groups (Nassau), 219
The Melungeons: Resurrection of a Proud People (Kennedy), 219
Member Welcome Center, AOL Genealogy Forum, 284-286
menu bars, browsers, 70
Message Board Center, AOL, 290-292
message boards
AOL Genealogy Forum, 289-293
defined, 232
FamilyHistory.com, 247
RootsWeb, 234-238
Message of the Day (MOTD), 106
Messages button
AOL Genealogy Forum, 290
CompuServe, 274
messages, e-mail errors, 356
Met Genealogy FAQ, newsgroup, 140-141
MetaCrawler, search site, 92
metasearch engine, defined, 81
The Métis of North American Genealogy Web site, 218

Mexico
North American Genealogy Forum, 270-271
online resources, 208
Our Spanish Heritage: History and Genealogy of South Texas and Northeast Mexico, 317
microfilm publications search, using NARA, 154
Microsoft IE (Internet Explorer)
choosing browsers, 70
CompuServe based on, 266
guided tour of, 70-74
reading newsgroups with Outlook Express, 134
tips and tricks, 74-78
Microsoft Meeting, 99
Microsoft Outlook Express
as dedicated newsreader, 131-132
layout, 132-133
overview of, 43
reading newsgroups, 134
reading Usenet with, 131-132
Mid-Continent Public Library Web site, 8
Migrations Web site, 317
military records, researching, 6
MIME (Multipurpose Internet Mail Extensions) files, 42
mIRC
how chats work in, 101
overview of, 105-106
spam prevention, 101
Miss Manners, 52-54
Missing Links newsletter, 124, 239
modems
cable, 25
DSL, 27
overview of, 23-25
software and, 33-35
thunderstorms and, 22
modulation, defined, 23
MOTD (Message of the Day), 106
Multipurpose Internet Mail Extensions (MIME) files, 42
My Sites link, MyFamily.com, 249
MyFamily.com portal, 248-252
MyRoots Web site, 29

N

N NOGROUPING, TT, 347
NAIL (NARA Archival Information Locator)
    defined, 151
    microfilm publications search, 154
    overview of, 153-155
NARA (National Archives and Records
    Administration), 151-157
    Genealogy page, 151-152
    help when using, 157
    overview of, 151
    Prologue page, 157
    recording research, 8
    Research Room, 151
    Web databases, Federal Register
        Publications, 155
    Web databases, JFK Assassination
        Records Collection, 155
    Web databases, Library Catalog,
        155-156
    Web databases, microfilm
        publications search, 154
    Web databases, NAIL, 153-155
    Web databases, overview of, 152
National and International Links Project,
    USGenWeb site, 330
National Archives, international
    genealogy, 194
National Archives of Australia Web site, 206
National Archives of Canada Web site, 207
National Archives of Ireland, 205
National Genealogical Society. *See* NGS
    (National Genealogical Society)
National Library of Australia Web site, 213
National Park Service, 14
National Union Catalog of Manuscript
    Collections (NUCMC), 191
Native American Heritage online book, 217
Native Americans, 217-218
navigation bar, RootsWeb, 230
NBCi, search site, 92
net etiquette. *See* online society
Netherlands
    Genealogy of the Royal Family of
        the Netherlands, 313
    online resources, 203-204
Netscape icon, 72
Netscape Navigator
    choosing browsers, 70

    guided tour of, 70-74
    reading newsgroups with, 134
    tips and tricks, 74-78
New England Historic Genealogical
    Society Web site, 317
news servers, 132
newsgroups
    categories of, 129
    interesting, 137-139
    moderated vs. unmoderated, 128
    structure of, 128
newsletters
    AfriGeneas Web site, 325
    RootsWeb site, 238-239
newsreaders, Usenet and, 131-134
Newton palm devices, 29
NGS (National Genealogical Society),
    221-226
    About us page, 223
    Contact us page, 225
    GEDCOMs and, 48
    home page, 222-223
    judging validity of information, 15-19
    library, 223-224
    membership, 225
    news and events, 223
    opportunities, 223-224
    programs, 224-225
NGS (National Genealogical Society)
    standards, 335-342
    guidelines for, 336-337
    overview of, 12
    publishing Web pages, 46, 341-342
    for records, repositories and
        libraries, 337-338
    sharing information, 340-341
    updates, 336
    using technology, 338-339
NNTP server error, browser error
    message, 353
North American Genealogy Forum,
    CompuServe
    overview of, 270-271
    tour of, 273-277
Northern Europe genealogy
    newsgroup, 139
Northern Light, search site, 92
Norton AntiVirus protection, 44-45
Norway, online resources, 205

Not found, browser error message, 353
NOT operators, using, 84
The Notary Protocols, 215
Notices button, CompuServe, 277
nslookup, FTP error messages, 354
NUCMC (National Union Catalog of
    Manuscript Collections), 191

O

Obituary Links search site, 90
Obituary Search pages, 90-91
offline reading, AOL, 293
Old Parochial Register (OPR), 10
online classes. *See also* NGS (National
    Genealogical Society)
        AOL chats as, 299
        DearMYRTLE, 288, 327
        Everton, 256-259
        Family History, How Do I
            Begin?, 311
        How Do You Start Researching?, 257
        Online Genealogy Classes
            Web site, 317
online forums, rules of, 55
Online Genealogy Classes Web site, 317
online society, 51-64
        chat etiquette, 61-63
        flames, 54-55
        forum decorum, 167-168
        getting along, 56-61
        manners, 52-54
        rules of, 55-56
        scams, 61
        for Usenet, 141-142
OPR (Old Parochial Register), 10
OR operators, using, 83
Our Family History, MyFamily.com, 251
Our Spanish Heritage: History and
    Genealogy of South Texas and
    Northeast Mexico Web site, 317
Outlook Express. *See* Microsoft
    Outlook Express

P

P PLACENAMES, TT, 347
Palm pilots, Internet connections, 29
palm-top computers, Internet
    connections, 28-29

Paper Roots, read-only mailing list, 125
Passenger Search, Family History
    Scrapbooks, 179
Patrin Web site, 216
PBS Web site, 8
Pedigree Resource Files, LDS site, 168-169
Pegasus
        blocking spam, 37
        overview of, 43
Personal toolbars, 73
Pitcairn Island Web site, 317-318
plus sign (-), using in searches, 82
Point-to-Point Protocol (PPP),
    choosing ISP, 31
Poland Worldgenweb Web site, 317
POPs (Points of Presence), choosing
    ISP, 31-32
portals, defined, 81
Portuguese, online resources, 205
Potowami Tribe Web site, 217-218
PPP (Point-to-Point Protocol),
    choosing ISP, 31
primary sources
        defined, 5, 13
        judging validity of, 15-19
        Repositories of Primary Sources
            Web site, 317
Prodigy
        Genealogy Newsletter, 122-123
        spam and, 37, 100
protocol, defined, 23
publishing, Web pages on Internet
        NGS research standards, 341-342
        overview of, 76-79

Q

queries
        conventions for, 11-12
        defined, 10
        GenServ Web site, 331-332
questions, posting on chats, 60
Quick Start, AOL's Genealogy Forum,
    286, 289-290

R

Random Acts of Genealogical Kindness,
    RootsWeb site, 240-241
read-only mailing lists, 124-126

reading offline, AOL, 293
records, NGS
    Records Preservation and Access
        Committee, 224-225
    research standards, 337-338
Relations 2.3 Web site, 29
religion, genealogy and, 4
repositories, NGS research standards,
    337-338
Repositories of Primary Sources, 317
Research Guidance tool
    FamilySearch Internet, 163
    international genealogy, 200
Research Helps, FamilySearch Internet, 164
Research Room, NARA, 151
Research Tools page, Library of
    Congress, 150
RLL (The Roots Location List) files, 118
Romani, online resources, 216
Romany, online resources, 216
Roots Cellar, Everton, 255
Roots Forum, CompuServe, 8-9
ROOTS keyword, AOL, 283
ROOTS-L mailing list, 115-122
    communications, 117-118
    files and databases, 118-119
    losing contact with, 121-122
    rules for, 117
    subscribing and unsubscribing,
        115-116
    using, 119-121
The Roots Location List (RLL) files, 118
The Roots Surname List (RSL) files, 118,
    231-232
RootsWeb lists, 199
RootsWeb Review newsletter,
    124-125, 239
RootsWeb site, 227-242
    Ancestry.com merger with, 228
    Ancestry.com vs., 244
    automated keyword search, 234
    automated surname search, 234
    Caribbean, 214
    chats, 109
    Doukhobors, 215
    getting started, 230-231
    HelpDesk, 241-242
    international resource, 201
    message boards and mailing lists,
        234-238

mission of, 229
newsletters, 238-239
overview of, 228, 230
search engines and databases,
    226-227
Social Security Death Index, 234
Surname List, 231-232
Web pages at, 239-241
World Connect project, 233-234
RSL (The Roots Surname List) files, 118,
    231-232
Russia, Doukhobors research, 215
Ruthenians
    Byzantine.net, 308
    online genealogy resources for, 204
RV-n-Genealogist Web site, Everton, 259

S

S SINGLELETTERS, TT, 347
SBt Genealogy Resources Web site, 318
scams
    Consumer Protection Committee,
        NGS Web site, 224
    online etiquette and, 61
    overview of, 19
Scandinavia, online resources, 205
Scotland, online resources, 206
scrapbooks
    creating with MyFamily.com, 249
    Family History, 177-182
search engines
    HistorySeek! History Search Engine
        & Historical Information, 315
    overview of, 80
    RootsWeb, 226-227
    searching Usenet postings with, 131
Search for Ancestors tab, FamilySearch
    Internet, 161
search sites
    defining terms, 80-81
    list of, 85-93
    tips for, 82-85
    White Page directories, 93-95
Search the Forum, AOL Genealogy
    Forum, 295
SearchBeat Web site, 213
searches
    American Memory link, 148-149
    AOL, 295, 297-298

browsers and, 74
Ellis Island Records Online, 176
NARA Web databases, 152-156
reading Usenet with Outlook
    Express, 134
Web-based card catalogs, 185-187
searches, RootsWeb
    automated keyword, 234
    automated surname, 234
    templates for, 230
secondary sources, defined, 14
security
    browser, 73
    IRC risks and, 102-103
    preventing spamming in chat
        rooms, 101
Sephardic Genealogy, 199, 217
Sephardim Genealogy, 199
Serial Line Internet Protocol (SLIP),
    choosing ISP, 31
servers, defined, 33
Share tab, FamilySearch Internet, 165-166
sharing, standards for information, 340-341
Shields Up Web site, 45
ships' passenger lists, 6, 194
Shopper's Guide, AOL Roots window, 298
shortcuts, bookmark, 72-73
slave data
    AfriGeneas Web site, 323
    tracking down, 210
Slavic genealogy newsgroup, 139
SLIP (Serial Line Internet Protocol),
    choosing ISP, 31
Slovakia, online resources, 204
smileys, online chats, 62
soc.genealogy newsgroup, 138
soc.genealogy.computing newsgroup, 138
soc.genealogy.hispanic newsgroup, 138
soc.genealogy.jewish newsgroup, 138
soc.genealogy.medieval newsgroup, 138
soc.genealogy.methods newsgroup, 138
soc.genealogy.misc newsgroup, 139
soc.genealogy.nordic newsgroup, 139
soc.genealogy.slavic newsgroups, 139
soc.genealogy.surnames.global
    newsgroups, 139
soc.genealogy.uk + ireland
    newsgroups, 139
soc.genealogy.west-indies newsgroups, 139

Social Security Death Index. *See* SSDI
    (Social Security Death Index)
Society of Australian Genealogists
    Web site, 206
society, online. *See* online society
software, 33-49
    e-mail, file attachments and
        formats, 41-43
    e-mail, filters, 35-36
    e-mail, spam protection, 36
    e-mail, spamming, 36-41
    FTP, 35
    inoculations, 44-45
    Internet mail clients, 43-44
    overview of, 33-35
    publishing on Internet, 46-49
    tracking information, 6
    Usenet, 131-136
    using FTP, 78
Software Center, AOL, 297
Somebody's Links newsletter, 239
Sons of the American Revolution
    Web site, 318
Soundex code, TT, 347-348
*The Source: A Guidebook of American
    Genealogy. 3rd Edition* (Szucs and
    Luebking), 18
South Africa, online resource (whites), 206
South America, online resources, 206
South Carolina State Library, 189-190, 318
Spain
    online resources, 204
    Spanish Heritage Web site, 319
spam, 36-41
    etiquette and, 53
    preventing on chats, 100-101
    protection from, 36-41
spammers, defined, 36
Spell Check, CompuServe 2000, 267
spiders, search sites, 80
splitters, DSL lines, 27
SSDI (Social Security Death Index)
    Ancestry.com, 245
    Everton Web site, 256
    RootsWeb, 234
St. Augustine Historical Society
    Web site, 214
standards, NGS. *See* NGS (National
    Genealogical Society) standards

standards, transmitting data, 343-350
  Ahnentafels, 344-346
  GEDCOMs, 344
  tiny tafels, 346-350
State Resources Pages, 241
StateGenSites Web site, 319
The Statue of Liberty-Ellis Island
  Foundation
    amateur genealogists and, 210
    American Family Immigration
      History Center, 174
    Family History Scrapbooks,
      177-178
status line, browser, 73-74
stored files, deleting browser, 75
subject line, posting on chats, 59-60
subscriptions
  Ancestry.com, 244-245
  AOL, 283
  DearMYRTLE, 327
  Everton Publishers, 261
  Global Gazette newsletter, 314
  mailing lists, 115, 122
  ROOTS-L, 115-116
Successful Links newsletter, 239
surge protectors, 22
surname searches
  AfriGeneas Web site, 323-325
  Everton Web site, 255
  FamilySearch Internet, 165
  gathering data on, 9-10
  genealogy forums, 273-274
  Genealogy Home Page, 328
  newsgroups, 139
  posting on chats, 60
  RootsWeb, 229-230, 234
  Surnames Center, AOL Genealogy
    Forum, 294
  Surnames.com, 319
  SurnameSite.org, 91
  SurnameWeb site, 91, 319
Sweden, online resources, 205
Switchboard Web site, 94

T

Task Force Russia, 150
Task menu option, 71
TCP/IP (Transmission Control
  Protocol/Internet Protocol)
    defined, 34
    error message, 353

technology, NGS research standards,
  338-339
The Telephone Book for Germany, online
  resource, 204
Telephone Search Facilities, AOL, 299
telnet, 188-190
terminology
  browser, 68-69
  Genealogy Dictionary Web site, 312
  search sites, 80-81
Texas
  Our Spanish Heritage: History and
    Genealogy of South Texas and
    Northeast Mexico, 317
  Texas General Land Office
    Web site, 208
thermometer bar, browsers, 74
thunderstorms, protecting computers, 22
Tiny Tafel Matching System (TTMS),
  348-350
tiny tafels (TT), 58, 346-350
toolbars
  browser, 71-72
  CompuServe, 274
  Personal, 73
Tracing Immigrant Origins Research
  Outline, FamilySearch.org, 199, 200
translations
  RootsWeb chat site, 109
  Web sites, 203
Travellers
  online resources, 216
  Traveller Southern Families Web
    site, 320
Treasure Maps, the How-to Genealogy
  Site, 320-321
Trojan horses
  overview of, 44
  virus protection using firewalls, 45
TT (tiny tafels), 58, 346-350
TTMS (Tiny Tafel Matching System),
  348-350

U

U. S. Civil War Units files, ROOTS-L, 118
UBE (unsolicited bulk e-mail). *See* spam
Ukraine, online resources, 204
Under One Sky newsletter, 219
United Kingdom. *See also* England
  The British Heraldic Archive, 307
  genealogy newsgroups, 139

online classes for vital records, 257
online resources, 205-206
United States
    American Civil War Home Page, 306
    AOL message boards, 290
    Census Bureau Home Page, 309
    Civil War Center, 321
    Daughters of the American
      Revolution, 310
    genealogy in, 4-5
    Mayflower Web Pages, 316
    New England Historic Genealogical
      Society, 317
    North American Genealogy
      Forum, 270-271
    Sons of the American
      Revolution, 318
    Traveller Southern Families, 320
    United States-Canadian Border
      Crossing Records, 259
    USGenWeb site, 328-331
University of Alabama, 185-186
University of Minnesota, 190-191
University of Texas, 185
Unknown user, e-mail error message, 356
unsolicited bulk e-mail (UBE). *See* spam
updates, NGS research standards, 336
URL box, typing GO words in, 274
URL (Uniform Resource Locator)
    copying to clipboard, 74
    Genealogy Home Page, 327
    guided tour of browsers, 70-74
    overview of, 68-69
    viewing recently visited, 75
U.S. Gazetteer Web site, 321
Usenet Web site, 127-142
    binary files, 139-140
    choosing ISP, 31
    error messages, 355-356
    FAQs, 140-141
    interesting newsgroups, 137-139
    net etiquette, 54-61, 141-142
    overview, 128
    software, 131-136
    spam protection, 36-37
    structure, 129-131
USGenWeb site
    Digital Census Project, 14
    online card catalogs, 190-191
    overview of, 328-331
    Special Projects, 321, 330-331
USRoots/Rootsquest Web site, 123
Utah State Archives Web site, 321
UUENCODE files, 42-43
UUE.ZIP, 43

V

Vietnam
    database, 255
    Vietnam Era Prisoner of
      War/Missing in Action, 150
View menu options, 71
Virtual Bouquets digest, 239
virus protection
    digital connections, 26
    downloading binary files from
      Usenet, 139-140
    Microsoft Outlook Express, 44
    overview of, 44-45
vital records
    Internet documentation of, 14
    online classes for England and
      Wales, 257
    researching with, 6
    where to write for, 196
Vive La Cajun Web site, 214
voice chats
    DearMYRTLE, 107-108
    overview of, 106

W

Wales, online classes for vital records, 257
Web browsers, 67-78
    choosing, 69-70
    defined, 68
    guided tour, 70-74
    terminology, 68-69
    tips and tricks, 74-78
    where to obtain, 68
Web connections. *See* Internet
  connections
Web pages
    changing browser's opening, 74
    defined, 69

publishing on Internet, 76-79, 341-342
RootsWeb, 239-241
translating into English, 203
Web sites. *See also* search sites
  alphabetical list of, 303-332
  census records from, 14
  for chats, 109
  choosing browsers for, 70
  connecting to with Palmtops, 28-29
  how to choose, 305
  international, 199
  judging validity of, 15-19
  junk e-mail and, 37-38, 41
  land patent information from, 14
  LDS and, 10
  locating ISPs for, 31
  online card catalogs, 190-191
  Pegasus, 43
  publishing information on, 46-47, 49
  recording research, 7-8
  RootsWeb, 239-240
  scams, 19
  security risks in IRC, 102-103
  standards for research, 12
  uncompressing files, 78
  virus protection using firewalls, 45
  writing for vital records, 196
West Indies genealogy newsgroups, 139
What's New on Cyndi's List?, 125
Where to Write for Vital Records
  Web site, 196

White Page directories, 93-95
WinZIP file, 43
WITH operators, using, 84
World Connect project, RootsWeb, 233-234
World Connect search site, 91
World Tree database
  Ancestry.com, 245-246
  FamilyHistory.com, 248
World Wide Genealogy Forum, 271
WorldGenWeb, international resource, 138-139
worms, 44-45
WS_FTP32, FTP program, 77

X

Xerox Map Server, 321
XXENCODE files, 42

Y

Yahoo!
  Australian genealogy resource, 206
  Genealogy page, 321
  mailing lists, 123
  search site, 80-81, 92
Yale University Library, online card
  catalog, 190-191
Yourfamily.com search site, 91

INTERNATIONAL CONTACT INFORMATION

AUSTRALIA
McGraw-Hill Book Company Australia Pty. Ltd.
TEL +61-2-9417-9899
FAX +61-2-9417-5687
http://www.mcgraw-hill.com.au
books-it_sydney@mcgraw-hill.com

CANADA
McGraw-Hill Ryerson Ltd.
TEL +905-430-5000
FAX +905-430-5020
http://www.mcgrawhill.ca

**GREECE, MIDDLE EAST,
NORTHERN AFRICA**
McGraw-Hill Hellas
TEL +30-1-656-0990-3-4
FAX +30-1-654-5525

MEXICO (Also serving Latin America)
McGraw-Hill Interamericana Editores S.A. de C.V.
TEL +525-117-1583
FAX +525-117-1589
http://www.mcgraw-hill.com.mx
fernando_castellanos@mcgraw-hill.com

SINGAPORE (Serving Asia)
McGraw-Hill Book Company
TEL +65-863-1580
FAX +65-862-3354
http://www.mcgraw-hill.com.sg
mghasia@mcgraw-hill.com

SOUTH AFRICA
McGraw-Hill South Africa
TEL +27-11-622-7512
FAX +27-11-622-9045
robyn_swanepoel@mcgraw-hill.com

**UNITED KINGDOM & EUROPE
(Excluding Southern Europe)**
McGraw-Hill Education Europe
TEL +44-1-628-502500
FAX +44-1-628-770224
http://www.mcgraw-hill.co.uk
computing_neurope@mcgraw-hill.com

ALL OTHER INQUIRIES Contact:
Osborne/McGraw-Hill
TEL +1-510-549-6600
FAX +1-510-883-7600
http://www.osborne.com
omg_international@mcgraw-hill.com